More Praise for
The Leadership Genius of George W. Bush

"Carolyn Thompson and Jim Ware's The Leadership Genius of George W. Bush *stands out from other volumes on the topic by its fresh perspective and unique insight. Its practical suggestions and diverse examples make the volume a must-read for anyone interested in building their own leadership qualities or developing that critical capacity within their organizations."*

David Beck, Group Publisher, Kennedy Information, Inc.

"The Leadership Genius of George W. Bush *provides a detailed and insightful look at what makes George W. Bush one of the strongest U.S. presidents in recent history. But perhaps more importantly, Thompson and Ware have given us an analytical framework and valuable set of tools with which to examine our own leadership style and skills."*

Margaret M. (Peggy) Eisen, CFA
Chair, The Institute for Financial Markets

"Thompson and Ware have combined to create a fascinating in-depth exploration of the strategies that have made George W. Bush an exemplary leader. This is a must-read for every executive and professional who wants practical, commonsense strategies for effective leadership."

Catherine D. Fyock, Author, *Get the Best*

"George W. Bush uses core values to define, superb communication to inspire, high performance teams to unleash creativity, and managerial focus to achieve results. This book offers unparalleled insight into the elements that make up his uniquely successful brand of leadership, and offers valuable lessons for all organizations."

Harvey Seifter, President of Seifter Associates
Author, *Leadership Ensemble: Lessons in Collaborative Management from the World's Only Conductorless Orchestra*

"No matter what your political sentiments are you cannot deny the leadership President Bush has brought to the world in the past two years. Now you can find out the inside story on what makes President Bush such a great leader. This book uncovers the practical commonsense genius of George Bush. If you want to learn how to lead like President Bush in whatever calling you find yourself then you need to read The Leadership Genius of George W. Bush."

Ralph Cochran, Executive Director, *Business Reform* magazine

The Leadership Genius of George W. Bush

10 Commonsense Lessons from the Commander in Chief

CAROLYN B. THOMPSON

JAMES W. WARE

John Wiley & Sons, Inc.

For general information on our other products and services, or technical support, please contact our Customer Care Department within the United States at 800-762-2974, outside the United States at 317-572-3993 or fax 317-572-4002.

Wiley also publishes its books in a variety of electronic formats. Some content that appears in print may not be available in electronic books.

For more information about Wiley products, visit our web site at www.wiley.com.

ISBN 0-471-42006-9

Printed in the United States of America.

10 9 8 7 6 5 4 3 2 1

Preface

A s longtime consultants in the area of leadership, we were fascinated by George W. Bush. How does a guy who seems so much
like the neighbor next door succeed as the most powerful leader in
the world? People underestimate him, but time and again he rises to
the occasion. Yet his style of leadership seems to contradict almost
everything we thought we knew about leadership.

Our task in writing this book has been to discover the secret that
makes Bush a leadership genius. We examined his leadership style from
what we considered a fairly well-rounded perspective. Our research
team (the two authors) consists of one male, one female; one conservative, one liberal; one traditional Christian, one nontraditional; one
more "right-brained" (creative and flexible), one more "left-brained"
(logical and organized). And yet we both came away with the same
admiration for Bush's leadership abilities.

Jim Ware's fascination with leadership dates back to his days as a
securities analyst, when he interviewed company leaders like Lee
Iacocca, Sam Walton, and Donald Rumsfeld. He and his colleagues
at Focus Consulting have developed various measurement tools
for diagnosing the effectiveness of leaders and the organizational cultures that they shape. He is interested in comparing business and
political leadership. Do the same principles apply? Can successful
business leaders cross over into politics, and vice versa? The study of
George W. Bush was a perfect opportunity to examine these questions. Bush considers himself a business leader, schooled at Harvard

and experienced as an entrepreneur. He clearly states that his approach to managing a political administration is based on his business training. Therefore, Bush's success in both business and now politics provides a resoundingly positive answer to the question: Are the timeless leadership principles applicable in all fields?

Carolyn Thompson gathers information, looks for trends, and turns them into something easy to digest in her sleep. It all started when, as a psychology major/history minor at Northwestern University, she discovered that she could turn the minor into a major simply by taking two more classes. The advisor pointed out that the two majors—history and psych—regularly produced authors of books about great leaders in history. Those authors gathered volumes of information on the leaders, analyzed their characteristics, culled the main principles, and put them into a format that is easy for readers to apply. Carolyn first used these skills not as an author but as the director of a human resources department. Now she uses them in customized training, focusing on how to meet organizations' business objectives through improvements in employee performance. Working with companies, their leadership, and their employees has given Carolyn a unique perspective on the subtle differences that often separate successful enterprises from mediocre ones. These experiences have led to extensive writing on the subjects of leadership and employee performance improvement.

By poring over research documents, reading books, and through experience, we have both discovered that leadership is core to a company's success. A plethora of books have been written on how to lead and on specific kinds of leaders, from Colin Powell and other military leaders to great business leaders such as Jack Welch. You won't find many, though, on great politicians who led entire countries to success, such as Ronald Reagan. Is it that the leap is too great, moving from how these leadership skills are used in the political arena to how they'd be effective in a business setting? Or is it strictly marketing—that is, most business people don't see the applicability of what they consider political principles to the skills needed in their businesses? The reality is that all business is politics and all politics is business. The only difference is where we get our operating capital from. The rest—negotiating one's way through shifting alliances, hiring people, gaining trust, being disciplined—is all the same. George W. Bush is an easy first study because his career as a leader includes both the business and political arenas. We learned an incredible amount that we've already applied to our own businesses, and we know you too will benefit from studying his tactics and applying them to yourself and your organization.

CAROLYN B. THOMPSON
JAMES W. WARE

Frankfort, Illinois
Glenview, Illinois
November 2002

Acknowledgments

T hanks to Pamela van Giessen, our editor, for presenting us with the fantastic idea for this book in the first place, and for her advice and support during the writing.

Our next big thanks goes to George W. Bush himself. When we say we enjoyed learning about him and applying his lessons to our work, we mean it. He inspired us on days when we lost computer files. He inspired our sense of family and the balance we needed to have on those days when we were racing for a deadline. One of the authors has been a daily exerciser for years, but under amazing deadline pressures has occasionally skipped the workout on a super-busy day. Not so this summer. You just can't write about the kind of discipline George exhibits and skip your exercise routine! The calming yet energizing benefits of the discipline of exercise saved many a frazzled day.

We really enjoyed reading the piles of books about Bush written by others. Many of them made for entertaining reading. And where would we have been without the Internet? Can one even do the kind of research we needed to do without it anymore? Our eternal gratitude, and that of our pocketbooks, goes to the staff of the Frankfort Public Library, who saved us time and money by quickly finding a copy of every book we asked for about or relating to George W.

Thanks to everyone at the White House for their help in getting us to the right people; getting Eric Draper's wonderfully inspiring photo; and confirming the dates, names, and places in Bush's life.

Lauren Topel was a last-minute lifesaver, making many, many changes to be rushed into production. Thanks also to Debbie Daw, who gave us countless ingenious ideas for dealing with Word when it wouldn't do what we needed it to. This easy-to-read format comes to you courtesy of Brooke Graves (copy editor) and Jamie Temple (compositor). Thanks for your expert production.

Jim specially thanks his wife, Jane, for her patience while he disappeared to work on this book. He also thanks his partners at Focus Consulting, Beth Michaels and Dale Primer, for their insights on leadership. And Barry Rustin for a great photo despite difficult odds.

Carolyn specially thanks Patti Lowczyk, for keeping her work flowing while she ran spell checks; Robin Pelfrey, for always asking how the researching and writing were going; Lynn Hauser, for taking over the job of editing Training Systems Inc.'s monthly e-zine, *Recruit, Inspire & Retain,* one week before the book's editing deadline; Don Page, for his incredible excitement at the thought that she was involved in writing a book on such a smart man in the first place; and David and Jennifer Thompson, who have the most amazing amount of trivia knowledge (when it couldn't be found on the Internet, they always had the information). Special, special thanks to Bill Kauzlarich, who went it alone in a family crisis while she was rushing for the deadline and because he just happens to be the love of her life. And to Jim—for his constant faith in her, his constant praise, and his excitement for the project; for asking her to work with him on this book; and for long conversations that led to the descriptions you are about to read of Bush's unique combination of leadership actions.

Finally, of course, thanks to the One who makes all things possible for us—God. For without that hourly guidance, we'd never have been able to keep our focus.

C.B.T.
J.W.W.

Contents

Photo credit: Eric Draper, White House.

George W. Bush

The Making of the Leadership Genius

Beliefs
- Compassionate conservatism
- Individual responsibility
- Proponent of limited government
- Opponent of government controls on business
- Proponent of free market

1930s	Samuel Bush (great-grandfather) serves as advisor to President Herbert Hoover.
1946	Born New Haven, Connecticut, July 6, 1946 (while George H. W. Bush was undergrad at Yale).
1948	Moves to Midland, Texas.
1950	Prescott Bush (grandfather) runs for U.S. Senate (loses).
1952	Prescott Bush elected to U.S. Senate.
1953	Sister Robin dies of leukemia.
circa 1953	Starts playing Little League baseball.
1958	Elected seventh-grade class president, San Jacinto Junior High School.
1959	Moves to Houston, Texas.
circa 1959	Altar boy in his church (first stirrings of his faith).

1961	Starts Philips Academy, Andover, Massachusetts (Dad went there).
1961	Works as clerk for Baker, Betts, Sheppard & Coates (summer job); customer service and quote desk for stock broker (summer job).
1963	Head of cheerleading squad at Philips.
1964	Creates intramural stickball league and announces himself "High Commissioner" of stickball at Philips.
1964	Helps Dad with U.S. Senate campaign in summer (Dad loses).
1964	Starts Yale (plays baseball, history major, fraternity president).
1964	Ranch hand (summer job).
1965	Roughnecks on oil rig (summer job; quits one week early).
1966	Sporting goods sales for Sears (summer job).
1966	George H. W. Bush elected to U.S. House of Representatives.
1968	Graduates from Yale in June.
1968	Basic training, Texas Air National Guard at Lackland Air Force Base, San Antonio, Texas.
1968–1969	Pilot training at Moody Air Force Base, Valdosta, Georgia.
1970	Promoted to first lieutenant at Ellington Air Force Base, Houston, Texas.
1970	Helps Dad with U.S. Senate race (Dad loses again).
1971	Management training for agribusiness company, Houston, Texas.
1972	Helps with Red Blount's U.S. Senate campaign (Alabama).
1973	Honorably discharged, Texas Air National Guard.
1973	Ran Project PULL, Houston (inner-city mentoring program).

1973	Starts at Harvard Business School.
1975	Receives MBA from Harvard University.
1975	Visits mother and father in Beijing for summer.
1975	Moves to Midland (teaches Sunday school at Presbyterian church and starts as a landman in oil industry).
1976	Sole proprietorship, oil and gas business.
1977	Business goes well; names it Arbusto Energy, Inc., Spanish for *Bush*.
1977	Meets and marries Laura Welch.
1978	Runs for 19th district Congress seat (loses).
1979	Helps Dad with presidential primary race (Dad loses and is chosen for vice president).
1981	Barbara and Jenna born (active dad to twins).
1982	Daughters are baptized in Laura's Methodist church; he becomes active member of finance committee.
1982	Renames Arbusto as Bush Exploration.
1984	Merges Bush Exploration into Spectrum 7 Energy Corporation.
1985	Recommits to Christ after weekend with Billy Graham and becomes active in a Bible study group of local businessmen.
1986	Sells Spectrum 7 to Harken Energy; gets seat on Harken's board and consults for Harken.
1987	Moves to Washington, D.C. to help Dad with presidential campaign (wins).
1988	Delegate to Republican National Convention.
1988	Moves to Dallas, Texas.
circa 1988	Coaches Little League.
1989	Buys Texas Rangers baseball team with partners (he is managing general partner).
1993	Decides to run for governor of Texas against incumbent Ann Richards.
1995	Moves to governor's mansion in Austin, Texas.
1995	Inaugurated as governor of Texas.

1995	Legislative session gets juvenile justice laws strengthened, tort reform, local control of education.
1996	Launches faith-based initiative task force.
1996	Launches literacy program (all children read by third grade).
1997	Legislative session gets tax reform with $1 billion tax cut, education funded by state, and welfare reform, patient protection insurance regulations.
1998	Runs for reelection (first Texas governor to win back-to-back four-year terms).
1999	Legislative session gets $2 billion tax cut and ends social promotion schools.
1999	Decides to run for president of the United States; raises $37 million.
November 2000	Election recount.
December 2000	Wins election (first president with MBA).
January 2001	Inaugurated as 43rd president of the United States.
January 2001	Establishes Office of Faith-Based and Community Initiatives.
February 2001	Gallup poll presidential approval rating is 62 percent.
April 2001	First 100 days passed.
April 2001	CNN poll approval rating is 62 percent.
May 2001	Bipartisan agreement on tax bill.
June 2001	Signs tax bill.
August 2001	Stem cell research funds allowed on small and existing lines only.
September 11, 2001	
September 14, 2001	Washington, D.C.'s National Cathedral leads nation in prayer with four past presidents.
September 14,	Visits Ground Zero.

September 2001 2001	*Washington Post* approval poll rating is 90 percent; Time/CNN poll, 84 percent; Gallup poll, 90 percent.
October 2001	Anthrax scares.
October 2001	Commences attacks on Afghanistan.
December 2001	Enron scandal breaks.
December 2001	Gets education bill passed.
January 2002	Signs education bill.
May 2002	Bush, FBI, and CIA accused of having prior warning of 9/11.
May 2002	Gallup poll presidential approval rating is 77 percent.
June 2002	Proposes Department of Homeland Security (to start operations January 2003).
July 9, 2002	Corporate trust speech on Wall Street (began talking about corporate trust in State of the Union address, January 29, 2002).
July 2002	Continuing drops in the Dow as concerns about corporate trust increase.
July 2002	*Newsweek* approval poll rating is 65 percent; Time/CNN poll, 70 percent; *Washington Post–ABC News* poll, 72 percent; Gallup poll, 69 percent.
November 2002	Midterm election aced for Republicans.

Introduction

I've never held myself out to be any great genius.

George W. Bush[1]

G eorge W. Bush may not hold himself out as a genius, but as the book closed on the 2002 midterm elections, it became abundantly clear that he is a brilliant leader. From the 2001 tax cut through terrorist and geopolitical crises, Bush's mandates have carried the day since the moment he entered the Oval Office.

It is therefore unfortunate that in modern politics no president has suffered as many jabs about his intelligence as George W. Bush. Although politicians are regular targets for comedians, late-night talk show hosts, and cartoonists, with "Dubya" the attacks have been especially vicious. During the 2000 presidential campaign, David Letterman one night wisecracked, "Bush has a new campaign slogan. It's 'Reformer with Results.' Which I think is a big improvement on the old one: 'A Dumb Guy with Connections.'" Jay Leno followed suit, "They finally found some dope in the Bush campaign. It's the candidate." Ridiculed and attacked repeatedly for his presumed lack of intelligence and leadership skills, as Bush attained national prominence during the Republican primaries, he quickly became the Rodney Dangerfield ("I don't get no respect") of politics. Political columnists and commentators passed around the stick, using Dubya as a piñata. In their eyes he was a lightweight worthy of little but scorn and contempt.

Bush entered Washington in January 2001 amid much heckling and derision. For the first nine months many Americans paid little attention to the usual Washington politicking about the administration's legislative agenda—the priority of which was to pass a tax cut, which was accomplished in short order.

Then, when the United States faced its greatest crisis since Pearl Harbor, Bush rose to lead the American people through one of the most horrific events in modern history. And he did it beautifully. The American people responded with approval ratings of 90 percent. Months after his courageous response to 9/11, Bush's approval ratings remained remarkably strong. In fact, through the summer of 2002, he stood as one of the most popular presidents ever, rivaling the Great Communicator himself, Ronald Reagan. In the fall of 2002, just as the media wondered if those high ratings could hold, and conducted new polls that presumably would show that the American people were beginning to question their leader, Bush delivered a brilliant speech to the United Nations. Even liberals had to concede that the message was compelling and authoritative—the very sorts of adjectives used to describe great leaders. As syndicated columnist Kathleen Parker pointed out in October 2002, though many say that Bush is stupid, time and again he's gotten what he wanted and done what he said he was going to do.[2] Which is what effective leaders do!

As if to prove the point, Bush then stumped for his fellow Republican candidates across the country during the midterm elections. Apparently many voters were listening, because on election Tuesday they came out and voted for the candidates of Bush's party.

How is it that this supposedly not-so-brilliant man leads so successfully time and time again? Even experts on leadership, such as Warren Wilhelm, professor at Harvard Business School and a top consultant, believe that "intelligence is the most basic leadership characteristic of all."[3] But Bush doesn't claim to be an intellectual genius. Nor is he academically inclined, as was his predecessor, Clinton, a Rhodes Scholar. President George W. Bush may have attended Yale University as an undergraduate, but he received a C-minus average in his four years there. His SAT scores were average as well: 566 on verbal and 640 on math (out of a possible 800 for each). A rough translation of SAT scores into IQ measures gives Bush an IQ of 119, a bit above average, but lower than his opponent in the 2000 elections, Gore, at 130. When it comes to intelligence, it appears that President Bush is much like most of us: everyday average.

How does one explain the huge gap between the media commentary (at least pre-midterm election commentary—after which even the liberal pundits had to admit that Bush was brilliant when it came to achieving his objectives) and public opinion as shown by poll ratings? Something was wrong with this picture. As authors and consultants in the field of leadership, we were knowledgeable about the subject. We've read the books and worked with real, live leaders. But we were not especially knowledgeable about George W. Bush or his approach to leadership. We asked ourselves: *What makes him so effective? How does he do it?*

We dove into the research: reading, listening to speeches, and talking to as many sources as possible. Our aim was to find out how Bush "does" leadership. We had our own opinions about what constitutes excellent leadership, but we purposely loosened our grip on our views to better examine Bush. We did not try to jam Bush into our mold of leadership. Rather, we studied his decisions and actions in college and graduate school, the National Guard, the oil business, professional baseball, Texas politics, the presidential campaign, and the presidency.

What we found, after months of study, were two key factors that explained Bush's success. First, he consistently employs what we identify in this book as "timeless principles of leadership." These principles have been used throughout the ages by leaders from Attila the Hun to Thomas Jefferson. They are time-tested and they work. Throughout these chapters, we highlight these crucial principles and show how Bush uses them.

Second, and just as important, Bush has what our grandfathers called "horse sense." Bush knows this about himself. Commenting on his competent handling of crisis, Bush said, "I've got good common sense and good instincts." He adds, "I've got confidence in my abilities. I love to be underestimated."

This one-two punch explains Bush's success. Timeless principles plus common sense equal leadership genius. Although some people may argue that genius means high IQ, there is another definition that fits Bush perfectly: *a single, strongly marked capacity.*

Capacity for what? For common sense. The difference is crucial to leadership. It's what author Dan Goleman calls "Emotional Intelligence" or EQ (Emotional Quotient as opposed to Intelligence Quotient, or IQ). EQ measures one's ability to work with people. It includes skills like reading people, communicating, motivating, and building trust. Peter Drucker, management guru, agrees with this distinction and says that leaders in the information age will rely more on people skills than on book learning or raw intelligence.

Through his skillful use of what we call the timeless principles of leadership, and his uncanny common sense (people skills), Bush has become a genius at leadership. Regardless of one's views on his politics and policies, it is clear that he has an intuitive ability to lead that helped him win the governorship of Texas from a popular sitting governor and then take the United States by storm.

Clearly, there is something to be learned from Bush and his leadership practices. It has been said that leadership is not a popularity contest, but it is important that people respect their leaders enough to follow them, particularly in a democracy. If approval ratings and the voice of ordinary, real Americans are any indication, it appears that people trust Bush. As one individual, a Democrat, told us, "He took my breath away when I heard him speak impromptu at the White House. His passion for the subject—education—and his eye contact with the small group . . . I got chills."

What can business people—the leaders of companies large and small—learn from this masterful leader, George W. Bush? Our goal is to spell out exactly how Bush leads so effectively and how you can learn from his techniques. We break his tactics down into bite-size pieces and provide context and background for each element. To use an analogy, imagine watching a brilliant quarterback in football. Each play involves hundreds, if not thousands, of variables: play selection, calling the signals, analyzing the defense, possibly changing the play at the line of scrimmage, executing the play, avoiding tacklers, handing off or looking for receivers, passing, and so forth. A great quarterback makes it look easy. When asked how he does it, he may be clueless. He simply has a ton of experience and awesome talent. Thank goodness for slow-motion replay! It allows us to carefully dissect what happens in the four seconds that constitute the average football play. We can then analyze the elements of greatness.

In a sense, we've used slow-motion replay to analyze Bush's style and uncover what he does that makes him so successful. We've examined different phases of his life, looking at major decisions, strategies, techniques, failures, and successes, all with the intent of seeing what practices endure. Each chapter reveals a leadership lesson from Bush and shows how he uses it. There are 10 key practices: identifying core values; having a vision; building trust; hiring the best; leaving them alone so they can do their jobs; building alliances; being disciplined; communication; intuition; and finally, getting results. From our own knowledge of leadership, we show how these practices are in fact timeless principles. Then we explain the components of the practice and help you learn how you can develop this skill.

Each chapter ends with a "how to" section. After we've slowed the tape down and analyzed what Bush is doing, this is where we provide tips and tools for developing these skills in yourself and putting them into practice. Whether you are running a Fortune 500 company, the local school board, or your condo association, these actionable suggestions will help.

In keeping with Bush's style, we've taken an everyday, practical approach to the subject (a style Bush likes) and one that's entertaining as well. Learning is easier when it's fun, which is why we provide this combination of biography, current affairs, and management how-to. For the serious students of leadership, we've included source material that will point you to relevant academic and management studies on leadership.

If the point of leadership is to know where you're going, know and be able to communicate your values, and be disciplined enough to carry them out, then Bush, like Moses, is a leadership genius. Moses used his leadership genius to best the mighty Egyptian pharaoh, bringing 600,000 slaves out of bondage into nationhood. His laws, created during the 40 years he and the Israelites spent in the wilderness, provide the ethical foundation for Judaism, Christianity, and Islam. Bush uses his leadership genius to push forward the philosophy of "compassionate conservatism" that he believes will improve the lot of all Americans. Shaped around a clear message, his agenda is to improve educational standards, bring about juvenile justice, eliminate burdensome taxes to help the U.S. economy, and ensure the security of the people of the United States. His leadership lessons, created over a lifetime, can provide the foundation for our own leadership genius.

CHAPTER 1

What Do You Stand For?

Identify Core Values

Here are the principles by which we operate and make decisions.

George W. Bush[1]

Quick: What were the values of the Clinton administration? What did Clinton stand for?

We've put this question to many people and, after the predictable intern jokes, the response has been, "I'm not sure." People know that Clinton was a Democrat, that he was liberal, and that he could "feel their pain" . . . but they are unsure of his deeply held beliefs.

Such is the difference between Bill Clinton and George W. Bush.

Our study of Bush starts with values because that's where leadership starts. Values address the question, "What's important?" A leader who tells you his values and what they mean is saying, "This is what I stand for. This is what I care about." Whether one is a leader of the free world, a business executive, a department manager, or head of a household, the job starts with values. They guide us and motivate us. They connect us in a way that a paycheck cannot. When the go-go years of the 1990s finally ended, many Americans were left to ponder, "What are my values?"

Bush knows what he stands for. He is serious about his values. He admires other leaders who feel the same. He likes Reagan for this reason: "He articulated the values that made America great."[2] He likes his dad for this reason also: "He is a product of a great generation that lived the values of duty, honor, and country. Those values, which caused him to hear the call to serve his country at age eighteen, are an indelible part of Dad's being. He is a principled man who has a clear view of right and wrong."[3] The younger Bush believes that clear, consistent values are a key to leadership. In fact, values are the reason a leader has followers in the first place. People are drawn to a person who stands for something—a person who courageously says, "I believe in this and I'll fight for it."

WHAT'S IMPORTANT TO BUSH?

The list of Bush's personal values is extensive: accountability, cooperation, freedom, fun, and others. At the top of the list, though, are three in particular. From our research, these core values assume primary importance for him. They are what really matters to him deep down. They are captured in two statements:

> You can enter the [political] arena, serve with distinction, absorb the slings and arrows, and emerge with dignity and integrity and the love of your family intact.[4]

and

> My family would love me, my faith would sustain me, no matter what.[5]

Bush's three personal core values are:

1. Family (mentioned in both statements).
2. Faith (belief in God).
3. Integrity (which, when intact, provides for dignity).

There is ample evidence from Bush's life that these three core values drive his actions. His devotion and loyalty to family are unquestioned even by his harshest critics. In the days that followed September 11, 2001, brother Jeb said, "George has not changed in my conversations with him"; he still talked "about the family things—how the children are doing, for example."[6]

Family loyalty is not something to fool around with in the Bush camp. During his father's campaign for the presidency, George "Dubya" was named the "loyalty enforcer."[7] Anyone displaying the slightest hint of disloyalty to the candidate (his father) was dealt with harshly, and the loyalty test used by George and his brother Jeb was extreme: *Would you throw yourself on a grenade to save Dad's life?* The least hesitation invited suspicion. Lee Atwater, chief strategist for the campaign, made this mistake when he first met the young George and incurred his wrath: "How do we know we can trust you?" barked Bush. Atwater, realizing that he hadn't scored well on the family loyalty scale, recovered enough to suggest that Bush come to Washington and watch him firsthand. Bush accepted the challenge and the two later became friends.

Another episode that highlighted family loyalty occurred when the media labeled Bush's father a "wimp." Feeling some personal responsibility for that *Newsweek* article of October 1987 (because he had scheduled the interview), young Bush took out his anger on media personnel. In one celebrated incident, Bush heard two broadcasters criticizing his father's choice of Dan Quayle as running mate. Young Bush stormed over to their booth and said, "I'm the Vice President's son and I want you to know I resent what you all said about my dad."[8] Bush called his own behavior the "fierce loyalty of a proud son."[9]

Bush says of his family, "We are a close family. I love my brothers and sister and count them among the most important people in my life."[10] Bush credits his parents with teaching him his solid values. A friend from Yale, Britt Kolar, agrees: "I think his values have been consistent from the word go, and those are the values he learned from his family."[11] The role of the family, in Bush's eyes, is to instill positive values. This belief influences his policy recommendations. For example, Bush favors reducing the marriage penalty in the tax code because it imposes a financial hardship on couples. His reasoning is that government should encourage sound family formation because that in turn supports healthy values. Therefore, leaders should do what it takes politically to make it easier to form and maintain families.

The integrity of politicians and business leaders is always under intense scrutiny, now more than ever. Cynicism is the order of the day. That's why, in our research, we looked for instances in which Bush's actions and his words lined up. For example, does he encourage his staff to spend time with *their* families? Or would he really prefer them to work evenings and weekends? A story from Karen Hughes about her son provides one example of Bush's genuine concern about families. Hughes's 12-year-old son was playing in a championship Little League game just when his mother, Karen, was in Iowa in the midst of an important campaign swing (just before the Ames straw poll). When Bush became aware of the conflict, he said to Hughes, "You need to get on the next flight home and go see that game." Reflecting on this incident, Hughes said, "My boss was running for president, but I made every game except one."[12] The message is loud and clear: Family is more important than a job.

The same is true of Bush's Christian faith. He reads the Bible, openly accepts Jesus as his personal savior, and attends the White House morning prayer meeting. When pressed by reporters to defend his fundamental Christian view, Bush responded, "It's me. It's what I'm all about. It's how I live my life. It's just a part of me."[13] In this way, Bush clearly prioritizes his values. Yes, politics and winning are important to him but, he says, "What I'm not willing to do is sell my soul to become president."[14] He is a major supporter of faith-based alternatives for helping people in need.

In the days that followed the terrorist attacks of September 11, Bush said it was his faith that sustained him and made him feel equal to the huge task at hand. In fact, the tragedy of 9/11 shows the importance of values in Bush's professional life. We are most powerful and effective when our personal values line up with our professional values—when we can take our true selves into work. For Bush, 9/11 did exactly that. Bush believes that leading the country against the terrorist threat is "God's mission for him. Bush has told many friends and advisors that he has never known such clarity of purpose, such certainty that he is the right person for the moment."[15] In the wake of 9/11, many of our friends said, "Wouldn't you hate to be the president right now?" Yet Bush embraced the role of leader with even more vigor and clarity of purpose than before 9/11. Such is the power of deep beliefs and the values that stem from them. Underlying any value you hold is a belief that explains why you have that value. For example, Bush values faith because of his underlying belief in God and Christianity.

How about integrity? Throughout this book we'll look at many instances of tough decisions that required Bush to choose the path of most resistance—decisions like the one he faced as governor of Texas when asked to sign the Patient Protection Act. In this case, Bush knew the politically smart thing to do was sign the legislation and move on. He also knew that a veto would call into question his leadership abilities and provide ammunition for his opponent in the next election. Nevertheless, Bush vetoed the bill, because his integrity was at stake. As he explained it, "I was willing to take the political heat rather than sign what I thought was a bad law."[16]

These three personal core values—family, faith, integrity—motivate Bush and fuel his success. To succeed as president, Bush needed to feel that these three core values aligned with his political ambitions. Early in the campaign, biographer Frank Bruni wrote, "I'm not sure [that being sworn in as president] was, really, a vision that danced through his head at night."[17] Bush himself admitted to this uncertainty: "Right now I'm determining the extent to which I have fire in my belly."[18]

As the campaign wore on, Bush found ways to align his personal values and the role of president. He saw how the position of president would allow him to champion the family values that he believed in and how he could restore integrity to the highest office. His faith would see him through adversity. Bruni commented on this change: "[B]it by bit, he was embracing his mission, buckling down to it."[19] Once elected, the events of 9/11 seemed to bring the final pieces into alignment, so that Bush felt he was exactly the right person for the job.

FROM PERSONAL TO POLITICAL VALUES

Personal core values describe what is most important to us at home. Professional core values describe what is most important at work. When the two are the same, as in the case of a full-time parent, the values are identical. When people leave their homes and go to a place of work, typically they shift to "workplace" or professional values. For example, most of us don't list "customer service" as a personal value (unless we were raised in the Nordstrom family), but at work it may become the most important value.

People who enjoy their work often find or make connections between the personal and the professional. For example, professional "customer service" may tie into a personal value of service to others. (Most religions include service to others as part of their credo.) Persons in customer service roles at work may feel that their role in the organization is in perfect alignment with their personal value, "being of service."

George W. Bush believes that his political agenda of compassionate conservatism aligns completely with his three personal core values of family, faith, and integrity. These personal values bring fulfillment and happiness to him. He believes that compassionate conservatism gives people the greatest chance for fulfillment and happiness. From a political perspective, Bush believes that his conservative views provide the best chance for families to prosper. Get government off the backs of people and businesses and they can succeed. Allow problems to be dealt with at the local level. Allow the free market to work. In Bush's view, all of these conservative approaches strengthen the economy and support the family—they are the compassionate thing to do.

Bush values integrity and it too plays a major role in his professional mission. Not only does he want to restore integrity to the Oval Office, but he also wants to promote a way of life that allows each person to live with integrity. Bush views traditional liberal solutions to the country's problems as promoting a hopeless mentality in which "we are all victims of forces beyond our control."[20] Liberals, in their efforts to help, have actually worsened the problem, in

Bush's eyes, by creating a society of blamers; *it's always someone else's fault.*

The following statement reveals Bush's political values, but note how his personal values are woven in:

> I am a conservative because I believe in the worth and dignity and power of each individual. My philosophy trusts individuals to make the right decisions for their families and communities, and that is far more compassionate than a philosophy that seeks solutions from distant bureaucracies. I am a conservative because I believe that government should be limited and efficient, that it should do a few things and do them well. I am a conservative because I believe in a strong national defense to keep the peace. I am a conservative because I support free markets and free trade. I am a conservative because I believe government closest to the people governs best.[21]

In this professional statement Bush has included his personal values of both family and integrity. Personal and professional come together in his view of compassionate conservatism. When people refer to him as a compassionate conservative, Bush embraces it: "I welcome the label. And on this ground, I will make my stand."[22]

This clarity is useful. In choosing staff, for example, Bush can build a unified team by searching out candidates who share his compassionate conservative view. It's not necessary to hire people who have the same personal values, because people can be motivated toward the same ends by different values. The key is that the team members feel strongly about compassionate conservatism. Bush explains his selection process as follows: "I select people who are qualified, who share my conservative philosophy and approach to government, and then I expect them to make the calls as they see them."[23] A case in point is Vance McMahan, a member of Bush's Texas staff. When Bush interviewed him for the staff position, Bush said, "I could tell from our conversation that Vance and I shared a conservative philosophy."[24] Bush understands that core values are the glue that holds a team together.

CORE VALUES: A TIMELESS PRINCIPLE OF LEADERSHIP

THE EXPERTS SAY

What the Experts Say

A strong positive culture is one in which values are shared.
Richard Barrett[25]

Core values are the organization's essential and enduring tenets, not to be compromised for financial gain or short-term expediency.
Jim Collins and Jerry Porras[26]

Values and culture are the foundation on which not only behavior but business plans are erected . . . . [T]hey drive everything in the organization.
Jac Fitz-Enz[27]

What the Leaders Say

We strive to uphold fiduciary values: candor, integrity, trust, and fair dealing.
Jack Bogle[28]

It's easy to have principles when you're rich. The important this is to have principles when you're poor.
Ray Kroc[29]

Richard Barrett, a consultant who specializes in helping leaders build values-driven companies, acknowledges the wisdom of Bush's strategy:

Research shows that companies that seek to align the values of the organization with the values of employees, and vice versa,

are more fun to work in, are more successful and are more focused on the needs of their employees and their customers.
Organizations that don't have this alignment tend to be more
inward looking, bureaucratic, and stressful. They may be financially successful, but find it difficult to hire and keep talented
people. Companies that seek to create a values alignment, on the
other hand, have very few problems attracting and retaining talented people. They know what their employees want and they
know how to provide it.[30]

Values are the glue that holds groups together, from families and
religions to organizations and companies.

Although values have always been perceived as being important in
leadership, Jim Collins and Jerry Porras highlighted that importance
in their best-seller, *Built to Last*. They carefully studied 18 outstanding companies and their mediocre counterparts (called "comparison
companies"). They identified the key components of the successful
organizations. Core values were at the top of the list: "Core values
are the organization's essential and enduring tenets—a small set of
timeless guiding principles that require no external justification; they
have intrinsic value and importance to those inside the organization."[31]
Importantly, these values stay the same over time, regardless of what's
hot and what's not. They are essential, enduring tenets, not strategies
or operating practices.

Look again at the professional core values that Bush has laid out:

1. Individual responsibility and choice.
2. Limited government.
3. Strong defense.
4. Free markets and trade.
5. Local government.

These values will not change for Bush as world events unfold. These
are his core beliefs and he uses them to shape all policy decisions. Any
bill brought before him will be tested against these values. Moreover,
he hires people who also embrace these values, and expects them to

use these values in their decisions and actions as well. Clear values allow a team to operate most efficiently. Like a flock of birds, a team can refer to its values and make midflight corrections while staying in close formation. Teams without common values experience more conflict and inefficiency.

Core Values in the Corporate World

Robert D. Haas, chief executive officer (CEO) of Levi Strauss, uses values to help his organization succeed. In the five years from 1985 to 1989, the time period in which Haas implemented his values approach, sales increased 31 percent and profits increased fivefold. Haas says, "Values provide a common language for aligning a company's leadership and its people . . . . Values are where the hard stuff and the soft stuff come together."[32] Here as an example are the guiding values of Levi Strauss, which they call their "Aspiration Statement":

1. New behaviors (openness, teamwork, trust, personal responsibility).
2. Diversity.
3. Recognition.
4. Ethical management practices.
5. Communication.
6. Empowerment.

These six guiding values were extracted from a longer statement, much as we did for Bush's values earlier. We include them to make the point that each leader and each organization will choose different core values that represent what that leader and organization embrace. Clients often ask us, after a day of wrestling among themselves to determine their own core values: "Don't all these values statements look pretty much the same?" Our answer is an emphatic no! Even within the same industry, companies will choose very different values.

Is there ever an instance when the members of an organization simply cannot agree on a set of core values? In our experience, no. Clients have always been able to identify and commit to a common set of values. Collins and Porras report the same experience: "We've never encountered an organization, even a global organization composed of people from widely diverse cultures, that could not identify a set of shared core values."[33] The most diverse group that the authors of this book have worked with was a global financial organization consisting of leaders from Switzerland, America, Germany, Britain, Australia, and Japan. In less than four hours they agreed on and defined these six values:

1. Disciplined and consistent processes.
2. Accessibility.
3. Teamwork.
4. Unique insights.
5. Integrity.
6. Results.

This group of 15 leaders moved through the steps of identifying their shared values smoothly, only bogging down when language became a problem. (The Europeans wanted one of the values to be *transparency*, meaning open and honest. Americans balked at the use of the word because of its connotations.) Since identifying and committing to these six values, these leaders have woven them into the processes of hiring, orientation, evaluation, promotion, and even compensation. They monitor these values over time, rating themselves as to how well they are living out a particular value. Scores for both the value ratings (that is, how well they are living the particular value) and overall corporate performance improved significantly in the period from 1998 to 2001.

Integrating Values into a Culture

A leader's role is to make the values live in the organization. It's not enough for Bush to talk about compassionate conservatism; he must personally walk the talk and make sure that everyone in his administration does so as well. Consider for a moment the following values and ask yourself, "How would I feel about joining an organization that espoused these values?"

Communication
We have an obligation to communicate. Here, we take the time to talk with one another . . . and to listen. We believe that information is meant to move and that information moves people.
Respect
We treat others as we would like to be treated ourselves. We do not tolerate abusive or disrespectful treatment.
Integrity
We work with customers and prospects openly, honestly and sincerely. When we say we will do something, we will do it; when we say we cannot or will not do something, then we won't do it.
Excellence
We are satisfied with nothing less than the very best in everything we do. We will continue to raise the bar for everyone. The great fun here will be for all of us to discover just how good we can really be.

Sound pretty good, don't they? (You can almost taste the apple pie.) Most people would feel okay about joining a company that had these values.

In fact, these are the stated values of Enron (prior to its collapse). Consider how the leaders of Enron put these values into practice. For example, Enron's definition of *respect* was similar to the "golden rule": Do unto others as you would have them do unto you. It's a good ethical litmus test. Yet how did Ken Lay and the other Enron leaders live it out? For starters, Ken Lay misled employees about the outlook for the company. He told them, in the fall of 2001, as people were getting nervous about the future for Enron, that it was bright. The message was: Hold onto your Enron stock, it's going to do fine. Lay gave this rallying cry even as he was *selling* his own shares of the stock. Of course, the much-analyzed story only gets worse from there, as Enron's eventual failure shattered the retirement plans and wrecked the finances of many older employees, who held substantial positions in Enron stock. In short, these stated values had nothing to do with the real culture of the firm. (In fact, the real culture was described to us by a former employee as so cutthroat that he wasn't just worried about getting stabbed in the back, he was worried about getting stabbed in the front!)

Moving from the extreme—Enron, where investors lost nearly $60 billion—to more typical examples, we see lots of organizations that fall short of their stated values. During a series of diversity training events at a large insurance company, we took an informal survey of how many employees could name the company's four core values. This firm had gone to the trouble of printing its four core values on plaques and paperweights several years earlier, so they were clearly established. The result of our survey showed, however, that fewer than 5 percent of the employees could state the firm's four core values.

This example is the rule rather than the exception. Most of the organizations that we work with have talked about values—perhaps even formally identified them, as in the case just cited—but they still need to bring the values to life. They need to make them an integral part of the everyday processes of the organization: hiring, evaluating, promoting, compensating. When we find the rare company that has established itself as truly values-driven, we can almost guarantee that it is enjoying good success. Alignment around common values makes for a strong culture. And strong cultures, as shown in studies by experts like Kotter and Heskett,[34] outperform weak ones.

Doing It Right

American Century in Kansas City has taken this message to heart. It has firmly established these five values:

1. Providing value for our investors.
2. Challenging and inspiring the best people.
3. Building a financially sound company.
4. Being adaptable and innovative.
5. Working with integrity.

The leadership at American Century is so serious about these values that the founder, Jim Stowers, Jr., meets with each new employee to explain them. Every year the company holds an annual conference honoring the five employees who best exemplified these values during the past year. American Century enjoyed tremendous financial success in the 1990s, growing from a relatively unknown investment company to a $100 billion powerhouse at the end of the decade. A significant reason for its success was the stability of key personnel; in the 10-year period of the 1990s, American Century lost only one key leader. Staff turnover at all levels for American Century is about half of the industry average. Because the company has clearly defined its culture, it can hire people who fit—and when employees "fit in" to the company culture, they enjoy themselves, feel connected and purposeful, succeed in their work, and remain with the company. That is why Charles Ellis, a recognized expert in the investment field, says, "Over the very long term, culture dominates."[35]

Much of George W. Bush's success comes from the simple fact that he knows his values and hires people who embrace them. This creates a strong culture. A group of people who have identified core values, defined them, and bought into them make a formidable team. It's the leader's job to make this happen. Not by telling people what their values "should" be. That never works, as seen in the case of Enron. The leader succeeds by surfacing what is really important to his team. What they will rally around. What they will fight for, and, in some cases, what they will die for. Strong cultures are highly motivating. The job at hand gets done.

So, how exactly does one do this "values" thing? Whether you are the leader of a family or the world's most powerful nation, the process is the same.

HOW TO BUILD A VALUES-DRIVEN TEAM

Bush has an advantage when it comes to building values-driven teams. As governor of Texas, and then as president of the United States, he got to choose his staff. Many leaders are not so lucky. You may be one of them! You are assigned a team, rather than having the luxury of handpicking the members. We'll cover both situations, starting with Bush, whose work was to pick people who fit into his conservative framework. Then we'll describe a process that works when you have inherited a team. We use corporate situations, but the process works just as well if you are the leader of a block party, church or synagogue committee, or a household.

Bush succeeds in building high-performance teams because he gets everybody on the same page. Once again, that process starts with clear values. Can you name your own personal values? Professional values? Do they tie together well? Successful leaders identify and clarify their values. Bill Lyons, CEO of American Century, has one written statement for his personal values in life and one for his professional values. The latter contains and reflects what is important to him personally.

If you have not done this work, now is the time. It's the first step to successful leadership. Consider the following list of 100 values and circle 10 of them that appeal to you personally.

Once you have circled 10 personal values, reconsider your choices, and narrow your list down to fewer than six, as Bush has done with his core of three.

1. Accountability
2. Achievement
3. Acknowledging
4. Adaptability
5. Autonomy
6. Balance (home/work)
7. Balance (physical/ emotional/ mental/ spiritual)
8. Being the best
9. Blame
10. Buck-passing
11. Bureaucracy
12. Caring about each other
13. Challenge
14. Clear performance goals
15. Client collaboration
16. Client satisfaction
17. Coaching/ mentoring
18. Collaboration
19. Commitment
20. Community involvement
21. Compassion
22. Competence
23. Conflict resolution
24. Consensus
25. Continuous improvement
26. Control
27. Cooperation
28. Cost reduction
29. Creativity
30. Curiosity
31. Diversity
32. Efficiency
33. Employee fulfillment

34. Employee health
35. Employee participation
36. Empowerment
37. Enthusiasm
38. Entrepreneur-ship
39. Environmental awareness
40. Ethics
41. External com-petitiveness
42. Family
43. Fast (speed)
44. Financial stability
45. Friendship
46. Generosity
47. Global leadership
48. Global perspective
49. Hierarchical
50. Honesty
51. Humor/fun
52. Independence
53. Information sharing
54. Information hoarding
55. Innovation
56. Integrity
57. Internal competition
58. Internal politics
59. Job security
60. Knowledge
61. Leadership development
62. Learning
63. Long hours
64. Long-term perspective
65. Loyalty
66. Making a difference
67. Manipulation
68. Open communication
69. Openness
70. Organizational growth
71. Passion
72. Personal development
73. Philanthropy
74. Positive spirit
75. Power
76. Productivity
77. Professional growth
78. Professionalism
79. Profit
80. Prudence
81. Quality
82. Respect
83. Results orientation
84. Risk-averse
85. Risk-taking
86. Service to clients
87. Shareholder value
88. Short-term focus
89. Slow-moving
90. Social responsibility
91. Spirituality
92. Strategic alliances
93. Teamwork
94. Territory
95. Thought leadership
96. Tradition
97. Trust
98. Vision
99. Winning
100. Wisdom

An exercise that may help in the narrowing process is to fill in a table like Table 1.1 with your values. One of Bush's values, family, is used as an example.

When you've pared the list down to five or six core values, then turn to this question: What values do I believe will make my work group

Table 1.1   Personal Values

Beliefs	Values	Behaviors
1. Family is the basis of a healthy life.	Value family members and time spent with them	Meals together, weekends and vacations together, and the like
2.		
3.		
4.		
5.		

a high-performing team? Some of the values may be the same. For example, in Bush's case, "integrity" is important both personally and professionally. The more closely your personal values and your work values align, the more productive and happier you will be.

Consider the list of 100 values again and choose 10 that you consider to be your top professional values. Use the same narrowing process, combining similar values into a common one. Again, when you've narrowed the list to six or fewer, use a table to fine-tune and better understand your choices. Table 1.2 uses one of Bush's compassionate conservative values as an example.

Table 1.2   Professional Values

Beliefs	Values	Behaviors
1. Free markets are the most productive.	Conservative solutions to to economic issues	Veto bills that increase regulations
2.		
3.		
4.		
5.		

Bush values free markets because he believes that they provide the most productive solutions. They result in greater wealth, so that people can take better care of their families (in particular, feeding, clothing, and educating their children). This value influences the behavior of Bush and his staff, in that they work on behalf of legislation that supports free markets.

When a leader has this sort of clarity concerning core values, he or she can assemble a team of people who not only have excellent skills and talents, but also "fit" with the culture the leader is creating. (We'll cover this in Chapter 4 on hiring the right people.) Importantly, a leader with a good team can go a long way toward heading off disasters before they happen. If Bush hired someone whose answer to every social and economic problem was "more government," they would be arguing constantly about their deeply held beliefs. Is *that* productive? Have you ever witnessed an argument between a conservative and liberal that ends with one of them saying, "Oh, I see your point. Thank you, I've been so blind all these years. I'll be changing my party affiliation tomorrow." (Can you say, "When hell freezes over"?)

Bush promotes efficiency on his team by aligning them around the same basic values. You can do the same, *if* you are lucky enough to get to choose your staff.

Identifying Values in a Previously Established Group

If you inherit a team, which is typical, you need to consider some additional steps for identifying and committing to common values.

First, go through the same steps described in the preceding section for yourself and your teammates. Identify personal values and professional values. Have each person narrow his or her professional value choices to five or fewer and fill in Table 1.2.

At this point you have a room full of teammates who have decided on their own core professional values. The goal is to end up with these people agreeing on five that they—and the rest of the team—can share and support.

To do this, ask each person to pair with another person and decide between themselves which five values are most important. If they have coincidentally chosen the same five (which is highly unlikely), they will have no work to do. Usually, each person has identified different values, so negotiations must begin. Exchanges are often quite animated. This is good. People are talking about what is important to them. They should be fighting for their positions. If the room remains quiet and flat during this part of the exercise, you should be concerned.

The process of pairing continues: When two people have agreed on five values that they both can support, they join another team of two and the negotiations continue. This pairing process goes on until the group is divided into two teams of roughly equal size, each of which has identified five values that all its members can support. List the five finalists from each large group on two flipcharts, so that you have ten values total, and let the teams have a look at what the other group decided.

This process, which was originated by Ken Blanchard,[36] works well because it starts with the individual and then moves toward having the whole group buy into a core set of values. The final list of 10 values is examined for duplicates or closely related values that can be combined under one heading. (For example, *honesty* and *integrity* could be combined into *trust*.)

The next step is to gain consensus from the group on five or fewer values. This narrowing discussion may take an hour or even longer. It's important to let people talk through the differences. After all, the team members are discussing what is deeply significant to them. If you shut down their conversation, you're bound to step on toes. The goal is to walk out of the room with core values that answer these two questions: (1) What do we stand for? (2) How do we want to work together?

When the team has identified its core values, which means that everyone can support the values chosen, then it is time to define those values. Beth Michaels and Dale Primer at Focus Consulting have done some good thinking about the values process and use the following exercise to define the core values.[37] The steps are:

1. Write the name of each core value on a flipchart page and hang the pages around the room.
2. Divide the team evenly into smaller groups. The number of these smaller groups will be one less than the number of core values. (For example, if your team picks five values, make four even-sized groups out of the participants.)
3. Arm each group with a marker and turn them loose on the charts with these instructions: Write down all your thoughts about what this value means to you. What does it look like in action? Give examples. What are the beliefs underlying it? Allot five minutes for each group to work on a value.
4. Have the groups switch to another flip chart after five minutes. (Because you have more value charts than groups, there will always be an open chart available for a free group. This keeps the faster-moving groups from getting bored. They can move as soon as they are done with their current flipchart page.)

If this process seems onerous, remember that you only have to do it once! Core values should stay the same over time. They may possibly be tweaked, or slightly reworded, but there should be no major overhauls. Perhaps now you can see how lucky Bush has been: He gets to bypass this process and go directly to choosing a staff with shared values. Smart organizations have figured this out and, similarly, hire people who fit into their culture.

When the smaller groups finish dumping all their thoughts about each value on the flipchart pages, then:

1. Ask people to stand by one of the values that is especially important to them. Usually the people will divide up fairly evenly around the pages. If one flipchart page is orphaned (nobody's first choice), ask a few people who selected it as a second choice to stand beside it. (If no one moves even then, the group should reconsider whether this value is really so important.)
2. Have the people summarize, in a short phrase or with bullet points, what is written on the flipchart page. How would we recognize this value or, for that matter, a violation of it? Specif-

ics are very helpful here. For example, the global financial firm discussed earlier took all the data on the flipchart page for "Teamwork" and summarized it this way:

Teamwork:

- We acknowledge and leverage cultural differences and capabilities.
- We practice open, global communications and cooperation.
- We encourage constructive criticism, collegiality, and mutual respect.
- We have fun!
- We align our work with our values and vision.

Defining the value helps bring it to life. When people understand what it means, there is greater likelihood of their using it in day-to-day behavior.

3. Have them use simple, everyday language. Harley-Davidson, the motorcycle manufacturer, gives a good example:
   - Tell the truth.
   - Be fair.
   - Keep your promises.
   - Respect the individual.
   - Encourage intellectual curiosity.

We showed Harley-Davidson's values to a team that was working on this exercise, and they were so moved by the language that they almost simultaneously yelled, "Yes, let's make those OUR values!" This was after three hours of selection work that had yielded a significantly different set of values for their team! We had to remind them that values, no matter how good they might sound, have to actually fit the group.

Don't underestimate the power of language, though. Encourage people to find compelling language to express their important values. Bush uses values as a motivational tool all the time. One teacher we know said that she got goosebumps listening to Bush talk about education. Like two tuning forks resonating with each other, when Bush talked about one of his deep passions, it touched the teacher's core value.

In light of the Enron, WorldCom, Arthur Andersen, and other corporate debacles, we have also moved toward having teams rank their values. The fall of Arthur Andersen, for example, can be attributed to a shift in the priority of its values. "In the 1990s, the firm embarked on a path that valued hefty fees ahead of bluntly honest bookkeeping, eroding Andersen's good name."[38]

Which is it for your team: hefty fees or honesty? Seems like an easy decision, but Andersen, whose core business was financial integrity, got it wrong and destroyed the company. Consider the values of your team. Which one comes first? Do any of the values conflict? Have you chosen two that are natural opposites, like "risk-averse" and "entrepreneurial"? Which gets top priority? Ranking values makes for interesting dialogue and constitutes important guidance for team members.

For Bush, it seems clear that family, faith, and integrity come before all else. These values form the core of what he considers personally important, and surrounding them are the conservative principles that he believes promote family, faith, and integrity. In valuing conservative economic principles, such as free markets and limited government, Bush makes a clear statement to his staff that guides day-to-day decisions.

These priorities, though, mean that some issues get pushed to the bottom of the list. The environment is one of them. When Bush took over as governor of Texas, "according to the tri-national North American Commission on Environmental Cooperation, set up by NAFTA, Texas pollute[d] more than any other state or Canadian province. That record include[d] air pollution and water pollution."[39] Ouch. This presented a major conflict in values for Bush, because personally he loves his 1,600-acre ranch. He takes visitors on a 4×4 off-roading tour. He hunts, jogs, and generally loves the outdoors. Despite these personal feelings, Bush did not campaign on the promise of improving the environment. Rather, he promoted his conservative economics, which supports business interests over the environment. Molly Ivins, who always treats Bush less than tenderly, says of his environmental record: "By no known standard has the air of Texas improved under

Governor Bush, nor has anything else involving the environment. He personally intervened to protect major air polluters in the state, and his appointees in this area are staggeringly dreadful."[40]

No one is happy about pollution, least of all Bush. But here's the point: All choices in life involve tradeoffs. Values guide us through the tough decisions. They allow us to say yes to one thing and no to another. Environmental groups may not like what Bush is saying yes to, but at least he is consistent with his own values. The environmentalists can protest, lobby, and support other candidates if they wish. They have different values and priorities. The true danger comes in a case like Andersen's, where the company leaders (and much of the staff) lost sight of their values and priorities. Think about it for a second. Here's a company whose core business is being a gatekeeper for public trust, and it places profits ahead of integrity. How long did they think *that* would last? For a while it worked, but eventually it brought down the entire company. This difference between Bush's clarity and Andersen's confusion is why we encourage you to go beyond just identifying your core values. You should define them and rank them. This is not merely a hypothetical issue—just ask any of the unemployed workers from Enron, Andersen, or WorldCom. Confusion about values can be fatal.

Rating Your Progress

For clarity, have your team members rate the values they've chosen. Ask them how well they are living the value as a team. For example, suppose your team picked "innovation" as a core value. People believe that to be a high-performing and successful team, they will have to be innovative. Fine. On a scale of 1 (lousy) to 10 (excellent), how well are you doing on this value? (That's why it's important to spend time defining these values, so you can evaluate yourselves more accurately.) Have each team member write down the values on a sheet of paper and give each a numerical rating from 1 to 10. The rating should reflect how the team is doing currently, not an aspiration for the future.

The chart in Figure 1.1 shows, on the left, the six values of the global financial firm mentioned earlier and how these value ratings improved over time. The rating for each of the six values has improved since the company started measuring them in May of 2001. Aligning around these six values has helped this organization's performance significantly. As with Bush and his clear priorities, these values guide the team's decisions and actions. The process involves an investment of time and effort, to be sure, but as Peter Drucker, management guru, says, "What gets measured, gets done."[41]

In summary, clear values make for strong cultures. Leaders of strong cultures have woven the values into the fabric of their organizations so that they truly live in the daily work. Further, the leaders in strong cultures know the importance of walking the talk (nothing is as contagious as example). Finally, rating values and monitoring them over

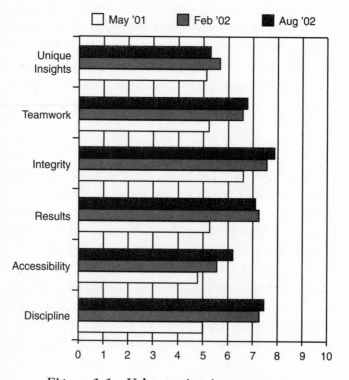

Figure 1.1   Value rating improvements.

time gives evidence of where the team is succeeding and where it needs work. One can only guess what a rating process like the one described previously would have revealed at Arthur Andersen. Perhaps they would have been able to avoid complete collapse.

What are the results from a strong culture? Members of the organization feel connected to their fellow workers and motivated to do the work at hand. They spend less time complaining at the water cooler and more time producing. Employee turnover drops. Evidence shows that the stock prices of publicly traded firms with strong cultures increase more than those of firms with weak cultures. The organization gains a reputation for excellence. It becomes easier for the organization to attract and hire the best people.

Bush understands the connection between values and results. He knows that getting all his team members on the same page enhances performance. Values drive behavior. He used this knowledge in choosing business partners, in governing Texas, and in running the country. Once Bush assembled a team that was clear about its core principles, his team was free to "make decisions based on [those] principles, which are very clear . . . . We don't have to run every decision up the flagpole," said McMahan.[42] Bush was then able to move to the next question, "Where are we going?" Bush answers this question in his vision, which is the subject of Chapter 2.

CHAPTER 2

Where Are You Going?

Inspire Through Vision

*I sought to let people know what was in my heart by
speaking plainly and simply about my vision for our
state's future.*

George W. Bush[1]

When assembling his team, Bush starts with core values and moves to vision. Though his father may have downplayed "the vision thing," "Dubya" understands it well: "I believe my job is to set agenda, to articulate the vision, and to lead."[2] Leaders must focus on the big picture and the overarching questions. Either by nature or through practice, they must learn to get high enough above the action to see the whole picture. There is a good reason why football coaches put some of their staff in the skybox looking down on the field: From this vantage point, leaders can then decide what is important. Bush criticized the Clinton administration on this very point: "For all the administration's rhetoric about reinvention, they never ask the fundamental questions about the purpose of government—what it is doing, or whether it should be doing it at all."[3] In other words, they never went up to the skybox and looked at the big picture to see what should have been changed. Bush consistently operates from the premise that he "must focus on the big picture, [and] let others worry about the details."[4]

Sometimes criticized for his emphasis on general concepts rather than specifics, Bush receives praise from staff members who claim that he effectively focuses on "the forest, and not the trees."[5] Vance McMahan, a staff member from Texas, said,

> There was a meeting in the State Capital [sic] one time in the middle of a drought. [Engineers and wonks] flashed a bunch of graphs and charts and they were talking about whether the state should build this reservoir. After that went on for fifteen minutes, the governor said, "Tell me how much water we have, how much water we're using and how much water we need."[6]

When leaders cut through the fog and identify the key issues, followers feel encouraged that they are making progress. Issues do not stay hopelessly mired in discussion. Priorities are set and orders given because the leader sees the big picture. Aubrey Immelman, an expert on the psychology of presidents, agrees that Bush excels at painting the big picture—in fact, he calls Bush "positively Reaganesque."[7]

Even before his entrance into politics, Bush had a skill for creating a compelling vision. His purchase of the Texas Rangers baseball team was the result of a dream that he would one day own a major league team. As the owner, he had another dream that he and his partners would build a new stadium for the Rangers. The new ballpark would be "an incredible place to watch a baseball game. The ambience [would evoke] a simpler time of family and fun." The fact that Bush and his partners had virtually no money to build the stadium did not faze him. Instead, Bush says, "[W]e had a vision, we developed a strategy, we picked good people like Tom [Schieffer] to manage the project, and the proof was in the results." Indeed, five years later Arlington Stadium was "an unqualified success, a win for everybody involved."[8]

You might suspect that Bush's successes are the product of excellent instincts, honed over time, but actually Bush is quite self-aware. He says specifically that it was his ability to see the big picture and craft an inspiring vision that accounted for much of his success in politics and business: "[W]e succeeded in baseball because we had a vision and a message."[9] The "we" that Bush refers to includes Tom Schieffer, who developed "an ingenious plan and sold it to another big thinker, the Mayor of Arlington."[10] Bush loves big ideas and big thinkers—he noted that his reading initiative in Texas was based on "an idea, a big, bold idea."[11] But we're getting ahead of ourselves; let's back up to his campaign for governor.

In his race for governor, Bush clearly set out his vision to the voters: "I campaigned on a platform of fundamental reform in four major areas: welfare, juvenile justice, tort laws, and education."[12] Running against a popular incumbent, Ann Richards, Bush was clearly the underdog. Governor Richards was not only the most popular governor in the history of Texas, but had also become a national celebrity. Her sixtieth birthday party, thrown by friends at the Austin Coliseum, was hosted by actress Alfre Woodard and included music by Don Henley, Lyle Lovett, and Willie Nelson. Richards could "talk Texas" with the best of them and had a gift for catchy sound bites (like the time she said that George W. Bush was born with "a silver foot in his mouth").[13] Despite this formidable opponent, Bush kept hammering home his vision, with special emphasis on education, for which he holds deep passion.

Eventually, Bush's articulated vision allowed him to defeat Ann Richards, notwithstanding her political skill and popularity. It certainly wasn't his political experience (he had run once for a legislative position and lost) or his war chest of campaign contributions (adequate but not excessive). Skeptics might argue that the Bush name got him elected, but we maintain that it had much more to do with his clear and compelling vision.

When Bush won the race for the governor's slot in Texas, he said that his first challenge of leadership was to "outline a clear vision and agenda." He painted a vivid picture of his goals to the new staff. He also provided them with a description of his core values, as described in Chapter 1: "[H]ere are the principles by which we operate and make decisions."[14] Once priorities and initiatives are agreed on, Bush delegates much of the implementation to his staff and trusts them to carry it out. Bush is a firm believer that a leader "needs to focus on the big picture, his message, and the agenda, and let others worry about most of the details."[15] Chapter 5, on "Leave 'Em Alone," elaborates on this aspect of Bush's leadership methods.

This pattern is characteristic of great leaders. On the battlefields of Europe, General Patton followed the same strategy: Tell your captains which hill to take, but not how to take it. This approach requires confidence in the abilities of one's staff. Bush cannily picks capable people and then lets them figure out how to realize the vision.

Bush's skill at creating a vision both motivates and focuses his staff. It is a powerful way of getting everyone on the same page, which is crucial when dealing with numerous government agencies. As governor, Bush met "regularly with the directors of the criminal justice, health and human services, education, environmental, workforce, and other major agencies, to set a strategic vision and mobilize all our resources toward the same goals."[16]

Later, as a presidential candidate, Bush used this same skill to craft a compelling vision of himself as a compassionate conservative:

> Compassionate conservatism is neither soft nor fuzzy. It is clear and compelling. It focuses not on good intentions but on good results. Compassionate conservatism applies the conservative, free-market principles to the real job of helping real people, all people, including the poor and the disadvantaged. My vision of compassionate conservatism also requires America to assert its leadership in the world. We are the world's only remaining superpower, and we must use our power in a strong but compassionate way to help keep the peace and encourage the spread of freedom.[17]

This vision, combined with the core values discussed in Chapter 1, made up what Bush called the winning formula for the 2000 election: a "positive and optimistic and conservative candidate."[18] Vision is the tool that Bush used to inspire his staff, voters, and even his opponents.

UNDER FIRE

The real test of a leader is what he or she does under fire—and nothing that Bush learned at Harvard, or as a fighter pilot, or as an oil executive, or as a baseball team owner, or even as governor of Texas, could have prepared him for the events of September 11, 2001. Having learned that the Twin Towers at New York's World Trade Center had collapsed, and that the Pentagon was burning, Bush conferred with Vice President Dick Cheney every 30 minutes from Air Force One. The kinds of questions that were coming at Bush were the type usually reserved for movie stars in action/thriller movies like *Armageddon*, such as questions from the Air Force: "Should we shoot down any commercial aircraft heading toward Washington, D.C.?" and "Should we plan a retaliation strike?" Bush cleared the cabin so that he could discuss these issues with the last president who had had to grapple with similar questions, his father.

In the 48 hours that followed the terrorist attacks, Bush responded like a CEO handling a crisis. He resisted the pressure from aides who wanted an immediate declaration of war. He sent senior advisor Karl Rove on a mission to tell professional football and baseball teams to start playing again as soon as possible, with beefed-up security at the stadiums. He demanded authorization of war powers before Congress could demand the right to supply one. And despite the public's initial confusion as to Bush's whereabouts immediately following the attacks, his leadership and actions in the days that followed won him a 90 percent approval rating.

True to form, Bush kept his eye on the big picture. When you consider the pressure he was under, this degree of focus in itself is remarkable. Even on the day after the attack, when his trusted advisor Karen Hughes tried to turn his attention to logistical planning for the morning's photo opportunities, Bush remained clear about his priorities. "We need to talk about the big picture," he told her.[19] Bush did exactly that. In his first speech following the attacks, he reminded the American people of the top priorities: "Our first priority is to get help to those who have been injured, and to take every precaution to protect our citizens at home and around the world from further attacks."[20] Great leaders bring order in the midst of chaos. They help people regain their footing by reminding them of the bigger picture and what must be done now to move toward it.

Time magazine praised Bush for his handling of the war and credited it in part to his clarity of vision: "He is, in a difficult time, what the nation needs in a Commander in Chief—simple in his speech, clear in his vision, confident in his ultimate success."[21]

VISION: A TIMELESS PRINCIPLE OF LEADERSHIP

The idea that vision is important is as old as the Bible: "Where there is no vision, the people will perish."[22] Given Bush's deep Christian faith, it is likely that he is well aware of these words and understands their significance. Centuries ago, someone chiseled these words in the stone walls of a church in Sussex, England:

A vision without a task is just a dream,
A task without a vision is drudgery,
But a vision and a task is the hope of the world.

Leaders provide the vision and workers get about the task. Various personality assessments indicate that a person tends to be stronger at one or the other: vision or task. "Vision" people are comfortable with complexity, dislike details, and use metaphors (Bush does so often: "I was a pitbull on the pant leg of opportunity"[23]; "I'm in charge of hats and bats,"[24] referring to his role with the Texas Rangers). Task people tend to like step-by-step instructions and deal better with specifics than with the abstract. It is clear that Bush's strength is vision. He lets his staff members translate the vision into specific tasks that they then implement.

The business world thrives on the dynamic interplay of vision and task. Southwest Airlines is a good example. This little Texas-based airline, founded by Herb Kelleher, now has the highest market value of any American airline, larger than United, American, Delta, and Continental combined. The stock return from 1975 to 1995 for South-

THE EXPERTS SAY

What the Experts Say

Leaders see the whole picture and articulate that broad perspective with others. By doing so, leaders create a common purpose that mobilizes people and coordinates their efforts into a single, coherent, agile enterprise.

Robert Rosen[25]

Nothing much happens without a dream. For something great to happen there must be a great dream—the dream of an individual person.

Robert Greenleaf[26]

What the Leaders Say

What we're trying to do here is very holistic. The whole company has to believe in the mission, be integrated on the vision and on using it to leverage the company. When it's for real, the suppliers know it, the employees know it, and the customers know it. You can't buy the kind of loyalty that creates.

Ben Cohen and Jerry Greenfield, founders
of Ben & Jerry's Ice Cream[27]

My first act after being named head coach of the Bulls was to formulate a vision for the team. I had learned from the Lakota and my own experience as a coach that vision is the source of leadership, the expansive dream state where everything begins and all is possible. I started by creating a vivid picture in my mind of what the team could become. My vision could be lofty[,] I reminded myself, but it couldn't be a pipe dream. I had to take into account not only what I wanted to achieve, but how I was going to get there.

Phil Jackson, coach of the Chicago Bulls,
six-time world champion basketball team[28]

west (brace yourself, especially if you didn't own any of its stock) was in excess of 21,000 percent! Herb Kelleher will tell you that a large part of the company's success is due to the dynamic tension between him—a visionary thinker—and his right-hand person, the company's president, Colleen Barrett, who is task-oriented. On a popular assessment instrument (the Myers-Briggs Type Indicator), the two of them scored as far apart as is humanly possible. (This story is a real testament to diversity!) As Kelleher put it, "One of our strengths is that we are so complementary."[29]

In some successful companies, the vision and task relationship is reversed: The top executive is more pragmatic and detail-oriented, and his or her right-hand person is visionary. This was the case with Brinson Partners, a global investment firm founded by Gary Brinson in the mid-1980s. Brinson worked closely with Jeff Diermeier, an intuitive, big-picture thinker, to craft a vision of what it would take to be a premier player in the money management business on a global scale. Brinson Partners became so successful that they appeared on the radar screen of United Banks of Switzerland, a giant financial concern, which eventually acquired them in the mid-1990s.

It is also possible for task-oriented leaders to succeed if their business largely depends on operational excellence. The president of one packaging company took the business from a small operation run from her garage to a multinational, $400 million enterprise. The core values of this company are:

- Speed
- Passion
- Operational excellence

This executive has also taken the Myers-Briggs Type Indicator test, and clearly scores as a "Colleen Barrett–Gary Brinson" type of manager: precise, detail-oriented, practical. This woman is a master at promoting focus and efficiency, which is why the company has grown rapidly. As the basic business slows, however, she is aware that the company leaders must enlarge their vision to include new channels of distribution, and possibly new businesses as well. In the traditional language of business, the woman described here has excellent management skills, whereas the Kellehers and Bushes of the world are excellent leaders. In simple terms, leaders plan the work, and managers work the plan. This woman will have to stretch her leadership skills and supply a vision and strategy to guide the company through its current slowdown.

What do today's experts say about vision? Interestingly, it may be the *only* timeless leadership trait they agree on. Peter Drucker, perhaps the top consultant to corporate leaders, believes that no single leadership style, proven or otherwise, works for everyone. He does argue, though, that any great leader must constantly ask, "What are the organization's mission and goals?" In other words, what is the organization's vision of the future? (Remember that Bush criticized Clinton for not asking the fundamental questions.) An article about leadership in *Fast Company* magazine put this point succinctly: "The most important ingredient is the vision. Without that, you're nowhere."[30] Ken Blanchard, another leadership guru, made the same point: "If you're lost, what do you start with? You start with vision."[31]

Consider the case of Ford Motor Company in the mid-1980s. The company was going through bad times, in which both market share and profits were declining, when Don Petersen took over as president and chief operating officer. By the time he retired in 1990, the company had turned around. How did they do it? When asked this question, Petersen said, "Ford's comeback stems from a management meeting in 1984 when the company's leadership adopted the Company Mission, Values, and Guiding Principles." In other words, a successful comeback began when Ford clearly identified its vision of the future.

Great leaders inspire us with their visions. Kennedy spoke of putting a man on the moon. King cried out for the realization of his dream that white and black children would walk hand-in-hand one day. In both cases, the vision energized people, instilled confidence, and invited wide participation.

So how do you develop the ability to create vision?

HOW TO CREATE AN INSPIRING VISION

What makes a great vision? The elements vary from one vision to another, but all truly inspiring visions share some of the same components. Based on their vision work with many companies, Interactions Associates, a global consulting and training firm, compiled the following list:

- **High standards.** Almost by definition, vision suggests a "stretch" goal, something that requires us to go above and beyond the call of duty and everyday pursuits. Collins and Porras, in their book *Built to Last,* call these BHAGs (Big Hairy Audacious Goals).[32] Examples range from Sony's vision of becoming the premier name in quality electronics, thereby transforming Japan's image as a maker of shoddy products; to Motorola's goal of winning the Baldrige Award for excellence (which it did). The purpose of setting high standards is to energize and encourage employees to reach beyond what they believe is possible. As Walt Disney said, "It's fun to do the impossible."

- **Unique attribute.** Visions inspire us because they highlight what is unique about our capabilities. They ask, "What are we truly best at?" Wells Fargo achieved excellent results in the banking industry because its CEO, Carl Reichardt, concentrated on streamlining its operations and remaining geographically focused in the western United States. One of his colleagues remarked on Reichardt's ability to stick to the company's unique attribute: "If Carl were an Olympic diver, he would not do a five-flip twisting thing. He would do the best swan dive in the world, and do it perfectly over and over again."[33] Visions highlight our brilliance.

- **Future focus.** Visions are about the future. They may indirectly extol the past, but they must direct our attention to unrealized possibilities. They excite our imagination about what has not happened but could. Often they include a timeline or date for completion, as did President Kennedy's vision of a man on the moon by the end of the 1960s.

- **Vivid imagery.** Visions paint a picture. Many visions fall flat because leaders do not infuse them with life and energy. As any writer will tell you, the way to do that is with details and stories. A leader at one of the major airlines was preparing to lecture a group of employees about the importance of customer service, a topic about which he cared deeply. In creating his vision statement, though, all he could come up with were stock phrases like, "The customer is always right" or "Treat the customer as you would a friend." These phrases had no juice. Finally, we asked him to tell a story about customer service at the airline. Without hesitation, he told a story about a pilot who stepped out of the cockpit of a 747, went to the gate area, picked up the microphone, and personally apologized to the restless passengers for the long delay. Bingo! Here was a real-life situation that people could immediately understand and relate to. Similarly, consider the vivid pronouncement from Sony, delivered in the 1950s:

> We will create products that become pervasive around the world . . . . We will be the first Japanese company to go into the U.S. market and distribute directly . . . . We will succeed at innovations that U.S. companies have failed at—such as the transistor radio . . . . Fifty years from now, our brand name will be as well known as any in the world . . . and will signify innovation and quality that rival the most innovative companies anywhere . . . . "Made in Japan" will mean something fine, not something shoddy.[34]

- **Unifying theme.** Great visions bring people together. Great leaders understand this. Bush has an instinctive grasp of this aspect of vision statements. In his campaign for the presidency, he stated, "You cannot lead by dividing people. I am a uniter, not a divider. My campaign will be positive, hopeful, and inclusive. I want to show that politics, after a time of tarnished ideals, can be higher and better."[35] Effective CEOs and politicians understand the importance of finding and focusing on common ground.

- **Shared values.** As discussed in Chapter 1, shared values are powerful. For this reason, vision statements often appeal to (and even directly include) values. Bush's unifying theme emphasized the values of positivism, hope, and inclusion. Sony's statement emphasized, in vivid imagery, the Japanese people's shared value of elevating their culture and national status, which had been devastated after World War II.

Let's test Bush's vision of compassionate conservatism using the preceding checklist. Great visions do not have to have each of these components, but typically include at least three. Here are the components he uses:

- *Unifying theme:* Compassionate people and conservative people can walk hand in hand. There's no need to choose sides.
- *Shared values:* Peace, free markets, and freedom.
- *Future orientation:* Encourage the spread of freedom.
- *High standards:* Maintaining peace and freedom in a turbulent world.

These are some of the components of an inspiring vision. Later we will see that Bush incorporates many of these components in the different visions he crafts: some for hiring the right people, others for inspiring those people, and still others for guiding them through crises.

Delivering the Vision

How does a leader deliver the vision? How does it strike the listener? Does the leader come across as intellectual? Emotional? Holier-than-thou? Effective leaders are aware of how they deliver a vision statement. Typically, a good leader recognizes what Freud told us decades ago: that each listener has a child, adult, and parent in his or her psyche. Children are emotional and animated. Parents are full of advice ("shoulds") and beliefs about right and wrong. Adults are objective and take a "grown-up" approach. To be effective, leaders must deliver their visions in a way that speaks to each of these parts of the psyche.

The 1996 presidential campaign with Clinton, Dole, and Perot provided a good example of this model. Clinton appealed to the child in us. He was clearly the most emotional of the three candidates, talking about poverty and racism and reminding voters that he could "feel their pain." Dole came across as the parent, talking about ethics and what was right for the country. Perot, with his charts and graphs, came across as the objective, "adult" personality, presenting the facts and providing logical solutions to the country's ills.

Leaders understand the need to cover all the bases as they deliver vision statements. The delivery must come from both the heart and the head. Leaders need to go beyond well-scripted speeches and *actually* care about their followers. Remember our friend who heard Bush deliver an impromptu speech on education exclaimed that "it took my breath away. He was magnificent." When we asked why, her response was, "He was so passionate and looked us right in the eyes." One of the most convincing instances of George W. Bush's sincerity is that, in the wake of 9/11, he shed heartfelt tears for the families who had lost loved ones—even as he continued to appear strong and resolute about his commitment to fight terrorism.

Some leaders are not especially emotional or imaginative by nature. How can they deliver a compelling vision? A case in point was an engineer at the Woodward Governor Company, which makes parts for jet engines. Stan, a classic task-oriented person, precise and careful, was much like George H. W. Bush, who questioned the "vision thing." When asked about it, Stan said, "I don't get it. My father taught me to work hard and take pride in my work. I have never missed a day of work in 23 years. I show up early each morning and work hard until closing time. My employees do the same. I don't have some grand vision of work." When Stan reflected on this simple, plain vision statement, he found that several of the components mentioned earlier were indeed part of it: high-quality products; the values of precision, hard work, and discipline; and the unifying theme of loyalty. He took these elements and constructed a vision statement that accurately conveyed his profound conviction about what it means to do an excellent job and how important that is. He liked the content of the vision and agreed that it conveyed the deep truth about how he felt.

The problem of delivery remained. Stan was a mild, soft-spoken man. He could not imagine himself jumping on a table, Tony Robbins–style, and delivering his vision in a soul-rocking fashion. From this perspective, he believed that his efforts would always be second-rate. But the truth is that vision statements draw their power from the speaker's authenticity. Once Stan understood this simple point, he was able to deliver his short vision statement with amazing power, because of his own level of conviction.

Personal Conviction and Power

Stan's story reveals an important aspect of vision statements: They are only as powerful as they are true for the leader. When executives cannot touch their own personal passion, they cannot hope to express a vision with fire and conviction.

When executives go on retreat, away from the culture of corporate America, it seems easier for them to tap into their truth and passion and deliver inspiring personal visions. Once they have had the experience of touching on some deep inner truth, they often find that their professional interests stem from the same core beliefs. John, an executive with a medical products company, found that his early childhood experience of losing his mother to cancer directly related to his personal and professional calling of health care. He had originally gone on a weekend "experience" because he was feeling burned out in his career. When he brought to consciousness both his personal mission and then his professional mission of healing, he returned to his work with new passion and a vision about health care for his employees.

But is this ability to create and deliver an inspiring vision really so important? Two experts on leadership, Kouzes and Posner, believe it is. According to them, leaders must have "a vision for the future. This capacity to paint an uplifting and ennobling picture of the future is, in fact, what differentiates leaders from other credible sources."[36]

Vision and the Big Picture

Another facet of visionary leaders goes beyond the creation of inspiring mission statements. Skill with vision implies a leader's ability to see the big picture—to see the forest for the trees. The downfall of Jimmy Carter, with his engineering background, was his preoccupation with details. Bush's style is just the opposite. He focuses on the big picture, leaving the details to others.

Seeing the big picture involves understanding priorities. Jokes about this are common: the fellow who is rearranging deck chairs on the *Titanic*, or the fellow who asks, "Aside from that, Mrs. Lincoln, how did you like the play?" In each case, the person misses the real import of the situation. In contrast, true leaders see what is important even in the midst of chaos. They cling tenaciously to their beliefs, given their better vantage point with a grasp of the bigger picture. An example from industry is Kimberly-Clark. In one of the gutsiest moves in the history of business, its CEO decided to sell the company's paper mills. He saw that, in the bigger scheme of things, this part of the business was doomed to mediocrity. Therefore, he decided to exit that business field and put all the company's resources into the consumer business (products such as Huggies and Kleenex), even though this meant competing against industry giants Procter & Gamble and Scott Paper. The business media and Wall Street did not see the bigger picture and sharply criticized the move. Twenty-five years later, Kimberly-Clark owns Scott Paper and beat P&G in six of eight product categories. Kimberly-Clark's stock price outperformed the general stock market during that time by a factor of four to one. (*Quiz:* Can you name the CEO at Kimberly-Clark who was responsible for these radical changes? See Chapter 10 for the answer.)

The Kimberly-Clark CEO employed an intuitive knowledge that many traditional managers ignore. Nevertheless, many top business leaders claim that their success is due to intuition, which is closely aligned with the skill of vision. It is simply an ability to see beyond what is right in front of our noses. Dr. Daniel Isenberg, a professor at the Harvard Business School who has performed elaborate studies on intuition and corporate success, concluded, "The higher you go in a company, the more important it is that you combine intuition and rationality, and see the problems as interrelated."[37] Bush seems to rely on this very blend of intuition and rationality, which allows him to see the big picture. We'll return to this aspect of Bush's leadership in Chapter 9, "Intuitive Wisdom: Trust Your Instincts."

Building the Skill: Big Picture and Vision

Some people have a knack for the big picture. Carl Jung, the Swiss psychologist, discovered this in the early twentieth century. Jung called these people *intuitives*. Their minds are naturally designed to see patterns, think about the future, imagine possibilities, and see the big picture. Jung called the opposite type *sensors*. They like details, tend to be pragmatic, and focus more on the past and present. Bush is an intuitive. As noted earlier, he states without hesitation that "a candidate needs to focus on the big picture, his message and agenda, and let others worry about most of the details."[38] When aides start to read a lengthy report to Bush, he often asks them to close the report and summarize the findings in a few minutes.

Those of you who are naturally intuitive may be thinking, "So what's the big deal?" Your mind works like this also, so you don't see Bush's approach as being anything special. Detail-oriented people, however, react quite differently. They may well say, "I can't think that way. I like a step-by-step, factual approach." The good news is that these factual thinkers can develop their ability to see the big picture. It just takes practice. Jung saw these mental preferences—for big picture or details—as being like handedness. That is, some of us are left-handed and some right-handed. When we use our dominant hand to write a check or eat a meal, it is quite easy. If we try to do the same with our "bad" hand, the task is much harder. The point is, though, that we can learn to use our "bad" hand. For example, basketball superstar Michael Jordan trained himself to shoot and dribble with either hand. If we are serious about becoming good leaders, we can develop our intuitive (i.e., big-picture) side. Conversely, if we are poor at details, we can work on strengthening those skills.

Whether you are naturally intuitive, like Bush, or more detail-oriented, the following exercises can help you stretch your intuitive abilities:

- Select a problem that you have been wrestling with recently. On a blank sheet of paper, draw a picture of the problem. Do not use words or numbers or people in your picture. If you can, draw a picture of the solution, too. Even if the solution does not make sense, just draw it and consider what relevance it might have to the problem you selected. (Many great thinkers had techniques like this for tapping into their intuitive minds. Thomas Edison used to place pans on the floor and then sit in a chair above them, holding rocks in either hand. When he eventually dozed off, the rocks would fall on the pans, make a racket, and wake him up. Then he would try to remember what he was dreaming about just before he was awakened.) In the same way, drawing helps pull us into the right side of the brain where the intuitive, "big picture" faculties live.

- Another intuitive approach to problem solving is to choose a problem and then ask the next five people you see—including strangers—what they would do in your situation. Take each person's comments seriously and find a common theme in what each has said. Intuitive thinkers are good at spotting the common threads in seemingly unrelated statements.

- Finally, choose an inner image that recurs in your nighttime dreams, or an analogy that you find yourself using frequently, and have a dialogue with it. Visualize it and then say, "Tell me about yourself." We often use this technique with corporate leaders. After the usual joking dies down, we have seen some remarkable breakthrough ideas as a result. Why? Because the technique taps directly into the intuitive powers of the unconscious. Bill Watterson, author of the *Calvin and Hobbes* comic strip, attributes his success to this inner dialogue process. He wrote in the preface to his last book that he let his characters "write their own material. I put them in situations and listen to them." Calvin's answers were things that Watterson, the rational adult, would never have thought of.[39]

Getting Real

Even if you are a fairly intuitive type, creating an inspiring vision can still be daunting. Rituals for assisting in vision creation range from Native American techniques, involving vision quests and sweat lodges, to corporate American leadership training, such as that conducted by Steven Covey and others.

Bush's vision, as presented in his autobiography, *A Charge to Keep*, is compelling because he makes it personal. It's unusual for corporate or government leaders to reveal much about themselves, but the great ones know that talking from the depth of one's being is the only sure way to build trust and inspire people. Bush shows the same openness. In describing the deepening of his faith, through his exposure to Billy Graham, Bush wrote that Graham "didn't make you feel guilty; he made you feel loved." Graham helped Bush to "find God's amazing grace, a grace that crosses every border, every barrier and is open to everyone."[40] Bush is equally candid about the love in his family. When his wife, Laura, gave birth to twin girls, Bush remembers hugging Laura, "both of us weeping with joy."[41] He declares, openly and with pride, that the Bush family is a close one, and that his brothers and sister are among his best friends. In addition, he is aware of and grateful for the unconditional love that his parents have always shown him.

Leaders need to be able to draw from their own passion so that the vision they base on that passion will reach and resonate with others. When corporate executives work on vision statements, they typically feel awkward sharing them with a group. The first few leaders who present their statements tend to play it safe, so their visions come off as tentative and wooden. Eventually, though, one executive will model what it means to speak from the heart. This person delivers his or her vision in a way that conveys power and passion and touches everyone in the room. Bush himself manifests these two different approaches. When he delivers a canned speech from a staff writer, he often appears wooden and unconvincing. But after 9/11, for example, when speaking from his heart about the horrible loss of life, his simple words and moist eyes touched the hearts of people around the world. Such is the power of authentic communication.

To develop your vision, follow these four steps:

1. Start with something personal. Find an object that has special meaning for you: a photo, a piece of jewelry, an heirloom. Talk to a colleague about why this object has deep significance. Allow your feelings to surface.

2. Shift your focus to your role in the organization and the work you do. (Assume for this example that you sell life insurance.) Answer this question: "Why do I come to work each day?" Write down your answer. For example, you might write that you come to work each day to provide customers with the right products for their needs. When you have written your answer, have the person you are paired with ask, "Why do you want to do that?" In other words, what is your underlying motivation to sell customers the right products? To this, you might answer: "Because it will give them financial security." Again, your partner asks, "Why do you want to do that?" You might answer this further question, "Because it gives them peace of mind."

   At this point you may feel that you've found the final underlying reason for your work: to provide peace of mind for people.

3. When you have dug down to the real reason why you do your work—and sometimes this requires as many as four "whys"—then have your partner ask: "How will you develop and grow this ability to provide peace of mind for people?" One possible answer is: "I will continue to study, learn all the new products, develop my interviewing skills," and so on. The answer that you give becomes your "internal" vision, that is, what you are personally doing to become the best that you can be. If you've really dug down to why your work is important, you should feel very motivated to do all the things you list as development steps.

   Bush, for example, really believes that compassionate conservatism will bring greater prosperity and happiness to the average American. He was so motivated by this vision that he was willing to go through the grueling campaign process to gain a place where he could implement it.

4. The final step in the vision process is defining an "external" vision that explains what service you provide to others. For this step, your partner asks, "Why do you want to achieve your in-

ternal vision?" In other words, what difference will it make in the world to accomplish your internal vision? Returning to our insurance example, you might say, "My external vision is to provide my clients with peace of mind through providing financial solutions."

This process helps leaders develop powerful guiding vision statements and avoid the endless wordsmithing sessions that have given vision work a bad name. The work that remains for a leader, after carefully thinking through these four steps, is to add life to the vision by returning to the components of an inspiring vision:

- High standards.
- Unique attribute.
- Future orientation.
- Vivid imagery.
- Unifying theme.
- Shared values.

The insurance executive in our preceding example might start with the external vision statement and then tell a story about a family that she helped, using vivid imagery and possibly describing a future in which all her clients enjoy the same success as that one family. Once the executive completes this fuller, richer statement, it is time to stand and deliver.

Stand and Deliver

The five steps for the final phase of vision are as follows:

1. Read your vision statement to several colleagues to get feedback about its content. Does it make sense? Does it contain components of an inspiring vision? Does it appeal to the emotions, the intellect, and the gut? If not, continue to rework it. If it does, go to the next step.

2. Memorize your vision. Practice it repeatedly until it is second nature. Say it hundreds of times (while shaving, or driving, or waiting in line).

3. If your vision contains a story, practice telling the story in the present tense. For example, "I am sitting with the Joneses and they are telling me that after years of trying they are finally expecting a baby." Stories told in the present tense are more powerful than those that merely recount the past. If your vision is a picture of the future, tell it as if you are in that future—as if the vision has been achieved.

4. Deliver your vision to colleagues. Do it by memory and be authentic. Feel the importance of it as you say it.

5. Have your colleagues rate you on this scale:
   - Engaged and enrolled? ("Yeah, let's go for it!")
   - Moderately interested? ("Sounds good. I can get behind it.")
   - Unmoved? ("Doesn't pass the 'so what?' test.")

Ratings from your colleagues should be recorded immediately. You are looking for an enthusiastic response, not an intellectual one such as, "Well, it all makes sense . . . ." If the feedback from your colleagues is the latter, you need to do some more brainstorming on your vision. Is the content compelling enough? Is it vivid and specific? Is the delivery authentic? Does the delivery address all three parts of the psyche (emotions, logic, and ethics)? What should be changed so that the vision genuinely captures the listener?

In most cases, the missing ingredient is not a detail or a voice inflection, it is simply sincerity. When Bush is handed cue cards to read, he sounds as flat as a Texas tortilla and receives a yawny "unmoved" rating. But when circumstances allow him to speak from the heart, Bush is eloquent and engaging. In remarks made in Sioux City, to a nearly all-white audience, Bush said:

I want to remind you of something about immigration. Family values do not stop at the Rio Grande River. There are moms and dads [who] have children in Mexico. And they're hungry . . . .

And they're going to come to try to find work. If they pay $5 in one place and $50 in another place, and they've got mouths to feed, they're going to come. It's a powerful instinct. It's called being a mom and being a dad.[42]

People want a ring of truth and sincerity from their leaders. To achieve it, though, you need to risk being real. You need the courage to be unguarded. You need the deep conviction that what you are fighting for is valuable.

Bush's skill level concerning vision is the product of his own soul-searching, persistence, and courage. Neither vision nor sincerity can be attained by shortcuts. Bush has deep feelings about what it means to be a compassionate conservative, which is why he can say with conviction: "My enthusiasm for our mission is exceeded only by my confidence that we can succeed."[43]

CHAPTER 3

Can I Trust You?

Become Credible

Now it is required that those who have been given a trust must prove faithful.

One of George W. Bush's favorite
Biblical passages[1]

E ven with values and a vision, a leader will fail if he or she is not trustworthy. A colleague jokes about a young man who is getting coached on leadership as part of being groomed for the top. His mentor says, "It comes down to one thing really: sincerity." The young leader responds cheerily, "Great! I can fake that."

But not for long. Eventually leaders have to deliver the real thing: trust. You can't build agreement around core values and an inspiring vision if trust is missing. Bush is aware of the sacred nature of trust. "Even after many months in the office, he could not stop pinching himself, misting up and reminding himself that he was in possession of something delicate and sacred: the people's trust."[2]

PRINCIPLED DECISIONS

The Karla Faye murder trial in Texas tested Bush's trustworthiness. Karla Faye Tucker had been sentenced to death, first in 1992 and then again in 1993; both times the execution was postponed. Her execution was rescheduled, during Bush's term as governor, for February 3, 1998. A *New York Times* headline captured the discomfort that Bush felt as he wrestled with the decision of whether to allow the death sentence to be carried out: "As Woman's Execution Nears, Texas Squirms."[3]

The case posed a number of problems for Bush. In the first place, Karla Faye was a woman and no woman had been put to death in Texas since 1863. Second, Karla Faye had found religion, in the form of a personal relationship with Jesus, while in prison. People who were concerned about putting a woman to death were doubly concerned about putting a born-again woman to death. The heavy media coverage included interviews with Karla Faye. Celebrities from around the world became involved in her plight. Bianca Jagger flew to Texas to argue on behalf of Tucker for Amnesty International. Pope John Paul II wrote to Governor Bush that Karla Faye was living proof of the redemptive power of faith—the same power that Bush relied on in the at-risk youth programs he supported. The situation turned personal when one of Bush's own daughters challenged him at the dinner table, telling him that she opposed the death penalty.

Bush's response to his daughter is an important lesson in building trust. Rather than defending his position or, worse yet, lashing out at her for holding a different opinion, he welcomed the fact that she was voicing her truth:

> I told her I was proud that she was thinking about the issue, that she had a right and a responsibility to make her own judgment, and she should always feel free to express her opinion. I welcomed that moment. Current events are great teachers, and I was pleased for the opportunity it gave her to express her opinion and independence.[4]

Bush has promoted a similar trust-building environment in his administration. He has made it clear to his staff that what he wants from them is

> thorough research and unvarnished opinion. I don't want them to tell me what they think I want to hear; I try to create an atmosphere where they feel comfortable expressing their ideas and opinions. Whether in a policy or appointments or legal briefing, I'll frequently stop, go around the room, and ask different individuals what they think and why . . . . I want members of my staff to know I think about what they say. It's important to listen, and I often call to follow up or ask about something someone said in a conversation. I do like people to make their points and express their opinions directly and concisely. If I know and trust someone, I would rather have him or her make the case in person.[5]

Persons in leadership positions often make statements similar to Bush's, but they don't mean it. Their underlying truth is captured in the joke attributed to Sam Goldwyn: "I don't want any 'yes' men working for me; I want people who will tell me the truth, even if it costs them their job."

Bush's statements and actions, both at home and with his staff, establish the foundation for safe communication. Trust cannot be held in an unsafe container. Bush does a good job of promoting honest and candid discussion by welcoming a diversity of opinions.

Returning to the case of Karla Faye Tucker: Bush was particularly moved by a letter that she sent him in late January 1998. In it, Karla Faye acknowledged her guilt and took responsibility for the horrible ax murders that she and her boyfriend had committed. Bush struggled with the part that described Karla Faye's conversion to Christianity:

> It was in October, three months after I had been locked up, when a minister came to the jail and I went to the services, that night accepting Jesus into my heart. When I did this, the full and overwhelming weight and reality of what I had done hit me I

began crying that night for the first time in many years, and to this day, tears are part of my life.[6]

Imagine Bush reading these lines! He himself had had a faith conversion, which he described as "the beginning of a new walk where I would recommit my heart to Jesus Christ . . . . Through the love of Christ's life, I could understand the life-changing powers of faith."[7] Presumably Bush could clearly understand Karla Faye's dramatic change in character—and yet, under state law, he was not allowed to grant a pardon unless new evidence indicated her innocence. And no such evidence had been presented.

Even more heartrendingly, Karla Faye went beyond simply admitting her guilt, acknowledging her shame, and claiming that she was a new person. She also vowed to dedicate the remainder of her life, if Bush commuted her sentence, to the benefit of others: "I can, if I am allowed, help save lives. That is the only real restitution."[8]

One way out presented itself to Bush. In Texas, there is a citizen's board of pardons and paroles. This board reviews all cases before the governor makes the final decision. Bush believes that if he had wanted to duck his responsibility in this case, he "could have tried to tell the board how to vote. The members were, after all, mostly my appointees. But that isn't how I operate."[9] Therefore, on February 3, 1998, Bush delivered a short, televised address stating that he would neither pardon her nor grant a 30-day stay of execution. Karla Faye Tucker was given a lethal injection at 6:35 P.M., and was pronounced dead 10 minutes later. Bush claims that that decision was one of the hardest things he has ever done.

Leaders have to demonstrate their principles in their decisions, despite their personal feelings. Clearly, Bush had enormous sympathy for this woman. As a Christian man, he listened to fellow Texans whisper, "She's a good Christian woman, surely you can spare her." Yet he stood fast by the laws of the state and did what he believed was the right thing. We trust people who are consistent and courageous and who, under fire, will do the right thing. Bush showed this in the Karla Faye Tucker decision.

He also showed it, from the opposite perspective, in the Henry Lee

Lucas decision. When arrested on a gun charge, Lucas began confessing to a host of grisly crimes, including having sex with female victims after he had murdered them. Far from the spiritual conversion that Karla Faye had experienced, Lucas remained mean and devious throughout his trial. One reporter who had been following the case closely wrote a letter to Bush remarking on just how difficult it would be to spare a man like Lucas:

> I am fully aware—as a journalist of fifty years—of the political ramification of whatever decision is made in the next few days. But I do have faith that you, of all people involved, have the courage to do what your heart believes is just and proper . . . . [T]he biggest problem here is that Lucas is not a man for whom most people would ordinarily go to bat. He is a colossal liar, a dirt-ball—and a killer.[10]

However, as this journalist went on to point out, there was absolutely no way Lucas could have committed the murder for which he had been sentenced to death. Others, yes, but not this one, the infamous "orange socks" murder (so named because the female victim was found on Halloween, wearing only orange socks).

After reviewing the case, the citizen's board of pardons voted to recommend that Lucas's death sentence be commuted to the lesser penalty of life in prison. The final decision, once again, lay with Bush. Would he spare the life of a serial killer, or would he overrule the board's decision? The Austin *American-Statesman* reported Bush's decision this way: "Gov. George W. Bush, in a rare and politically risky decision, on Friday spared the life of Henry Lee Lucas, once considered the nation's most prolific serial killer."[11]

These two decisions highlight an important reason why Bush has successfully built trust with his political colleagues and opponents alike: He is a man of principle. In his own words, "I base my decisions on principles that do not change. And whether they agreed or not, in the end, I think my fellow Texans knew that in each case, I had tried to do the right thing for the right reason."[12]

Doing what is right is called *integrity*. People with integrity consistently live their values. They are principled. In short, they walk the talk. If they promise to be punctual, then they show up on time. If they promise to be discreet, then they don't blab secrets all around town. You can trust that they have principles and live by them. They are consistent and often they are also courageous.

BUILDING TRUST THROUGH RESULTS

Leaders must also get results or all the integrity in the world will not be enough. When we think of leaders who could not get results, invariably we think of Jimmy Carter. Perhaps no modern president has earned the respect for integrity that Carter has, but history remembers Carter as a president who just couldn't get beyond the details and get the job done. The reverse is true of Nixon and Clinton. Both of them were acknowledged as highly proficient deal-makers, men who could make things happen. In each of these cases, though, their integrity left much to be desired.

Bush has succeeded where these presidents failed because he manages to get results with his integrity intact. Bush uses a classic CEO style to get results: He brings in strong people, lays out a clear vision with specific and measurable goals, delegates the tasks, provides resources and encouragement, and then follows up with accountability and rewards for success.

When Bush took over as governor of Texas, he needed to make good on his campaign promises that he would reform education in the state. He named Mike Moses as education commissioner. Moses had a strong background as a classroom teacher, principal, and finally superintendent of three Texas school districts. Moses shared Bush's insistence on results, saying, "Texas has great teachers and great educators, but we aren't getting the results we want in Texas schools today. We need to be innovators and creative thinkers to achieve excellence."[13]

Moses' innovative approach fit perfectly with Bush's hands-off leadership style. Bush outlined the objectives and let people like Moses carry them out, in whatever fashion they could devise that worked.

Bush and Moses agreed that you "cannot solve a problem until you identify it, so we would develop a teacher-and-child-friendly diagnostic tool to help districts monitor and measure and make sure students were developing building-block reading skills between kindergarten and second grade."[14] While leaving the details of the reform program to Moses, Bush worked to rally resources from businesses, foundations, and other state agencies to support the cause. Bush kept pushing for innovation, not the same old techniques that had resulted in 25 percent of the children in Texas failing their reading exams. Because the priorities were clear—reading was the number-one goal—Bush said that he would consider any new approaches that got results. Bush made it clear that his "interest is not the means, it is the results. If drills get the job done, then rote is right. If it is necessary to teach reading all day long—fine by me."[15] Importantly, Bush added that he would not dictate how the teaching should be done. Rather, he would take very seriously the measurement of the results.

Again, while Moses addressed the problem head-on, with the freedom to do whatever worked, Bush spoke with parents and teachers and community leaders to gain support. He built momentum behind the program. He got professional football and baseball players to give motivational talks in classrooms. The Boy Scouts jumped on the bandwagon and provided more than 1 million volunteer hours of literacy tutoring, inspiring Boy Scouts in other states to do the same.

As dramatic validation of Bush's claim that he is a "results-oriented" leader, the literacy program in Texas paid off handsomely:

- Texas Assessment of Academic Skills (TAAS) test scores increased across the board, for every ethnic group, in every subject, at every grade level tested over the past five years—even though the schools have expanded the universe of children who are taking the test.
- Math scores showed double-digit improvement rates.
- Minority achievement improved dramatically.
- TAAS scores in 2002 broke records, particularly in third-grade reading.
- A "report card" from the National Association of Educational Professionals on math achievement showed that African-American

fourth-graders in Texas ranked first in the nation, as compared to other African-American students around the country.

- Another national report card named Texas as a national leader in improving public schools.[16]

The centerpiece of Bush's reelection campaign in 1998 was additional emphasis on accountability, which included not promoting students who were not prepared for the next grade. Again, Bush focused on results.

Focus and successful results build trust. Although we may like and believe a leader like Jimmy Carter, we ultimately may not trust him because we doubt his basic ability to get the job done. To be trusted, leaders must pave the way for their staff to get results. Bush instinctively does the right things. By setting out clear goals, avoiding the temptation to micromanage, rallying outside resources, and rewarding the winners and result-getters, he builds trust that he and his team can be successful.

Moreover, Bush understands that trust is a two-way street. The more you extend trust to others, the more they will trust you in return. Bush says, "I put a lot of faith and trust in my staff."[17] In the frightening days following the 9/11 attacks, Bush told military staff who were constantly bringing him updates, "Don't bring this to me. I've given you a task, and I have full confidence in you to carry it out."[18] In this way, Bush demonstrated the trust that he was expecting his staff to put in their own people.

TRUST IN PRACTICE

The formula for trust may look easy, but putting it into practice is difficult. During a four-hour session involving the president of a not-for-profit organization and his senior staff, the president several times remarked that, "I am the one who makes things happen." The senior staff members had occasionally voiced objections to these grandiose statements, but seemed to be taking them in stride overall. This idiosyncratic behavior on the part of the leader was apparently acceptable. After all, this organization had achieved tremendous success and status in its field. There was no reason to feel discouraged about its results record.

However, when the president left the meeting early, the members of the team vented their frustration, fuming, "He has to run everything. He treats us like we're all idiots and that nothing would happen if he were gone." One senior team member threatened to quit and another chimed in with, "Me too." And then one of them had the key insight: "He just doesn't trust us." Unlike Bush, who really does trust his staff, this president still wrestles with the trust issue. Leaders gain our trust by first trusting us.

TRUST AND EMPATHY

Yet another way in which Bush builds trust is by being genuinely open and caring with people. Leaders can be honest and competent but heartless. Such a leader may earn the respect of employees, but will rarely garner their loyalty and trust. When Bush was in the oil business, he said "I felt responsible for my employees and tried to treat them fairly and well."[19] It is one thing to say this during good times and another to live by it during hard times. In 1985, Bush's oil business was suffering along with the rest of the industry. The price of crude oil had dropped from $18 a barrel to almost half that level ($10) in just 6 months. Exploration stopped, firms failed, and Bush was forced to sell his small oil business to a larger concern that could better weather the tough times. Thereafter Bush decided to move to Washington to help with his father's presidential campaign. Before he left Texas, though, Bush showed his caring side: "I wanted to help every one of my employees find another job, and I did so."[20]

This action sent the clear, unambiguous message that Bush cared about the well-being of his employees over and above what they could do for him. His actions said, "We're all in this together." This genuine concern for others is a powerful component of building trust.

Another aspect of building trust is simply the willingness to be open, vulnerable, and real. Tears may have ruined other candidates' bids for the presidency, but for Bush, tears are a sign that he cares. In his biography of Bush, Frank Bruni wrote:

> Bush cried when he spoke at the Southern Methodist University event in honor of Laura Bush in October of 1999, and he cried months later when he told an audience in North Carolina how much she meant to him, how much she had sacrificed for him. He cried on about half of the occasions when he talked about how supportive his father had been. He had a soulful, deeply emotional streak, and it grew more pronounced as the [presidential] campaign intensified and the pressure mounted.[21]

Bush's tears in the days that followed 9/11 also showed the nation that the president could be vulnerable. Desert Storm hero General Norman Schwarzkopf once said, "I don't trust a man who doesn't cry." Bush took it to heart when an aide confirmed what he already knew, saying, "The American people need to see you, and you need to show them that you care."[22] In showing his vulnerability, Bush has surpassed the father whom he much admires. George H. W. Bush appeared to the public as a very decent man, but also wooden and detached from real emotion. Quite to the contrary, the younger Bush lays it all on the line when it comes to an emotional issue like trust. "How do we know the United States won't abandon us?" [Pakistani President General Pervez Musharraf] asked. "You tell your people," said Bush, leaning forward and raising his finger as if testing the wind, "that the President looked you in the eye and told you that he would stick with you."[23]

Finally, Bush builds trust with his simple willingness to poke fun at himself. During the infamous "killdee" incident in Texas, in which Bush accidentally shot and killed a bird that was on the protected species list, the media jumped all over Bush. The governor had mistaken this protected bird for a game bird and shot it dead. Rather than dance around the incident, Bush confessed his mistake at a Dal-

las news conference, adding this humor to the situation: "Thank goodness it wasn't deer season; I might have shot a cow."[24] Reflecting back
on this incident, Bush said,

> I think it showed a side of me that voters had not seen. I was
> able to laugh at myself, to make a mistake, admit it, and poke
> fun at it. People watch the way you handle things; they get a
> feeling they like and trust you, or they don't. The killdee thing
> helped fill in blanks the voters may have had about what type of
> person I was.[25]

Biographer Bruni expressed the same sentiment about Bush. Once
while traveling with Bush, Bruni tried to do an end-run around Karen
Hughes, who handled all requests for interviews. Hughes caught Bruni
in the act of asking Bush for an interview and shot him a disapprov-
ing look. Bruni smiled awkwardly and said, "You can't blame me. He
complimented me, and I had to seize the window" (as in "window
seat of the airplane right next to Bush").

Bruni admits it was a silly thing to say. Bush realized it as well and
repeated, "Seize the window?" with a huge grin consuming the entire lower half of his face. "You're talking like me!"

Bruni says of moments like this:

> This was the thing about Bush—whenever you wanted to dis-
> miss him as slow-witted or unreasonably pleased with himself,
> he would do something along these lines. He would show, in
> an instantaneous response, a flash of cleverness and a clear self-
> knowledge about his own failings. And he would be likable,
> just as you were dwelling on aspects of him that weren't so lik-
> able at all.[26]

In researching Bush's leadership, we made it a point to ask friends,
neighbors, strangers on airplanes, "What do you think of President
Bush?" In the responses, we noticed a common theme: "You can trust
him." If you've ever heard Lou Holtz, the famous former coach of

the Notre Dame Fighting Irish football team, talk on leadership, his first question of a leader is, "Can I trust you?" One reason why Bush has had extraordinary popularity ratings in the year-plus following the 9/11 attacks is that people trust him. He instinctively knows how to build credibility.

TRUST: A TIMELESS PRINCIPLE OF LEADERSHIP

Many readers may be wondering why we make such a fuss about trust. "Of course, trust is important to success. Tell me something I don't know!" In fact, trust seems to be so obvious a requirement for the leadership of great organizations that even Jim Collins, in his excellent books on the topic, doesn't discuss trust. It's as if Collins simply assumes that trust is necessary, in the same way that we assume that oxygen is necessary in employees' work spaces.

But world events paint a very different picture. Enron, WorldCom, Arthur Andersen, and other companies are putting trust to the test in the new century. Their actions suggest that they operated from a double standard. They seemed to believe that one can succeed by merely showing an ethical front to the public, while operating unethically behind the scenes. They based their operations on a belief that being honest and being successful don't mix. Competitive advantage is gained by flouting the rules and not getting caught. Marianne Jennings, a professor of legal and ethical studies at Arizona State University, uses the term *ethics creep* to explain this phenomenon. Leaders take small steps over the ethics line until gradually they are way into the territory labeled *corruption*.[27] This is similar to the well-known study in which frogs are placed in a pot of water that is then slowly heated. The frogs never jump out, because the increase in temperature is so gradual, and eventually they are boiled to death. Likewise, leaders who get scalded in their own ethical waters often express disbelief at what has happened. "How did it go this far?" they wonder. Same way—a gradual increase in "temperature." Those of us watching our waistlines can certainly relate to creep. It applies to overeating as well: a sliver, a slice, a slab, a slob!

THE EXPERTS SAY

What the Experts Say

Organizations are no longer built on force but on trust.
Peter Drucker[28]

Trust is the highest form of human motivation. It brings out the very best in people. But it takes time and patience, and it doesn't preclude the necessity to train and develop people so that their competency can rise to the level of that trust.
Stephen Covey[29]

Successful risk management is built on trust. Top executives must learn to trust their people. Throughout our research, we found both small and large examples of risk taking that were based on trust.
Jac Fitz-Enz[30]

What the Leaders Say

Good teams become great ones when the members trust each other enough to surrender the "me" for the "we."
Phil Jackson, coach of the six-time world champion basketball team, the Chicago Bulls[31]

Individuals want leaders that they can trust . . . people in whom they can believe. Trust involves affirmative answers to such basic questions as, "Can I count on you?" "Will you keep your commitments?" "Can you hold sensitive information in confidence?" etc. Skillful leaders inspire trust in their followers.
Brian Billick, coach of the world-champion Baltimore Ravens football team[32]

In the political arena, Presidents Nixon and Clinton tested the trust principle, discovering in the former case that it cost him the office altogether and in the latter that much time, effort, and political capital were wasted sorting out the mess and trying to rebuild trust.

Actually, the ethical debacles in business make the case for trust better than any piece of academic research could. Investors watched nearly $200 billion of market value evaporate as the truth about Enron and WorldCom surfaced. It's impossible to ignore calamities of that magnitude. Even the most profit-driven bosses are taking steps to make sure that their businesses are clean. Values, ethics, and trust are becoming a hot topic as Wall Street struggles to regain credibility and President Bush insists on tougher sanctions for white-collar crime.

Let's not ignore academia, though. What does the research show about trust and leadership? Is trust a timeless principle in effective leadership?

The Center for Creative Leadership, in Greensboro, North Carolina, has been researching the topic of leadership for decades and has concluded that the best predictor of success in an organization is leadership that behaves with integrity and honesty. In addition to these two core traits, three other related traits were identified: "loyalty, trustworthiness, and pride."[33]

Alfred DeCrane, Jr., chairman of Texaco, Inc., reached a similar conclusion from his own experience in business:

> Real leaders are fair and honest, and not just because of laws and regulations; they are ethical, open, and trustworthy. These basic roots of character, perhaps more than any others, garner the respect that is needed in order for an individual to be called a leader. I've been in business long enough to see that short-term "wins" can be achieved without these qualities, but I've also seen that lasting leadership and success—at whatever level—is impossible without them.[34]

More evidence of the importance of trust comes from a study performed by Bruce Pfau at Watson Wyatt Worldwide. He and his colleagues studied 750 North American and European companies to discover the relationship between various human resource practices and stock prices (details are provided on their website: www.watsonwyatt.com/research/). The study by Watson Wyatt showed that "leaders play a key role in the establishment of a collegial company culture. Improving the trust and integrity associated with company leadership builds shareholder value by 2.3%." Now, you might think that 2.3 percent doesn't sound like much. Well, pick a company at random—say, Allstate Insurance Company. Its market value is around $30 billion. A 2.3 percent increase represents a dollar gain of $690 million. That will pay for a few bent fenders!

Another piece of evidence is provided, indirectly, by Collins and Porras's study of visionary companies in *Built to Last*. As noted earlier, Collins and Porras don't examine trust explicitly, but they do name "consistency" between core values and actions as one of the characteristics of visionary companies. Trust is the byproduct of companies that are consistent in this way, companies that "walk their talk." In fact, this criterion of consistency is the most dramatic difference between the visionary companies and the list of comparison companies that Collins and Porras chose for the study. Thirteen of the visionary companies (out of eighteen selected) met this criterion, whereas none of the eighteen comparison companies did. The visionary companies outperformed the comparison companies in the stock market more than sevenfold in the period 1926 to 1990.[35]

An example of integrity comes from the visionary company Johnson & Johnson. Its response to the Tylenol crisis in the 1980s was completely consistent with its values. When it was discovered that a few of the bottles had been intentionally tampered with (outside of company control), Johnson & Johnson pulled *all* the bottles off the shelves, despite the high cost, to keep any other users from being harmed. Another, more recent example of integrity comes from Baxter, which manufactured a faulty kidney dialysis machine that resulted in the death of several patients. The CEO, Harry Kraemer, immediately assumed responsibility and shut down all production, setting up a relief fund for the victims. At the same time that Baxter was taking these actions, Arthur Andersen's leaders were saying, "We didn't do anything wrong" (with straight faces). Given that Baxter had only recently acquired the company that actually produced the dialysis machines, Kraemer could have excused himself and Baxter and blamed it all on the "new" subsidiary. Instead, he didn't even mention that fact, taking complete responsibility and the full brunt of the bad publicity and liability.

A survey conducted by the International Association of Financial Planners in the financial services area showed that the primary factor in people's choice of a financial advisor is trust—way ahead of performance, credentials, or accessibility. This survey was performed before the Enron and WorldCom debacles, so we can only assume that the results would be even more dramatic today. The average American is yearning for a square deal, a fair shake, and a level playing field (and fewer clichés).

We know that trust is important, even critical. But what exactly *is* trust? The dictionary defines it as "assured reliance on the character, ability, strength, or truth of someone."[36] Robert Bruce Shaw, author of *Trust in the Balance,* has broken it into three components. Leaders who do well in all three areas are considered trustworthy:

1. Achieving results: Following through on goals and commitments.
2. Acting with integrity: Behaving in a consistent manner.
3. Demonstrating empathy: Respecting the well-being of others.

Shaw poses specific, behavioral questions to reveal whether a firm's leaders are enhancing or eroding trust. For example, in the area of "Achieving results," Shaw asks respondents to identify which of the following statements is more true for their leadership team:

- There is little agreement on our key performance targets and measures (low trust).

or

- Everyone understands our "vital few" performance targets and measures (high trust).

By translating the concept of "achieving results" into these specific behaviors, Shaw created a survey that provides a very useful barometer for the trustworthiness of a leadership team. In this way it is possible to measure and diagnose trust.[37]

The results of a survey by Focus Consulting Group completely support the contention that trust is a key component of successful financial organizations. Excellent firms—defined as those that had two times the asset growth of the industry, half the staff turnover, and top quartile fund performance—showed strong trust ratings. Comparison companies, with only average performance, rated average to low on the trust scale. Figure 3.1 shows the results of the study, comparing the trust index of high-performing (good results) and low-performing (poor results) companies.

In the beginning of this chapter, we reviewed some of the ways in which Bush builds trust in each of the three critical areas. In the case of Karla Faye Tucker, Bush showed that he is a man of integrity. We can trust him to act in accordance with stated values and principles, even when doing so is painful and difficult. The Karla Faye Tucker

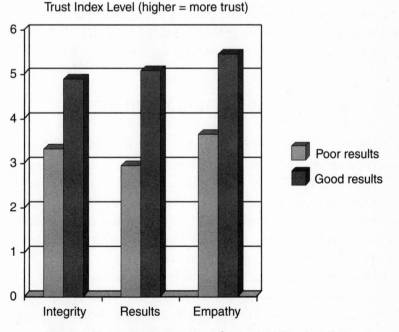

Figure 3.1   Comparison of trust index levels.

decision was hard for Bush. In fact, Clay Johnson, a staff member, saw how deeply the event affected Bush and said to him, "You should worry if you didn't think this is a hard thing to do. It's a good thing, not a bad thing, that this affects you this way."[38] Bush himself had this to say after he heard the announcement that the prisoner was dead: "I sighed and picked up the phone to call Laura. I said I called to tell her I was on my way home, but the truth is, I wanted to hear her voice."[39] We trust leaders who make the right decisions under pressure. These leaders have integrity.

Bush also builds trust by getting results and by helping his staff get results, as demonstrated in the previous example of his initiatives for reading and education in Texas. We trust leaders who are competent and who know how to get the job done. This aspect of trust and leadership is so important that we dedicate the whole final chapter of this book to it.

Finally, Bush builds trust by being open and caring with people. After listening to Bush deliver an impromptu talk at the White House to a small group of visitors, a friend told us that it gave her shivers. His eye contact, sincerity, and passion left her completely convinced of his honesty and trustworthiness. His genuine tears of grief after 9/11 showed the same openness and vulnerability.

HOW TO BUILD TRUST

Leaders build trust by understanding the three pillars of the trust platform: results, integrity, and empathy. Each leader tends to have strengths and weaknesses among these three. The good news is that often the weak areas can be strengthened simply by awareness and attention. It usually represents a blind spot rather than some character defect. If leaders devote a small amount of effort to it, they often improve their "trust ratings" dramatically.

Before looking at some ways to reinforce the three pillars of trust, consider that many trust issues are simply the result of poor communication. A leader may have the best intentions, be very competent, and be extremely honest, yet still be mistrusted. Why? Because of a simple misunderstanding. It happens all the time. The joke about the three elderly British gentlemen on the train is a classic about poor communication:

First Gentleman, looking out the window: "Is that Wembley?"

Second Gentleman, looking at his watch: "No, it's Thursday."

Third Gentleman, looking at his paper: "So am I. Let's get a drink."

This joke may be far-fetched, but everyday trust is often eroded because of similarly botched communications.

Leaders can reduce the danger of miscommunication by following a simple formula when making agreements:

1. Make a proposal.
2. Clarify.
3. Get agreement.

As simple as this formula looks, it can help enormously to build trust and avoid many embarrassing moments. For example, at one point in our career, the authors of this book were asked by a government agency to do some conflict resolution work. We met with the head of the human resources department and some of his in-house staff. They put us through the paces as far as probing our background experiences, competencies, techniques, and so forth. Finally, they decided that we passed muster and said the all-important words, "Let's look at some dates." Six of us in the room opened our calendars and performed the "open date" dance for ten minutes until finally we had agreed on six dates to meet and work with their team. So, as a group, we completed the steps of:

1. Proposal (i.e., propose dates to do the work).
2. Clarification (i.e., double-check to make sure we had the dates correct).
3. Agreement (i.e., write them in our calendars).

Simple, eh?

Not so.

The first of these meetings, called "All Hands on Deck," was a short session to explain to the 60 staff members why we had been hired and what they could expect. The date was set for October 5, about two months in the future. As time passed, we received several offers from prospective clients to do work on October 5, which we (of course) declined because we were already booked. Finally, on October 3 we called the head of HR at the agency to ask about preparation for the first session. He responded, "Well, the money never came from Washington, so we'll have to postpone those sessions." We were so shocked that for a moment we didn't know what to say. (We had turned down other clients to save these dates!) We were angry, but we did our best to employ Stephen Covey–style wisdom: Seek first to understand, then to attack . . . er, we mean, then to be understood. The agency leader went into a long description of how funds are allocated in the federal government, which really didn't strike us as need-to-know information. When he finished, we asked what we thought was the obvious question: "When were you going to tell us that the job had been postponed?" (After all, it was two days before the scheduled start time.) His response? "Well, we were hoping right up to the last that the money would come, but now we have to assume that it isn't."

The conversation was so strange that neither of us knew how to respond. Oddly, but importantly, the man at the agency did not seem evasive or apologetic. He sounded as though his conscience were perfectly clear. We finally stumbled on a good question, which we recommend to anyone in a similarly awkward situation. We started by saying, "Could you help us?" This opening immediately puts people at ease. You, the questioner, are making yourself vulnerable. You are saying, "I need help from you." Most people will drop their guard and hear your next question—which for us was, "What could we have done differently to avoid this outcome?"

The agency leader responded, without missing a beat, "When the other clients called you, you should have phoned us and asked if this job was still on track." To him, this made perfect sense. For us, it was the craziest thing we'd ever heard. Was he suggesting that every single project on our calendar was tentative, and that we should always call clients back to see if they really want us to show up on the agreed-on date (or whether they were just kidding)?

Ever since this incident occurred, we've used it as an example to show the importance of clarity in building agreements and trust. In the instance with this agency, we had not clarified exactly what it meant to agree on a date. For us, it meant "Done deal; turn away other business." For them it meant, "Check back and see if the money has arrived." This misunderstanding cost us a significant sum of money. More importantly, this example shows that two competent and honest people with good intentions can still miscommunicate and damage trust levels.

To avoid making agreements that later blow up and damage mutual trust, try this exercise with your team. It will highlight the need for clarity. On a sheet of paper, write down the italicized words:

- *Late?* (How many minutes must pass until a person you are waiting for is late?)
- *Medium-priced dinner?* (How much does a medium-priced dinner for one person cost in this town, including cocktail, dessert, and tip?)
- *Crowd?* (How many people constitute a crowd?)

After each of the three items, ask your team members to write a number. Poll the room to find out the high–low spread for each item. Write the high and low numbers on a sheet of flipchart paper, as shown in Table 3.1. (We've used numbers that represent the biggest spreads we've seen.)

Once you have created a grid like the one in Table 3.1, tell your team that a client has asked you to set up a dinner to meet members of the team. The client's expectations are: "Be punctual, medium-priced dinner, and not a big crowd." What she means by this is given on the left: –5 minutes, $12 each, and 8 or fewer people. Your interpretation is on the right: 20 minutes late is acceptable, $65 per person is reasonable, and up to 1,000 attendees is fine. Your team will

Table 3.1   High–Low Estimate Spreads

	Lowest Number	Highest Number
Late?	–5 (you must be there 5 minutes early or you are late!)	20 minutes
Medium-priced dinner?	$12	$65
Crowd?	8 people	1,000 people

get the point quickly: Checking for clarity of understanding is critical. In this case, your client expects to spend less than $100—but based on your understanding, the dinner tab may be more than $60,000! (Can you say *unemployed*?)

The point, again, is that trust has everything to do with expectations and clear communication. Performing the second step—clarify—can help in this regard.

The final step of the process—check for agreement—is also critical. Many leaders do a good job on the first two steps but fall down on the final step. They make a proposal, explain it carefully, ask for any clarifying questions, and then (here's the mistake) they simply say to a roomful of people: "Okay, everybody on board?" This form of agreement usually leads to the "20-Step Agreement." When people leave the meeting, they appear to be in agreement. After all, nobody voiced disagreement. But 20 steps down the hall they say to their colleagues, "Nah, I don't buy that!"

Leaders need to use skill in finding out how much agreement really exists.

- First, they need to create a sense of safety so that people can disagree without fear. (Remember Bush's comment to his daughter when she disagreed about the Karla Faye Tucker decision?)
- Then they need to use an appropriate question to determine the level of agreement. A negative poll is more effective than the proverbial, "Does everyone agree?" approach. A negative poll turns the question on its head: "Is there anyone who does not

agree with this proposal?" or a variation, "I'd like to invite different opinions at this time. Does anyone see it differently?" (The ultimate negative poll is heard at weddings: "If anyone objects to the union of this man and this woman, speak now or forever hold your peace!")

Watch how decisions are reached in the next meeting you attend. Rarely does a leader use the negative poll, even though it is a very useful tool for building trust and agreement.

Another tool for building trust is the one provided by Shaw. Leaders must inventory themselves on the three scales: results, integrity, and empathy. Leaders can survey their colleagues and staff using the following statements. Respondents can answer using a scale from 1 (strongly disagree) to 7 (strongly agree).

Results:
As a leader, I . . .
1. have articulated a clear strategic direction that will enable us to achieve our objectives.
2. gain widespread agreement on necessary roles and accountabilities.
3. make decisions on tough issues in a timely manner.
4. hold people accountable to the highest standards of performance.
5. create a sense of urgency and a drive to succeed.[40]

Successful leaders, like Bush, will score high on these items. Bush has made "get results" his mantra. Strong leaders must get results to be trusted. (We'll cover this more fully in chapter 10.)

The second part of the trust inventory involves integrity. In this survey, leaders ask:

Integrity:
As a leader, I . . .
1. act in a manner that is consistent with our organization's values and beliefs.

2. am committed to a well-known strategic vision and set of values.
3. "walk the talk" in following through on my commitments to others.
4. hold people in the organization to the highest ethical standards.
5. deal with reality as it exists, facing the hard truths and difficult situations.

This set of statements tests whether the leader is consistent and courageous in action. Leaders at Enron were skillful at getting results, it is true, but they took shortcuts and talked out of both sides of their mouths. (As we noted earlier, Kenneth Lay told employees that Enron's business prospects were strong, even while he was selling his own Enron stock.) In the Karla Faye Tucker trial, Bush made a decision that was hugely unpopular but was consistent with his set of values and his understanding of the law. It took courage to do the unpopular thing.

Finally, leaders must also show that they care for their associates. The simple image here is that of a captain and his crew. In this image, everyone is literally on the same boat. If the boat sinks, the captain and crew all go down with it. This is the ultimate trust scenario, where each person's fate is tied to the others'. Quite the opposite happens in many corporations. The Enron executives jumped off that sinking ship with millions of dollars, leaving many of the crew members financially bankrupt. There was no sense of caring; rather, it was every man for himself. (The same thing has happened on ships, we might add. *Titanic* owner Bruce Ismay did not like the cluttered look of 48 lifeboats on deck, so he ordered 28 of them removed. When the ship sank on its maiden voyage, there were not nearly enough lifeboats for the 2,228 passengers and crew, but Ismay found room on one.)

When Bush's oil company failed, he made it a point to help each employee find new work. He did not abandon them. Another CEO on the west coast was told by his board of directors to lay off 30 employees. That CEO agonized over the decision, but finally agreed. He then personally met with every one of the designated people, explained the reason for the layoff, and apologized. We've since spoken with some of those employees, and every one of them would like to work for that CEO again if they had the chance. Caring builds trust. The attitude of caring is, "We're all in this together."

The third part of the trust survey measures a leader's ability to empathize with employees:

Empathy:
As a leader, I . . .
1. care about people and treat them as more than a means to an end.
2. treat others as partners, sharing both risks and rewards of performance.
3. believe all people are capable of great accomplishments, and empower them to act.
4. strive to provide the support (training, advice, etc.) needed to be successful.
5. remain accessible to people and open to discuss key business issues.

Leaders who receive high scores on all three scales are rare indeed. Bush is one of those leaders who clearly excels at building trust. Even with a tough character like Russia's Vladimir Putin, Bush has built the level of trust to the point where Putin said, "Over the last year and a half or two years, what we've experienced is a huge growth in confidence and trust manifested between our two countries."[41]

CHAPTER 4

Bring in the Right People, Part One

Don't Be Afraid to Hire People Smarter Than You

The next challenge was to build a strong team of effective people to implement my agenda. I worked hard to recruit the very best.

—George W. Bush[1]

Q: What do the following words and phrases have in common?

sought advice from close associates
Bush's team of headhunters
choosing
had come highly recommended
I found him
I put on a full-court press
recommendation from
convinced . . . to join our team
recruited
persuaded

A: They are all words used by George W. Bush, or about him,
    in any discussion about bringing in the right people.

In most organizations, we say that we're going to "interview someone"; Bush says he's going to "recruit someone." We say we're going
to "decide on who we want to hire"; W. says he's going to "choose."
We say we're going to "offer the person the job"; he says he's going
to "convince the person to join our team." We say we're going to
"advertise the position"; Bush says "I found the person."

What's the difference between George's words and ours? His are
about selling himself, the organization, the cause, and the position to
the right person for the situation. Ours are about the person's selling
themselves and us deciding to buy or not.

Bush's process is about research, personality fit, and persuasion.
G.W. determines what's needed for a particular position and who has
those skills, characteristics, and attributes. He discovers whether the
position and organization match someone before he interviews that
person. Bush's interviews thus can focus on how the person's personality melds with his own, and he prides himself on being a good judge
of people. Between the extensive upfront research and the early parts
of the interview, Bush is rarely presented with a person who is not a
perfect match for the position. All that's left—and he's a master at
this—is persuading the person that this is the right position for him
or her.

Well, you think, "Who wouldn't want to work with a candidate for
governor or president? Who wouldn't want to work for the governor
of the state of Texas? Who wouldn't want to work for a major league
baseball team? Who would say no to working for the President of the
United States?"

PERSUASION

"I asked Mike Weiss, a longtime friend and accountant from Lubbock,
who had valuable experience with state government as a member of
the governing board of the massive Employees Retirement System,

to come to Austin to help me get a handle on the state budget," first-term Governor-elect Bush said.

> Mike quickly identified the brightest budget mind in the state of Texas, Albert Hawkins, and told me I needed to persuade Albert to join my office as our budget director. Albert had been with the Legislative Budget Board for more than twenty years, and he was reluctant to leave the relative security of the role. When Albert came to the transition office to meet with me, he told Joe Allbaugh that he had come as a courtesy, indicating he probably wouldn't accept the job, but I put on a full-court press. I outlined my vision for Texas and told Albert it was time for him to put his years of experience to work in a leadership role that would help set the tone for all state government. I assured him that not only would he have the freedom to run the Governor's budget division, he would also be part of the decision-making process on every major issue in the Governor's office. Albert joined our team.[2]

When you're looking for people who are smarter than you—which is what you will be looking for—you'll be selling instead of buying.

Dick Cheney began by supervising the selection of Bush's vice presidential running mate. He had said that he didn't, under any circumstances, want to be considered for the job. However, he found that the more time he spent with Bush, the more confidence in and excitement for Bush's plans he developed, and that made him want to be VP. Bush still had to persuade Cheney to take the job. He wanted Cheney because of Cheney's experience in foreign affairs (which Bush lacked). He wanted Cheney because Cheney had had a long career in politics (which Bush lacked). He wanted Cheney because Cheney was patient and calm (which Bush struggled with).

Bringing in people who are smarter than he is requires Bush to know his own skills, characteristics, and attributes, as well as the ones needed for the position. That's how Bush knows what he's looking for: the person he needs to bring in will complement Bush's own abilities. Bush has said he couldn't possibly know all the information necessary to make good decisions.[3] No one can. Part of the leadership genius of George W. Bush is just that, knowing that no one can know everything—and further recognizing that leaders *shouldn't* know everything. Chapter 5 gives examples of leaders whose decision making (and in fact, whole organizations) have been bogged down by their trying to know everything and make every decision.

Bringing in people who are smarter than you keeps decision making and operations moving forward, because they are not dependent on a single person's knowledge and skills. This independence also helps you persuade those smart people to come and work with you. The following statements could be about you and your organization:

- When Bush was governor of Texas, he invited cooks, security officers, and personal staff of the governor's mansion to a private holiday party, where he gave out funny awards for unusual events that had taken place during the preceding year. Each year he invited his senior staff and major appointees to a formal holiday dinner to thank them.
- "He has assembled a great team of quality people, and it has been an honor for me to work with all of them."[4]
- "My first impression was one of tremendous energy."[5]
- "George W. Bush was the kind of candidate and officeholder political hacks like me wait a lifetime to be associated with."[6]

Persuasion is about what you have to sell and how you sell it.

RESEARCHING

Much has been said about Bush's deficiencies in foreign policy, lack of attention to detail, and big-picture orientation. Doris Kearns Goodwin, author of *No Ordinary Time, Franklin and Eleanor Roosevelt: The Home Front in World War II,* said of George W. Bush after September 11:

George Bush has around him a strong group of foreign policy advisers. They had worked together in the past, they had experience, they knew this part of the world, they knew these problems. That put him in a better position than a rookie President with rookie advisers. But it also showed a strength, that he was willing to put people who had a stronger reputation and more experience into his Administration than he himself had. That action shows a certain self confidence on the part of a leader. That's what Lincoln did in spades when he put into his cabinet all the rivals who thought they should have been President instead of him.[7]

"Governor," reminded a reporter on the presidential campaign trail, "you said you would always have people around you, as president, who would fill in any gaps in your knowledge of the world and the players on the world's stage."[8] So who did he find? For starters, Colin L. Powell. Secretary of State Powell was a professional soldier for 35 years, during which time he rose to the rank of four-star general and served as the 12th Chairman of the Joint Chiefs of Staff, the highest military position in the Department of Defense. During this time, he oversaw 28 crises, including the highly successful Operation Desert Storm in the 1991 Persian Gulf war.

George W. has always researched to determine what he needs for a particular position and who has those skills, characteristics, and attributes. Many times those skills are ones he doesn't have. He's a good judge not only of people, but also of his own skills, characteristics, and attributes. He knows what he needs to complement himself.

"I needed someone educators would trust to lead them in a new direction," said then-Governor Bush. "My staff and I were involved in the selection process, which resulted in the naming of my first choice. Mike Moses." In Chapter 3 you read about how Mike's innovations helped Bush deliver on his campaign promise to reform education, so you already know that he turned out to be the great hire Bush thought he'd be. Why? Because, as Bush says,

He shared my philosophy of local control of schools and high standards, and education was in his blood. His father was a long-time teacher who had retired as a professor and head of the Education Administration Department at Stephen F. Austin State University. Mike started his career as a classroom teacher, became principal, then worked as a superintendent in three different Texas school districts. He had earned a reputation as an innovator, someone who was not afraid to try new things. I liked what he had done in Lubbock, where he advocated early intervention of at-risk students and established an alternative boot-camp school staffed by drill instructors to try to redirect the lives of students with discipline problems. He also gave parents and students greater choice and flexibility in selecting which schools to attend, created a new parent training program and worked to increase parental involvement in the schools. His strong financial management had turned the school district's debt of $4 million to a surplus of more than $12 million in 4 years. I also liked the fact that he had experience in three very different school districts. Experience that would offer a lot of insight into the problems and proper role of the state education agency.[9]

Bush knew that educators would trust an educator—and Bush wasn't an educator. He didn't have the credentials, the job experience, or the skills. So he went out and found someone who did. That someone also had to fit the position (Texas Education Commissioner), the organization (the people and government of the state of Texas), and the personality of the boss (Governor George W. Bush).

The perfect person—the one you really want to go pursue—may not always be recommended by others, as was the case with George Tenet, director of the Central Intelligence Agency (CIA) since 1997. Others may have regarded Tenet as an unlikely choice to run the war on al-Qaeda, but Bush didn't see it that way. He knew Tenet was obsessed with Osama bin Laden ("almost abnormally obsessed," said former Oklahoma Senator David Boren, Tenet's mentor). Most importantly, Bush knew Tenet had a plan. Over the summer of 2001—

"when we were getting a lot of chatter in the system about potential threats," National Security Council (NSC) chief Condoleezza Rice recalled—Bush ordered the CIA and the NSC to draw up a comprehensive proposal for breaking al-Qaeda for good. "I feel like I'm swatting at flies," Bush complained. "I want a way to take the network down." Tenet's team was working one up when al-Qaeda attacked. Bush trusted Tenet, even liked him. The president matches his desire for loyalty with an unshakable faith in his ability to judge people instantly; to "look them in the eye," as he likes to say, and size them up. Despite being a Clinton appointee, Tenet had passed those tests months before.[10]

Clearly, Bush's leadership genius in bringing in the right people lies not just in his research and persuasion abilities, but also in his willingness to hire people who are smarter than he is—no matter whose appointee they were. So check your ego at the door, and then get on with the recruiting!

PERSONALITY FIT

Because Bush has already done the research on fit for skills, characteristics, and attributes, his interviews can be conversations to determine personality fit:

I was looking for a travel aid[e], someone whose personality would meld with mine, someone young and hardworking and willing to spend long hours on the road. We spent the next hour and a half talking about family and business and religion and politics. [The interviewee] told me about growing up in Eagle Pass, a small Texas border town, and about being the first member of his family to graduate from college. I always want to know about people's backgrounds and families. I like people, and I'm interested in learning more about them, plus I believe people's values and priorities are rooted in their upbringing.[11]

Wait a minute.

- Ask about family and religion?
- Look for someone young?
- Someone "whose personality would meld with mine"?
- Put on a full-court press?

Up until this point, we've all been thinking, "Yes, yes, let's do it George's way. My goodness, this is sensible." But if you weren't getting a knot in your stomach while reading what Governor Bush talked about with his potential new travel aide, your labor attorney was. Every attorney, every consultant, every human resources (HR) professional, every book on finding the right people says, full-court press? No way! You should play hard to get (act like you have other candidates); only ask things you need to know (and you'll be hard pressed to prove to the Equal Employment Opportunity Commission that you needed to know about the family or religion of a candidate for the job of gubernatorial travel aide); and never select by age.

We believe that Bush's way works (and believe us when we say we're not using information about people's backgrounds to discriminate against them; one of us is an HR professional). Like Bush, we use such information to understand where the person is coming from. Doing that allows Bush to get a sense of what a person believes and where he or she is going. He hears people's core values and learns their priorities by asking about their background and family. Core values and priorities rarely roll off the tongue in response to a question like "What are your core values?" (They will, of course, for you, now that you've read Chapter 1, "What Do You Stand For?" In fact, you need to know your values so that you can determine whether a person's match well with yours.)

Learning peoples' core values and priorities by talking with them about their backgrounds in general is legally risky. You'll have information that can't easily be proven to be related directly to the skills needed for the position. Nevertheless, this information will tell you things about the person's characteristics and attributes that are hard to verify through research alone. An interview of this sort tells Bush, and it can tell you, the person's core values. Knowing that their values match yours is crucial to bringing in the right people. Bush takes the legal risk that he might be called upon to prove that he didn't use information about a person's background to discriminate against that person. We take that legal risk too, and we take it every time because the benefits (a match with our core values) outweigh the risk (hiring the wrong person). Bush's thorough researching before interviewing keeps the legal liability down. By learning what he needs for a position and only talking with people who have those skills, characteristics, and attributes, he only interviews people who are so close to right that all it takes is the persuasion.

The May 1999 issue of *Texas Lawyer* said, "The Governor chose people as if running a business (whether appointments or direct staff)."[12] So hold on with your "is this legal?" questions; we'll look at how we can make this work in your world in a few pages. Labor attorneys, humor us. Keep reading. First we'll explain the unique combination of activities that George W. Bush uses to bring in the right people (see Figure 4.1 along with examples of each activity). Then we'll work on how you and your organization can apply these activities to get the people you need to bring in.

So you've just gotten the leader's job. Most people get 10 weeks to find the right people for 1,125 posts requiring Senate approval, and for 5,000 other jobs as well. This time, you have 5 weeks. No problem; you have 18,000 résumés. Using only the activities noted in Figure 4.1, you find all the people you need—and you can bet that lots of them are smarter than you are. They have to be. They have to do their jobs and you have to do your job. Each person, if chosen well, is uniquely qualified for that job. When time is short (and isn't it always?), you need to rely even more heavily on George W.'s tried-and-true methods that get you the right people—really smart people.

"Those who cannot remember the past are condemned to repeat it," asserted George Santayana, the American philosopher. George W. Bush will rarely commit heedless errors, because of the extremely smart, been-around-the-block people he has hired along his leadership route. As president-elect and as president, he has taken full advantage, in hiring, of institutional memory. In fact, he's now hired enough people from his father's administration that his own is being called the "Restoration."

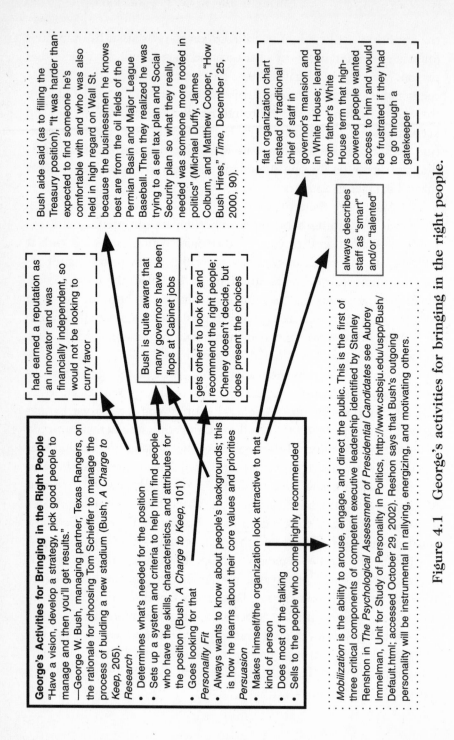

George's Activities for Bringing in the Right People

"Have a vision, develop a strategy, pick good people to manage and then you'll get results."

—George W. Bush, managing partner, Texas Rangers, on the rationale for choosing Tom Schieffer to manage the process of building a new stadium (Bush, *A Charge to Keep*, 205).

Research

- Determines what's needed for the position
- Sets up a system and criteria to help him find people who have the skills, characteristics, and attributes for the position (Bush, *A Charge to Keep*, 101)
- Goes looking for that

Personality Fit

- Always wants to know about people's backgrounds; this is how he learns about their core values and priorities

Persuasion

- Makes himself/the organization look attractive to that kind of person
- Does most of the talking
- Sells to the people who come highly recommended

---

had earned a reputation as an innovator and was financially independent, so would not be looking to curry favor

---

Bush is quite aware that many governors have been flops at Cabinet jobs

---

gets others to look for and recommend the right people; Cheney doesn't decide, but does present the choices

---

always describes staff as "smart" and/or "talented"

Bush aide said (as to filling the Treasury position), "It was harder than expected to find someone he's comfortable with and who was also held in high regard on Wall St. because the businessmen he knows best are from the oil fields of the Permian Basin and Major League Baseball. Then they realized he was trying to a sell tax plan and Social Security plan so what they really needed was someone more rooted in politics" (Michael Duffy, James Colburn, and Matthew Cooper, "How Bush Hires," *Time*, December 25, 2000, 90).

---

flat organization chart instead of traditional chief of staff in governor's mansion and in White House; learned from father's White House term that high-powered people wanted access to him and would be frustrated if they had to go through a gatekeeper

---

Mobilization is the ability to arouse, engage, and direct the public. This is the first of three critical components of competent executive leadership identified by Stanley Renshon in *The Psychological Assessment of Presidential Candidates* see Aubrey Immelman, Unit for Study of Personality in Politics, http://www.csbsju.edu/uspp/Bush/Default.html; accessed October 29, 2002). Reshon says that Bush's outgoing personality will be instrumental in rallying, energizing, and motivating others.

Figure 4.1 George's activities for bringing in the right people.

Figure 4.2 gives examples of the caliber of people he has recruited for his time in the White House. Look at the amazing diversity in just these few examples: diversity in ethnicity, in education, in sex, in geography, in experience, in age. His has been called the most diverse administration ever in the White House. Bush's process for bringing in the right people has led him to one successful hire or appointment after another. Had he not taken the risks associated with learning about their backgrounds, he would have missed some really smart, supremely capable people. Had he not ignored the jibes about "can't find your own people," he would have missed many of the tried-and-true, really smart people—the best kind.

George W. Bush brings them in and inspires them to want to stay with him. Remember Bush's travel aide? He was with Bush since that first interview in 1993 for the gubernatorial campaign staff. Karen Hughes has been with Bush since that campaign, too. Joe Allbaugh has been with him since that campaign. Karl Rove has been with him since that campaign. There are plenty of others, but you get the idea. New blood is important because it keeps an organization from being change-resistant. However, building a team with low turnover is paramount. Having the same people working together for years has created some wonderful efficiencies for the Bush team. Karen Hughes knows him so well, it's said she can finish his sentences. You'll see in Chapter 5, "Leave 'Em Alone," that Bush's staff can guide, support, and coach each other, simply because they know one another so well. These can be efficiencies only because Bush brought in the right people. Keeping the same people, if they are the wrong people, is not only inefficient for you the leader, but also damaging to the future of your organization.

"A governor's appointments are a lasting legacy. Long after you leave office many of the people may still serve. I believe I have helped put in place a new generation of leaders of my state" (Bush, *A Charge to Keep,* 109).

- *Andrew H. Card, Jr., Chief of Staff*
U.S. Secretary of Transportation under President George Bush. Coordinated administration's Hurricane Andrew disaster relief efforts. Directed Bush administration transition office. Assistant to the President and Deputy Chief of Staff to President Bush. Special Assistant to the President for Intergovernmental Affairs and subsequently Deputy Assistant to the President and Director of Intergovernmental Affairs to President Reagan. General Motors Vice President of Government Relations. President and CEO, American Automobile Manufacturers. Massachusetts House of Representatives. National Republican Legislators Association Legislator of the Year. Massachusetts Municipal Association Distinguished Legislator. University of South Carolina, B.S. (Engineering). Attended United States Merchant Marine Academy and the John F. Kennedy School of Government at Harvard University.

- *Richard (Dick) Cheney, Vice President of the United States*
U.S. Secretary of Defense. U.S. Congressman (House Minority Whip). White House Chief of Staff to President Ford. Deputy Assistant White House Chief of Staff to President Ford. Nixon administration staff member. Chairman/CEO, Halliburton Company. Attended Yale University, B.A. (Political Science); University of Wyoming, M.A. (Political Science); University of Wyoming, doctoral studies. Chair of National Endowment for the Humanities. Author. Educator.

- *Ann M. Veneman, Agriculture Secretary*
USDA Deputy Secretary. Deputy Undersecretary of Agriculture for International Affairs and Commodity Programs. Associate Administrator of USDA's Foreign Agricultural Service. Actively involved in the Uruguay Round of GATT negotiations, NAFTA, and the United States–Canada Free Trade Agreement. Secretary of the California Department of Food and Agriculture. Member of board of directors for Calgene Inc. Board member of the Close Up Foundation. International Policy Council on Agriculture, Food and Trade, a group funded by Cargill, Nestlé, Kraft, and Archer Daniels Midland. University of California at Davis, B.S. (Political Science); University of California at Berkeley, M.S. (Public Policy); University of California, Hastings College of Law, J.D.

- *Joe Allbaugh, FEMA Director*
Chief of Staff to (Texas) Governor Bush. Campaign manager for George W. Bush's campaign for governor. Deputy Secretary of Transportation for Oklahoma. Part of the "iron triangle" (with Karen Hughes and Karl Rove). Governor George W. Bush's point person for 9 presidential disaster declarations and more than 20 state-level emergencies. National Campaign Manager for Bush/Cheney 2000. Oklahoma State University, B.A. (Political Science).

- *Karen Hughes, presidential counselor*
Communications Director for George W. Bush for Governor campaign (Texas), Communications Di-

rector for Governor George W. Bush. Communications Director for George W. Bush for President campaign. Executive Director of the Republican Party of Texas. Television reporter. Southern Methodist University, B.A. with honors (English and Journalism).

Hughes is fiercely loyal to Bush; she's among the few who can get him to insert something into a speech that he didn't originally want to.

- *Karl Rove, Chief of Staff*
Manages the Office of Political Affairs, the Office of Public Liaison, and the Office of Strategic Initiatives at the White House. Chief strategist for George W. Bush's presidential campaign. Deputy Chief of Staff to Governor William Clements. Executive Director of the Fund for Limited Government. Special assistant to Republican National Committee Chairman George H. W. Bush. President of Karl Rove Company, an Austin, Texas-based public affairs firm that worked for candidates, nonpartisan causes, and nonprofit groups. Attended University of Utah, the University of Texas at Austin, and George Mason University. Taught at LBJ School of Public Affairs and in the journalism department at the University of Texas at Austin.

- *Donald L. Evans, Commerce Secretary*
Chairman of the Bush/Cheney 2000 campaign. Worked for George W. Bush's congressional campaign and Bush's successful gubernatorial campaigns. Oil rig roughneck for Tom Brown Inc. CEO,

(continued)

Tom Brown Inc. Chairman of the Board of Regents of the University of Texas. Board member of the Scleroderma Research Foundation and TMBR/Sharp Drilling. President of the United Way. Jaycees Man of the Year. University of Texas at Austin, B.S. (Mechanical Engineering); University of Texas, M.B.A.

- *Joshua Bolten, Assistant to the President and Deputy Chief of Staff for Policy*
Executive Director for Goldman Sachs International in London. General counsel to the U.S. Trade Representative in President George H. W. Bush's administration. Deputy Assistant to the President for Legislative Affairs in first Bush's administration. International Trade Counsel to the Senate Finance Committee. Worked in the legal office of the U.S. State Department. Princeton University, B.A.; Stanford Law School, J.D.

- *Paul O'Neil, Treasury Secretary*
Chairman and CEO, Alcoa. President and Vice President, International Paper Company. Deputy Director, OMB. Computer systems analyst, U.S. Veterans Administration. Board of Directors of Lucent Technologies and Eastman Kodak. Fresno State College, California, B.A. (Economics); Indiana University, M.A. (Public Administration).

O'Neill's unique experience in transforming an old-economy firm into a new-economy success has been chronicled as a study by the Harvard Business School, and studied in business schools across the nation.

- *Condoleezza Rice, National Security Advisor*
Director and Senior Director, Soviet and East European Affairs in the National Security Council. Special Assistant to the President for National Security Affairs for President George H. W. Bush. Special Assistant to the Director of the Joint Chiefs of Staff. Stanford University, Provost and Professor of Political Science. Stanford Center for International Security and Arms Control, Senior Fellow of the Institute for International Studies. Board of Directors for Chevron Corporation, Charles Schwab Corporation, University of Notre Dame, International Advisory Council of J.P. Morgan, San Francisco Symphony Board of Governors, Center for a New Generation, Transamerica Corporation, Hewlett Packard, Carnegie Endowment for International Peace, and National Council for Soviet and East European Studies. University of Denver, B.S. (Political Science); University of Notre Dame, M.S. (Graduate School of International Studies); University of Denver, Ph.D. Author of *Germany Unified and Europe Transformed* (with Philip Zelikow), *The Gorbachev Era* (with Alexander Dallin), and *Uncertain Allegiance: The Soviet Union and the Czechoslovak Army.*

- *Elaine Chao, Labor Secretary*
President and CEO of United Way of America.

Director of the Peace Corps. Deputy Secretary at the U.S. Department of Transportation. Chairman of the Federal Maritime Commission and Deputy Maritime Administrator in the U.S. Department of Transportation. Vice President of Syndications at BankAmerica Capital Markets Group. Board of Directors for Dole Food, Clorox, C.R. Bard, and HCA. Distinguished Fellow at The Heritage Foundation in San Francisco. White House Fellow. Transportation Banker with Citicorp. Mount Holyoke College, B.A. (Economics); Harvard Business School, M.B.A. Studied at M.I.T., Dartmouth College, and Columbia University.

- *Norman Mineta, Transportation Secretary*
U.S. Secretary of Commerce under President Clinton. Vice President at Lockheed Martin Corporation. U.S. House of Representatives (for California's Silicon Valley district). Chairman of the House Public Works and Transportation Committee and Aviation Subcommittee, 1981–1988; chair of Surface Transportation Subcommittee. Co-founded the congressional Asian Pacific American Caucus and served as its first chair. Chaired the National Civil Aviation Review Commission. San Jose City Council and Mayor. University of California at Berkeley, B.A. Served in U.S. Army as intelligence officer. Awarded the Martin Luther King, Jr. Commemorative Medal by George Washington University for his contributions to the field of civil rights.

Source: Bush White House biographies come from the Center for Responsive Politics, Politics1.com (accessed July 14, 2002); *Directory of Major US Officials* (Denton, Tex.: University of North Texas, 2000); and Bush, *A Charge to Keep.*

Figure 4.2 Biographies of selected White House appointees.

HIRING PEOPLE SMARTER THAN YOU: A TIMELESS PRINCIPLE OF LEADERSHIP

George W. Bush's way works—even though some of the activities are totally contrary to the current wisdom about attracting and hiring the right people. Let's take a look at what that current wisdom is.

☑ *For the Bush Way:*

- Set up a system and criteria to help find people who have the skills, characteristics, and attributes you need for the position.

Carolyn B. Thompson, in *Straight Talk for Employers*, says, start with a plan that targets people who will be successful at meeting your customers' and organization's needs—and then recruit only that type of people. The upfront planning is time-consuming, but if you figure out who will be successful and pursue only those people, you will not have to waste time interviewing or responding to people you don't want.

Recruitment is a marketing and sales process, something most of us are very familiar with. The only difference is that instead of marketing and selling your products and services, you are marketing and selling yourself, and your company as an employer, to potential applicants. You'd never waste your organization's time and money marketing to customers who didn't need your product/service, so don't do it with potential employees.

The product/service marketing and sales process begins with a marketing plan. What should we sell? Who wants to buy it? Where are they? What will attract them? Your recruitment plan (the way to market you as an employer to potential employees) will be the same.[13]

- Determine what's needed for the position.

Write a job description that lists every task the individual will be doing, throughout the entire work day. Brian Tracy, in *Hire and Keep the Best People*, wrote:

THE EXPERTS SAY

What the Experts Say

I follow the precept taught in Proverbs 22:29[:] "Do you see a man skilled in his work? He will stand before kings. He will not stand before obscure men."

Larry Burkett[14]

Employers don't have time to waste with unproductive employees, or even people who have to be coddled, coaxed and disproportionately supported to get their jobs done.

Roger E. Herman, strategic business futurist[15]

What the Leaders Say

I assigned company execs to make note of talented people they meet and actively maintain the contacts. When a position opens, they pass the name to the HR department.

President of a fast-growing technology consulting company[16]

When you're hiring, you want people who love you and love the values of your company.

Anita Roddick, The Body Shop[17]

What will the person be expected to do? Think of the job as a production process and identify each step in the process as a task that must be completed to a particular standard of performance. Identify the key result areas of the job and write them down. A single omission can lead to a hiring error.

We hired an Account Executive with a great track record in sales and account development for another company. We felt lucky to have her but within two weeks she fell apart. What went wrong? When we looked into it we found that the previous company had advertised heavily and generated a continuous supply of leads which she followed up on. At our company she had to generate her own leads. She just couldn't do this and we'd not made it clear to her that she needed to. We assumed she knew that prospecting was part of the job.[18]

- Go looking for that person.

In *Winning the Talent Wars*, Bruce Tulgan said, "Once you have a clear picture of the work itself, the remaining questions are obvious: Who is the best person to do the work? Where will you find the people you need? And are they available when you need them?"[19]

- Get recommendations.

In *Get the Best*, Catherine D. Fyock tells us that "[y]our goal is to build relationships with others who will share your commitment to finding the best candidates for your organization."[20] Even if you don't currently know people who can make recommendations, you can set a goal and implement it to build that network of recommenders. (Bushisms have been incredibly successful in bringing W. to fame, so we thought we'd try it.)

- Make yourself and your organization look attractive to that kind of person.

"Understanding and appreciating what good people want from their managers and employing organizations is the important first step to meeting those expectations," says Roger E. Herman in *Keeping Good People*.[21]

☑ *Against the Bush Way:*

- Learn about people's backgrounds (personal).

The website of Fairfield & Woods recites the labor attorney's conventional wisdom:

Federal statutes prohibit employment discrimination based on race, color, religion, sex, national origin, age, and physical or mental disability. Local ordinances may add marital status, sexual orientation and many others to the protected classes. Employers should take care not to run afoul of these laws when interviewing job applicants. During interviewing, no questions should be asked which directly seek information about the applicant's inclusion in any of the protected classes listed above. Questions which indirectly might elicit such information should also be avoided. For example, questions about where an applicant's parents come from may seek information about national origin, questions about the applicant's date of graduation may get you information about age, and questions about which organizations an applicant belongs to may get you information about religion, race, or national origin.[22]

George W. Bush knows that the basic rule is this: Only get the information you need to know to determine if the person will be the right one to handle the job. He has found that success in choosing the right person comes from knowing the people's backgrounds. "I believe people's values and priorities are rooted in their upbringing," he says. Yes, it's true that gaining such information about candidates' backgrounds can cause you to run afoul of the law. We'll show you how to plan and safely execute such conversations so you can get the benefits of the George W. way without running afoul of the law, your HR staff, and everyone's attorneys. (We're not just blowing smoke or using "fuzzy math" here; remember, one of the authors of this book is an HR professional who wrote a book saying "don't do it.")

- Do most of the talking.

"Since we are born with two ears and one mouth we should listen twice as much as we speak. . . . Do you spend more time talking than listening when you interview? Interviewing experts say that the most effective and efficient interviews are those in which the interviewer talks only 25% of the time," says Carolyn B. Thompson in *Interviewing Techniques for Managers.*[23]

Later, when we tell you how to do most of the talking, you'll think we're talking out of both sides of our mouths; that was the same Carolyn Thompson who wrote this book. Keep reading— we'll explain.

✓ *Undecided about the Bush Way:*

- Sell to the right people.

In most of the places we looked for the current wisdom on selling to the right people, we found only sentences (not Chapters, not even paragraphs). Among the few we found is a snippet from Stewart and Cash's book, *Interviewing Principles and Practices*: "Sell the advantages of your position and organization. Do not lie to applicants, intentionally hide negative aspects of the position or organization, or inflate applicant expectations."[24] This is certainly useful information on what not to do, but lacks anything on the "how" of selling the advantages.

Robert W. Wendover, in *Smart Hiring*, tells us that "[t]hroughout the interview process, remember that you need to sell the company as much as the candidate needs to sell to you. The candidates you want do their homework, investigate your organization, and ask tough questions when their turn comes."[25] This, however, suggests that your only role in selling is to be able to answer candidates' questions.

Catherine Fyock's *Get the Best* says that recruiting is marketing and selling, and she gives lots of examples of actual marketing campaigns. In regard to selling, though, she only tells us about some managers who weren't good at selling their companies. Even Carolyn B. Thompson's *Straight Talk for Employers*, which describes how to develop a recruiting marketing plan and how to make yourself attractive to the people you want to hire, doesn't specifically deal with how to sell yourself and your organization by persuading people.

Given this obvious gap in the literature, we synthesized a "how-to" method. We've created a system, including tools and strategies, for applying Bush's successful actions to bring in the right people in a way that works for you, your organization, and the people you need to bring in.

HOW TO HIRE PEOPLE SMARTER THAN YOU

We know you want to be as successful in bringing in the right people as W. has been, but you're concerned about that ugly "Against" list—especially the conventional wisdom on learning about people's personal backgrounds and doing most of the talking. We'll show you how to apply Bush's unique combination of activities for bringing in the right people to the specific people you need to bring in. This will allow you to do everything G.W. does while staying within your organization's policies and your attorney's comfort zone.

George's Activities for Bringing in the Right People

Researching
- Determines what's needed for the position.
- Sets up a system and criteria to help him find people who have the skills, characteristics, and attributes for the position.
- Goes looking for those people (gets recommendations).

Personality Fit
- Always wants to know about people's backgrounds, to learn about their core values and priorities.

Persuasion
- Makes himself and the organization look attractive to that kind of person.
- Does most of the talking.
- Sells to the people who come highly recommended.

Researching

- G.W. determines what's needed for the position.
- G.W. sets up a system and criteria to help him find people who have the skills, characteristics, and attributes needed for the position.
- G.W. goes looking for those people (gets recommendations).

You begin researching by determining what's needed for the position and setting up a system and criteria for finding people who have the skills, characteristics, and attributes that match the requirements of the position. You already know how to do this research. It's exactly like the research you do to determine which customers will want to buy your organization's services and products, and when setting up a system and criteria for finding those customers. You probably call it a marketing plan: What should we sell? Who wants to buy it? Where are they? What will attract them? A "Right People for This Position" marketing plan (see Figure 4.3) leads you easily through determining what's needed for the position and discovering the criteria for finding people whose skills, characteristics, and attributes match the position. You are marketing you as an employer to those people. Figure 4.4 shows what the plan would have looked like that led Bush to bring in Mike Moses.

We know you already have two questions:

1. How can I fit this into my already-beyond-reason schedule?

First, read Chapter 8 on being disciplined.

Second, recognize that, yes, upfront planning takes time. Then answer these questions:

What will the people need to know and be able to do, including things we can't? *(skills needed)*

What should these persons' core values and priorities be? *(characteristics and attributes needed)*

Who are the potential people whose skills, characteristics, and attributes match the ones needed? *(target market)*

Where will we go looking for people like this? *(who to approach to get recommendations)*

Figure 4.3 "Right People for This Position" marketing plan.

TX Education Commissioner POSITION

What will the people need to know and be able to do, including things we can't? *(skills needed)*
    Someone educators would trust to lead in new direction
    Past experience as teacher/administrator focusing on core curriculum
    Creative
    Flexible
    Strong financial manager (including budget setting/management)

What should these persons' core values and priorities be? *(characteristics and attributes needed)*
    Autonomy Direct interaction with policy maker (Governor Bush)

Who are the potential people whose skills, characteristics, and attributes match the ones needed? *(target market)*
    Superintendents of school districts getting high academic results from recent changes implemented

Where will we go looking for people like this? *(who to approach to get recommendations)*
    Those currently working as superintendents in Texas

Figure 4.4 "Right People for This Position" marketing plan for Texas Education Commissioner post.

Which takes longer, upfront planning and researching that helps you determine the requirements of the position, and setting up a system and criteria for finding the right people, or hiring the wrong person?

Which takes longer, upfront planning or wasting time on interviews with and responses to people you don't want?

2. Many of my positions have the same or similar tasks, so the target markets will be the same. Do I have to write out a plan for every single position?

   Develop a plan that covers multiple positions for which you need to bring in the right people now. This responds not to the number of positions or people the plan should cover, but to the just-in-time nature of our needs. If you develop a plan now and think it will apply in six months (or even three), you're working in a different world than most of us. Note: As a shortcut, we develop plans first; then, when we need to bring people in for that position again, we whip out the old plan and update it.

The research and the plan together are the key to getting recommendations. Once you research what's needed for the position, and know what kind of person will have the right skills, characteristics, and attributes for the position, you'll tell others (the recommenders). Give the written plan to people who are likely to know the right people for the position. Bush could have given the sample plan from Figure 4.4 to current and past superintendents in Texas when he needed to fill the education commissioner position.

Even better, stay in contact with recommenders constantly, not just when you need to fill a position. The organizations that are fully staffed with the right people take recommendations continuously, not just when there's an opening. Doing this will help you to build a pool of right people whom you can interview for personality fit as positions come open.

Personality Fit

- G.W. always wants to know about people's backgrounds. This is how he learns about their core values and priorities.

The research you do to determine what skills, characteristics, and attributes are needed for a particular position tells you what core values and priorities you're looking for. Bush's belief that you can learn people's core values and priorities by learning about their backgrounds is echoed by many of the companies described in Collins's *Good to Great*. In determining who would be "the right people," the companies Collins described placed greater weight on character attributes than on specific educational background, practical skills, specialized knowledge, or work experience. It's not that specific knowledge or skills are unimportant—far from it. These companies, however, viewed knowledge and skills as more teachable (or at least learnable), whereas traits such as character, work ethic, basic intelligence, dedication to fulfilling commitments, and values were seen as more ingrained or inherent. Here are a few examples:

- Dave Nassef from Pitney Bowes said, "I used to be in the Marines and the Marines get a lot of credit for building people values. But that's not the way it really works. The Marine Corps recruits people who share the corporation's values, then provides them with the training required to accomplish the mission. We look at it that way at Pitney Bowes. We have more people who want to do the right thing than most companies. We don't just look at experience. We want to know: Who are they? We find out who they are by asking them why they made [certain] decisions in their life. The answers to these questions give us insight into their core values."

- Another company, Nucor, goes as far as building its plants where their target candidates (people with the core values and priorities Nucor wants) live. Nucor says you can teach farmers how to make steel, but you can't teach a farm work ethic to people who don't have it in the first place.
- From yet another company, Collins learned that their best hires often were people with no industry experience. That company hired a manager who had been captured twice in World War II and had escaped both times. "I thought anyone who could do that shouldn't have trouble with business."[26]

To discover core values and priorities, Bush learns about background by asking about people's families—a bit scary for the HR professional who wants you to get only need-to-know information. Do what Pitney Bowes does: Ask for specific past decisions that relate to the skills/tasks to be done and knowledge that the person must have. You still have to extrapolate their core values and priorities from what they say, just as Bush does, but you'll be getting "need to know" information—in the legal sense—to do it from.

For example, you need someone who's flexible. Ask the people you interview to describe a decision they made in their lives that made them feel they were very flexible. After they respond, ask why they felt this decision required or demonstrated flexibility. The things you hear in their words, their tone of voice, the pacing of their speech, and their body gestures and facial expressions will tell you if flexibility was hard for them, easy, they liked it, they hated it, they were forced, and so on.

Now, match what you extrapolated about their core values and priorities to your own core values and priorities; Bush describes this as looking for a fit with his personality. If the core values and priorities match, and the skills match, you indeed have the right person here and you must get ready to persuade.

Persuasion

- G.W. makes himself and the organization look attractive to that kind of person.

Your research helps you discern what skills, characteristics, and attributes are needed for the position and who has the personality fit. But will the people you want want you? Now you need to know what will make you and your organization attractive to the people you want to bring in. You need to know it so you can create it. As with customers, you have made and will continue to make changes to your products and services to meet your customers' needs, so they'll buy initially and continue to buy. You don't make every change that customers suggest, but you discover what they want and then you go out of your way to make the changes that you can without hurting quality. (Reducing quality would, of course, make your customers unhappy!)

Once you know what will make you and your organization attractive to the people you want to bring in, go out of your way to make any necessary changes without being immoral, illegal, or creating a bad return on investment in dollars and time.

Use the tool shown in Figure 4.5 to discover, specifically, what you are currently "offering" to candidates. Then you'll know what you need to change to make you and your organization attractive to the people you want. You may even find that you have more to offer than you think. In fact, you may be really attractive until you and others in your organization open your mouths. Many times we use words that are less than appealing when we describe ourselves, the position, and/ or the organization. Let's see what you discover.

Assess these eight areas of your organization. Do your own looking and writing, or have others do the looking and writing, or discuss the assessment as a group, or any combination of the three. Write specific examples for each of the eight areas. This way everyone will be able to see concrete facts with their own eyes, as opposed to generalities that don't paint a picture and will cause people to say, "We don't do this."

1. *Values, mission, vision.* Can you recite your organization's mission, vision, values? Can your employees? If you can't, or they can't, or no one can, how can you possibly tell them to the people you want to bring in? Make your mission short, like these two: "ABC Company will be a customer-focused organization," "Quality of employee, quality of workplace, quality of customer."
2. *Fiscal status.* Is your organization healthy, or a bit under the weather? Tell the truth, especially if there are problems. Most of the people you want to bring in will be attracted by your honesty.
3. *Organizational structure.* Make sure the organization's structure fits your current size and needs. If it has grown, or you have changed the way you do business (for example, by instituting teams), you need to change both the structure (who's responsible to whom and how) and the graphic representation of that structure. The people you want to bring in will get the wrong message from an inaccurate representation.
4. *Policies/procedures.* Regularly reexamine your organization's policies and procedures. Things are changing so fast today that last year's procedures and policies will be holding your employees and your organization back. When written, policies and procedures serve as a persuasion tool to let the people you want to bring in see what you're all about, what will be expected of them, and the benefits of working with you.
5. *Compensation and benefits.* Benchmark against your competitors and region to make sure the compensation and benefits you offer are appropriate for the position, your organization, your industry, and the job market.
6. *Staff development.* Many organizations think they have to have a whole Training and Development Department to do staff development. In reality, though, all of us train and develop people in some way, often through ongoing supervision and co-worker help. What if you don't have formal staff development? Describing what you *do* have for the position is more attractive to potential employees than telling what you don't have.
7. *Management philosophy.* Do you use baseball-bat management, or a hands-off approach, or a guide-and-support approach? Whichever you choose, choose one that fits both the people you want to bring in and your organization's needs, so that people can see that they'll be able to be productive and enjoy what they do. Whatever you choose, *be consistent* and use it with all employees.
8. *Physical workspace.* It doesn't have to be beautiful (if the person you're bringing in is Ainsley Hayes for Associate White House Counsel and the organization is "The West Wing," then the Steam Pipe Trunk Distribution venue will be fine). It does have to be well lit, comfortable, and functional for the person and the position.

Figure 4.5   Organizational assessment tool: The eight areas.

More Persuasion

- G.W. does most of the talking.
- G.W. sells to people who come highly recommended.

Doing most of the talking only works if you have done all the research Bush does up front.

What you'll be talking about is anything the person you want to bring in (target market) needs to know to be sold on the idea that you're the employer for her. That the position you're offering is the best thing since sliced bread. That this is the opportunity she's been waiting for and she shouldn't dream of passing it up. You'll be talking about your core values, explaining the organization's vision, sharing stories about clients and customers, recounting successes, giving examples of what's important to you. You'll be talking about the eight areas of what you offer them. No lie: What you talk about when you're persuading/selling is what your prospect needs to hear, not what you want to tell him or her (back up and reread the first sentence of this paragraph).

Persuasion is getting people to do what you want them to do (take the position) because they want to do it (get all the things you're offering them). It's very personal (notice that *person* is the root of the word *personal*), so you have to know what the person's core values and priorities are—and you can only get those from thorough research. The candidates have to be excited about what you're offering (things that make them want to take the position), and these things are personal. Therefore, you have to know what they would feel is a good offering for them (again, this comes from research). Of course, you also have to have made the necessary changes to the eight areas of your organization so that what you describe and offer now matches things that make the people want to work with you. And one other detail: What you describe has to be true.

Armed with all this information, you still have to be able to deliver the information in a way that makes your target market want to buy. You have to have the interpersonal skills and the sincerity of a good salesperson/persuader. Here are three time-tested (meaning they've helped salespeople for hundreds of years and will continue to help you) techniques to practice.

1. *Shift your focus to others.* A woman was seated at a dinner one night with William Gladstone and the following evening with Benjamin Disraeli (both famous British statesmen). "When I left the dining room after sitting with Mr. Gladstone, I thought he was the cleverest man in England," she said. "When I left the dining room after sitting with Mr. Disraeli, I thought I was the cleverest woman in England."

Practice listening to others. Listening will increase your persuasiveness because people love to feel listened to. It happens so rarely that the focused attention makes them want to do anything you say. Also, because you're listening, they'll talk more, and then you'll know what excites them (research). Because you're really listening, you'll remember it and then you'll talk about it and they'll be persuaded. Wow—all this from simply listening to someone! Might be worth trying.

People who feel you're listening say they see you or hear you:

Leaning forward.
Looking them in the eye.
Nodding.
Asking questions about what they just said.
Paraphrasing.
Taking notes.

These actions cause other people to feel like you're listening (because you are). These actions also actually help to focus you on what the other person is saying, as opposed to getting yourself ready to talk.

Bush listens with his eyes and his ears. He pays attention, so he remembers things about people. Frank Bruni, a reporter for the *New*

York Times, tells of books he'd mentioned he'd like to read suddenly appearing after George was done reading them. Bruni tells about the time he offhandedly mentioned to Bush, while on the presidential campaign trail, that he was going to visit his father on his dad's birthday weekend. George took out an official Governor of Texas card and wrote a "Happy Birthday" note for Bruni to give his father. After Bush became president, Bruni interviewed him at his ranch. One of the first things George did was ask about Bruni's father. As Bruni emphasized, these are the kinds of gestures that are important to George W. Bush—birthday cards, caring, and remembering things about people.[27]

2. *Appreciate others' abilities.* Skillful persuaders send out the message, by means both spoken and unspoken, that they appreciate your abilities. The act of really listening can do this all by itself, as we just discussed. In addition, Bush always uses the words *smart* or *talented* as adjectives before a person's name when talking about that person. When you read about or hear him saying this about others, you get the feeling he'd say the same about you. Again, saying the words insincerely won't do it. You have to really appreciate other people's abilities.

"smart"
"talented"

Keep a small pad in your pocket (or make a place in your personal digital assistant) so that wherever you are, you can write notes to yourself when someone does something you appreciate. First off, this will help you remember it later. Second, every time you come across that pad in your pocket (or that file in your PDA), you'll think, "Oh, better notice and write something about someone else." Third, after you do it a few times it'll become a habit.

3. *Hone your sense of humor.* People who laugh, who are quick enough to pick up on something humorous, and who poke fun at themselves make us feel good. They make us feel comfortable. They also make us feel that they're real. Frank Bruni wrote about a time on the campaign plane when Bush walked back to the door between the forward cabin and the cabin where the reporters were. George placed one foot into the reporters' cabin, teasingly said, "Off the record," and grinned. He pulled his foot back into his own cabin and, banishing his smile, said, "On the record." Another step into the reporters'

cabin: "Off the record." Another step back into his own cabin: "On the record." Then George laughed his head off.[28]

Play it again, Sam. Bruni recounted yet another incident that displayed Bush's willingness to poke fun at himself—and let others do it too. On the plane at the end of the presidential campaign, Bush showed videotapes of *Saturday Night Live* skits that ridiculed his campaign debate performances.[29]

Laugh! Pick up on humorous things by listening and paying attention. Poke fun at yourself. Great persuaders have fine-tuned their sense of humor. Well, you say, I'm not funny. Fine; at least laugh when other people or things are funny.

Remember, the best humor is about you and is relevant to the current subject and the people present. (It's called "getting it," and it's tough to get it if you can't relate.)

Will applying George Bush's unique combination of activities get you the right person every time? Sorry, no. Sometimes the situation changes and the person doesn't. Sandy Kress (lead negotiator and chief policy maker for President Bush's national education-reform package) was chosen for his Democratic credentials, so that he'd attract bipartisan support for the legislation. He did. After the bill passed, he resigned.[30] Kress is a moderate, and continuing to work in Bush's conservative administration wasn't a good fit for him.

Will applying George's unique combination of activities help you bring in the right people the vast majority of the time? Yes, and it'll help you save time and gain recognition for your efforts to boot. In a July 2002 poll taken in Iowa, Bush was recognized for his ability to bring in the right people. That poll showed that Bush would have won the presidency handily if a rematch election had been held in July 2002. "I had no faith in Bush when he was running, but he has surrounded himself with men and women of character and vision," said Rhonda Lane of Eldrige, a registered voter who voted for Gore in 2000.[31] Remember July 2002? Approval ratings were going down, due to the failing stock market, and the media were saying that Bush's economic advisors were no good—but this voter said her newly found faith in George W. Bush was based on his ability to bring in the right people.

Bush works hard to build a strong team to implement his agenda. People say yes to working with George W. Bush because Bush helps them see that it's the right job for them. Then they stay with him because he assures them that he respects their talent and will leave them alone to get their jobs done—and he makes good on that promise.

CHAPTER 5

Bring in the Right People, Part Two

Leave 'Em Alone!

I know that I cannot possibly know all the information necessary to make good decisions about all the matters that come before different agencies, boards, and commissions. I select people who are qualified, who share my conservative philosophy and approach to government, and then I expect them to make the calls as they see them.

George W. Bush[1]

Once upon a time there was a really special President who knew there was too much information in the world for someone in his position to know it all. So the really special President hired really smart people. He told them his core values. He told them his vision and their role in achieving it. He supported them and disciplined himself to let them do their jobs without interfering. And it was a happy and productive group.

In another land, called NaySayer, there were a great number

of Loud Leaders who must not have hired really smart people who could do their jobs by themselves. Or maybe the Loud Leaders did hire really smart people, but the Loud Leaders believed that, because they were "the leaders," they needed to know everything and make all the decisions.

One day the Loud Leaders from NaySayer cast a spell on all the really smart people. The spell made them believe that the really special President was letting them do their jobs not because it was a good way to lead, but because the really special President just didn't know enough to do his job by himself, and that's why he had to hire all the really smart people.

Some of the really, *really* smart people started reading this book. They learned how the really special President hired smart people. How he supported people. How he created trust. How he created a vision and gave it to people straight. How he held people accountable to get results. These really, *really* smart people said, "I can choose to ignore the spell cast on me by the Loud Leaders of NaySayer. I can tell other people to read this book so they can ignore the spell too. We can all watch and learn from the really special President and get the benefits of happy and productive staff."

And so they did.

And the Loud Leaders from NaySayer? Well, they were heard from again and again, but their spells had lost their power.

Not only does Bush have the courage to hire experts who are smarter than he is on various topics, but he also has the common sense and discipline to leave them alone to do their jobs. Bush was praised widely after 9/11 for delegating the conduct and tempo of the war in Afghanistan to his military advisors and then getting out of their way. Cheney became a behind-the-scenes advisor. Powell took over as chief diplomat, and Rumsfeld led his generals into battle.[2]

Cheney, Powell, Rumsfeld, and everyone else George W. works with do their jobs well because Bush set it up so they can.

They understand that their job is to do their job.

They understand why they, specifically, were hired for their jobs (that is, they know where they are smarter than Bush so they can guide him):

- Karen Hughes has a gift for channeling Bush's voice. Her trademark line (as we noted in Chapter 4) is that she has worked with Bush so long she can finish his sentences.[3]
- Dick Cheney's experience in foreign policy and executive branch management allows him to offer high-quality, well-informed advice and counsel to Bush. He and President Bush meet every morning.
- You can see in Andy Card's ascent all the habits and practices that George W. most prizes in aides and advisors: the family connection, the first-term credentials, complete loyalty, uncommon discretion, and the diligence of a draft horse. Says Bush, "Andy Card is an experienced, low-keyed person who understands the definition of chief of staff is not junior President, but is the chief of a staff of very high-powered people whose job is to never deny access but to enhance access to me, and if there is a tie to be broken, he can break it in a good thoughtful way."[4]
- Colin Powell is described as the ultimate staff guy. He is the good soldier who punched four stars in 35 years in an organization that rewards loyalty and prizes the chain of command—just as his boss, Bush, does. Powell sees himself as the one who carries out the vision, not the one who imagines it. "My job," Powell said, "is to make sure the President gets what he needs to make proper decisions."[5]

Bush's staff do understand when it's time to pull their boss in: "You don't get the President involved at the start," says a White House official. "You set the table and insert him at key points in the process to get key things done, to make key calls to certain people to tell them that it's time to get off the dime, time to hold hands and jump."[6]

They want to do their jobs because they're appreciated. As George W. Bush's chief strategist, Karl Rove is supposed to keep the president in a healthy political glow. Rove does solid public relations (PR) work. No one, with the possible exception of President Bush himself, is more responsible for the success or failure of Bush's presidency. So when Bush sits down with congressional leaders, he can nod at Rove and say, "You all know the Boy Genius"—and they all do.[7]

Why do the staff understand these things? Because Bush tells them when he's recruiting them and when they start their jobs. And because he shows them every day after that by his actions.

BUSH LEAVING 'EM ALONE (THAT'S CODE FOR LETTING THEM DO THEIR JOBS)

You're thinking along these lines: "Fine! Bush got to bring in people who *could* be left alone. He started the businesses so he could bring in only people who could be left alone. He was the governor and president, so he could pick staff from scratch. Me? Well, I have the ones I have."

"Leave 'em alone" doesn't always mean left alone to make their own decisions or take action without guidance. The way Bush leaves staff alone is different in different situations. Look at these examples and see which ones you could apply to the people you have right now.

Example 1. Vice President Dick Cheney asked American investors to buy when the stock markets reopened on Monday, September 16, 2001.

We know you have at least one person other than you who can speak for the organization. When they're given that kind of authority, the rest of their abilities tend to rise to the same high level on the next occasion that calls on them to exercise it. Other staff members begin to look for ways they can show you that they're capable of handling things for the organization. It's a self-feeding growth cycle. No one but Bush and Cheney knows for sure if Cheney was told by Bush to ask investors to buy or if he just knew it was his job to say it. No matter. The leave-'em-alone point here is that *Cheney* delivered the message to American investors.

Example 2. Sometimes Bush starts the delivery of messages to the American public and his staff follows suit in their own spheres of influence.

"BUSH KNEW": The headlines appeared just before Bush's lunch with Senate Republicans in the Mansfield Room. They got to hear his first response to the accusation that he knew of specific terrorist plots before 9/11: "I would never sit idly if I'd known what was coming on September 11! Had I known about the plot I would have used the whole force and fury of the United States to stop them!" VP Dick Cheney telephoned Bush and asked whether he should turn up the heat at a fund-raising dinner in New York. The answer was simple: Do your job. At that dinner, Cheney warned critics not to make "incendiary comments" that are "totally unworthy of national leaders in time of war." He did it again at an event the next day. Laura Bush, who was traveling in Budapest, commented to reporters that it was "very sad that people would play upon victims' families' emotions, or all Americans' emotions."[8]

Example 3. Cheney reviews the president's daily schedule and decides which meetings to attend. Aides say he attends most policy discussions and meetings with Cabinet officers, in addition to his weekly lunch with the president. In the Oval Office, he sits in the chair to the right of the president.

Bush's staff can do their jobs, most times without surprising the president, because they listen, watch, and learn about what would be an appropriate direction for action. They know his mind from being around him and working with him.

Example 4. Bush ticked off points he wanted Cheney to make in a speech about the administration's position on Saddam Hussein. Cheney's speech infuriated many of America's allies, who were upset by his declaration that a "return of inspectors would provide no assurance whatsoever" of Saddam's compliance with United Nations resolutions. To them it sounded as if Cheney were saying the only way to neutralize Iraq was war, and these allies had already clearly said they weren't in agreement about going to war. The president hadn't told Cheney to say this.[9]

In this instance, even though Cheney listened, Bush was surprised. (Stuff happens.) But this didn't cause Bush to shut Cheney in a room for the rest of his term. They talked about it and then went on.

Example 5. "When military details were brought to him, [Bush would] say, 'Don't bring this to me. I've given you a task, and I have full confidence in you to carry it out,'" said a senior U.S. military officer.[10]

Some staff still want Bush's blessing, or want to check things out with him. Bush's telling them how much confidence he has in them may be all they need to be able to go off and do their work on their own from then on. Many, *many* staff people have worked for other leaders who made every decision, including how many pencils to buy. Dependence is a hard habit to break. When Bush says to make the decision on your own, these staff members have a hard time believing it, so they keep checking in with him. Bush gives compliments when they take action on their own, he tells them directly when he feels they do need to run things by him, and he is patient in giving the time it takes staff to really believe him and go it alone. This helps the staff, who want his blessing but don't really need it, get to "leave 'em alone" faster.

Example 6. At news conferences throughout the weeks after 9/11, Secretary of State Powell detailed an endless round of diplomacy.[11]

This is Powell's job. Imagine what would have happened if Bush had had to do all these news conferences and his own job too. Sometimes the magnitude of a situation makes you want to do all the work, just because it's good for the leader to be seen. Yes, it *is* good. Bush was "seen" through his staff representatives, and he did his job all the better because others were doing theirs.

Example 7. Bush received only one formal progress report from the group planning the new Department of Homeland Security before May 22, 2002, the day Andy Card presented him with the final options.

"He's not paid to work out the technical details of policy proposals," says a senior White House advisor. Another senior official who worked on the plan says that Bush peppered his aides with questions about how the new agency would function in practice: "Have you thought about how putting these different cultures together is going to work?" the president asked.

But by that point, Bush was only fine-tuning a machine whose design had already been determined. By handing the task of devising a vast new Cabinet agency to a few trusted aides, Bush ceded much of his own power to shape the policy. He could have picked the lesser of the options that Card provided him, but his reliance on his aides made it almost certain that he would approve their recommendation.[12]

Bush has never been one to sweat the details; he prides himself on setting clear goals and letting his lieutenants achieve them. They'll only keep achieving your goals, though, if you accept their recommendations the vast majority of the time. "Leave 'em alone" only works when you show you have confidence in their work. It takes discipline. It takes allowing a few errors. The end result—you can do your job because they do theirs—is part of the leadership genius of G.W. It's crucial to the success of a leader.

Example 8. For many years, there has been a standard ritual for the preparation of a president's budget. The Office of Management and Budget (OMB) offers the agencies initial spending levels, and the agencies howl in protest. Weeks of negotiations follow. Most disputes are resolved peacefully, but in the end the president sits as a court of one to adjudicate final appeals.

No such thing happened this year. Not a single Cabinet officer took his or her case directly to the president. Bush provided the overall spending guidelines to the OMB and a process was established to force resolution of differences before the final budget went to the president. First there was the normal give-and-take between the OMB and the agencies. Then there was a kind of appellate procedure that was run by Cheney and included White House Chief of Staff Andrew H. Card, Jr.; Treasury Secretary Paul H. O'Neill; budget director Mitchell E. Daniels, Jr.; and economic advisor Laurence Lindsey.

Health and Human Services Secretary Tommy G. Thompson said he never considered appealing to the Cheney group, let alone the president, despite sharp differences with the OMB about initial funding levels. "Mitch [Daniels] didn't want us to go to the president and I didn't want to go to the president," Thompson said. "I wanted to work it out." He did so in a series of meetings with Daniels. Thompson said he had no direct discussions with Bush about the details of the budget of the largest domestic agency in the government.

The Bush White House is designed to work the way the president wants it to work: with harmony, collegiality, and respect. Expect people to work it out together and they will.[13]

Example after example proves it. Bush carefully constructs an environment that invites the leave-me-alone people to come and makes them want to stay. He maintains the leave-'em-alone environment even though it occasionally results in a few staff members saying things they have to retract. He keeps the environment even though a few staff still can't bring themselves to believe that his hands-off approach is for real, and he keeps it no matter what the naysayers have to say.

BUSH CREATES AN ENVIRONMENT THAT LOOKS LIKE "LEAVE 'EM ALONE"

Clearly, Bush has to bring in the right people first, that is, people who *can* be left alone. Or does he? This is a chicken-and-egg problem: How can he bring in people who can be left alone without first proving to them that he will leave them alone? Leave-'em-alone people are attracted to work where they'll be left alone. Here's the unique combination from Bush's leadership genius again. Bush has a long record of leaving staff alone, he publicizes it, looks for people who would be interested in it, and sticks to it.

Bush Does Bring in the Right People

In Chapter 4 you learned exactly how Bush first decides who would be right for a position, and then goes out and finds those people and gets them to say, "Yes, I want to work with you." Much of his success at this comes from his personal knowledge of and interactions with the people he wants to bring in and the people who might recommend those people. Bush has been made fun of for choosing people he knew personally from his father's administration (as though he couldn't find his own people) and from his Texas gubernatorial staff (like he had to recycle).

Frankly, we're mystified. If you are looking for people who you're sure share your core values, and are able to be left alone, it would seem to follow logically that you would feel the most confident with people whom you had already seen do the job (or whom someone you knew had observed). Past staff, staff of other leaders whom you trust—this sounds like an internship for Bush's administration. Of course he has brought in some people who weren't past staff or staff for another leader he knows well. But there aren't many, and Bush follows his formula—research, personality fit, persuasion—rigorously.

He Sets up the Systems so "Leave 'Em Alone" Will Work

The right system, of course, attracts people who want to be left alone. Bush decided on a flat organizational chart rather than the traditional chief-of-staff approach. He did this both as governor of Texas and as president. The key word here is *decided*. This was not the system that existed in his industry (government). He changed it. Bush wanted senior managers of different divisions to report directly to him. "I like to get information from a lot of people," he said. "Plus, I knew that high-powered people [leave-'em-alone people] would be frustrated unless they had direct access to the boss. I had seen that problem in my dad's administration. Key members of his staff felt stifled because they had to go through a filter."[14]

G.W. saw organizational problems in his father's administration that he didn't want to repeat. Now, how did a big-picture guy, who leaves the details to others, know that lack of direct access was the problem?

Most big-picture leaders see *only* the big picture—the outcome—not the underlying cause. Bush, however, loves problem solving. He loves working with a group of people, asking questions, analyzing, coming up with solutions. Where did this passion come

> His favorite class at Harvard was Human Org & Behavior (Minutaglio, *First Son*, 157).

from? "I was fascinated by the case study method that Harvard uses to teach," Bush said.[15] He was even more interested when a case study had to do with the way businesses were organized, their structural semantics, their pecking order, the way management was structured.[16]

Because Bush lets senior managers of different divisions report directly to him, a lot of people have direct access to him and he *has* to leave them alone. There are just too many people reporting to him to second-guess them all, even if he wanted to. He'd never be able to keep his disciplined schedule and he would end up working all the time. When you work more hours doing your staff members' jobs, other things that are important to you (both at work and outside of work) begin to fall apart. That's the beauty of living your core values. It's easy for Bush to stick to "leave 'em alone." Any time he's tempted to do a staff person's job, all he has to do is take a look at what will happen to his core values: family (he needs that time with them); faith (he needs time for Bible reading and being still to listen to God); integrity (punctuality and truthfulness might suffer).

Bush's system includes a way to be sure that the information his staff people bring him is thoroughly researched and unvarnished (we also learned, in Chapter 3, that this is how he creates trust in his staff). "I don't want them to tell me what they think I want to hear," Bush said. That's why, at every turn, he asks the staff, "What do you think?" He knows that his give-it-to-'em-straight communications can cause people to clam up. He creates an atmosphere in which they feel comfortable expressing their unvarnished thoughts and opinions, partly by just asking them what they think.[17]

This comfortable atmosphere is also created, in part, by Bush's disciplined efforts never to behave as though he's better or more knowledgeable than anyone else.[18] Of course, given who he is as a person—his enthusiasm, his humorous nature, and his genuine humility—how hard could this be for him?

President Bush peeked into an early morning meeting of his senior staff, where eighteen to twenty of the most influential White House officials gathered to discuss the day's business. They were sitting and chatting when the door abruptly opened and Bush stuck his head in. They immediately stood in deference to the presence of the President.

"Sit down," Bush told them, shrugging off the courtesy. He left.

Moments later the door swung open and he was back. His aid[e]s stood anew.

He smiled, chuckled and told them that he just wanted to see them do that again.[19]

Bush Gives It to 'Em Straight about How It's Going to Work

Bush tells staff, "My job is to set the agenda and time and framework. To lay out the principles by which we operate and then delegate as much of the process as possible. The final decision often rests with me but your judgment has a big influence."[20]

He didn't just do this one day and think, "Cool, this works," and then expect staff to know. He had to tell them. Bush thought about all the things they'd need to know about how his leave-'em-alone system works. Because he's a straight talker, staff receive the information in a clear, concise, understandable way.

Bush also tells them, "I rely heavily on you. I trust you to bring me quality information and advice and I'll act decisively after weighing the options you present."

And he tells them, "I'm not going to make decisions in your area of expertise but I am going to hold you accountable for your decisions."

And he tells them, "You worry about doing your job. I'll take care of the politics." Then Bush stands up to the critics when they complain about something a staff member did.[21]

And he tells them, "Always return each other's phone calls first. It'll foster good communication and make sure you seek each other's advice

> I trust you.
> I rely on you.
> I'll set the agenda and time.
> I'll set the principles.
> You bring me quality information.
> Your judgment has a big influence on my decisions.
> I'll act decisively.
> I'll hold you accountable for your decisions.
> I'll stand up to the critics.
> You'll seek each other's advice.

and guidance." Did it work? Bush says that many of his staff have told him that it set the tone and was key to the team approach they developed.[22]

People believe Bush when he tells them about "leave 'em alone" during the recruiting process. They believe him when he tells them how it's going to work. The Millon Inventory of Diagnostic Criteria (MIDC) showed that Governor George W. Bush's main leadership strengths were "the important political skills of charisma and interpersonality, which will enable him to connect with people and retain a following."[23] In job after job, Bush's hands-off leadership system builds confidence and trust among his staff. They see it as he lives it.

A Side Benefit

The environment Bush creates rubs off on his staff and they use "leave 'em alone" with their own staffs. For example, "Powell," his State Department aides say, "is a man who looks after the basics, allotting specific tasks to his team."[24]

After 9/11, Bush needed Powell's knowledge of foreign affairs for support. That knowledge allowed Bush to feel comfortable having Powell tell Pakistan's leaders that they would have to choose sides, just like everyone else: "They're either with us or against us." And where did Powell get *his* support? Powell leaned heavily on his deputy and close friend Richard Armitage in dealing with Pakistan. Armitage, in turn, went for advice to Anthony Zinni, the retired Marine four-star general who had come to know Pakistani President Musharraf well, general to general, when Zinni held the Centcom post.[25]

Bush doesn't always leave it to chance that his staff will have the successes he has enjoyed with the leave-'em-alone approach. That's why he fought so hard for the employees of the Homeland Security Department to be exempted from the federal labor-management relations statute: Application of that law would have hampered the departmental leaders' wartime flexibility in hiring the right people.[26]

You can lay out the organizational structure, tell people that you want them to do their jobs on their own, and assure them that you won't interfere. You can even walk the talk and actually not interfere. But if results aren't achieved, you are ultimately responsible—you have to take the heat. Part of creating the environment for "leave 'em alone" is standing behind your people. When they achieve results, Bush gives them all the credit. When they don't, he defends them in public and then coaches, guides, and supports them privately, rather than tossing them straight into the street.

BUSH IS LOYAL TO HIS STAFF

Defend 'Em and Coach

When his staff members make mistakes, Bush's first action is to stand behind them. It's part of trusting his staff. George Tenet was so sure he had Bush's confidence that he never even made the ritual offer to resign after 9/11. He didn't even apologize. Furthermore, when Tenet came under fire from others, Bush was there with the hose. "We cannot be second guessing our team," Bush told a group of lawmakers aboard Air Force One on September 27, 2001. "And I'm not going to. The nation's at war. We need to encourage Congress to frankly, leave the man alone. Tenet's doing a good job. And if he's not, blame me, not him."[27]

Later Bush faced a sudden collapse of public faith in the men he had picked to run things on the home front, particularly the former swing-state Governors Ridge and Thompson. Despite days of briefings, neither had been able to get his arms around the crisis, and both had the bad habit of raising more questions than they answered. They were each responsible for coordinating the efforts of agencies, from the FBI to the CDC to the Army's biowar researchers, that seemed unable or unwilling to share what they knew with the

What happened to George that made him want to be so loyal to people?

"During the summer of 1965 George W. went to work for a drilling company in southern LA. He was a roughneck, a member of a crew on an offshore oil rig. 'It was hard, hot work,' he said. 'I unloaded enough of those heavy mud sacks to know that was not what I wanted to do with my life.' George was to work all summer, but quit a week early. He wanted to spend time in Houston with his TX friends before he went back to Yale.

"When his father heard what George had done he called him to his office in Houston. 'You agreed to work a certain amount of time and you didn't,' said George H.W. Bush. 'I just want you to know that you've disappointed me.'

"That was the worst punishment George W. could imagine. He had disappointed his father, the man he admired the most in the world. He later said, 'When you love a person and he loves you, those are the harshest words someone can utter. I left that office realizing I had made a mistake.'"

For his father the situation was over and he went on to the next topic—an invitation to a ball game.

—Beatrice Gormely, *President George W. Bush* (New York: Aladdin, 2001), 49–50.

others. "The Toms let him down this week," said a top administration advisor, "but the President is adamant that nobody say anything bad about them, and the VP has a big stake in them too."[28]

Well before he arrived at the White House, Bush had established his preference for delegating. He said over and over that the secret to making government work was putting together a great team and then demanding results. The critics said that was a sensible approach with veterans like Colin Powell and Donald Rumsfeld, but not for new people. This kind of comment caused Bush to redouble his public defense of his staff, and immediately declare that he was satisfied with the pace of the homeland security effort.[29]

Even veterans such as Powell can, in Powell's words, "get a little far forward on [their] skis." The leave-'em-alone policy allows staff to do their jobs—but even though you believe you know the mind of your boss from listening and watching, like Cheney, you sometimes miss. Powell said the Bush administration would "pick up where the Clinton Administration left off" in negotiating a missile-proliferation deal with North Korea. Whoops. The White House was annoyed that South Korea had just sided with Russia against Bush's missile shield proposal, and uttering "Clinton"-anything so near the beginning of the Bush presidency was less than popular. Needless to say, some coaching went on. The next day Powell retracted his position.[30] Note that *Powell retracted.* Your mother said, "You make your bed, you lie in it," and that's what Bush does. He publicly defends when what the staff person did or said is either not an issue or isn't actually incorrect. He then coaches in private. If a retraction is needed, Bush lets the erring person do it himself or herself.

George knows he must stand behind people if they are to have any hope of success. He demonstrated this steadfast loyalty as early in life as his time at Phillips Academy, when he was in charge of stickball. Alan Woofs remembers being unable even to catch the ball. (So what was George thinking? Bringing in a person who can't even catch the ball isn't exactly hiring people smarter than you, but Alan's story is a good example about sticking with a person once you've brought him in.) The other guys kept coaching Alan to just close his hands if the ball came near him. One time he did just that, causing him to catch it, and made an out. George stopped the game and led everyone in a standing ovation.[31]

The loudest "throw him to the lions" cries have come for Bush's Treasury secretary, Paul O'Neill, particularly as the markets continued to plummet in July 2002. This situation may have been a bit tougher for Bush: If all accounts are true, Bush has been a little put out with O'Neill from time to time because of blunt language that makes Bush's own straight talk look wimpy by comparison. Nevertheless, Bush shows us his discipline and convictions about defending his staff. "I have all the confidence in the world in the secretary of the Treasury. I understand one newspaper was calling for his scalp," Bush said.[32]

The emphasis here is on publicly defending staff and privately coaching them, which Bush does. Of course Bush has fired people. This is what you have to do when a person is unable to change even after private coaching. Remember, though, when you bring in the right people—people who are smarter than you in their jobs—they have a lot to offer. Bush goes out of his way to guide, support, and coach so that he doesn't have to lose those resources. Look at why Bush hired Paul O'Neill. He has true credibility with corporate America. He has been vital in pushing for tough corporate reform. As the former head of the aluminum giant Alcoa, O'Neill was widely credited with running a tight and honest ship. He even put workers' safety ahead of the bottom line. His foursquare, Midwestern sensibility is a good antidote to all the slick corporate dealing being exposed nowadays.[33] That sure sounds like the right person to be Treasury secretary during a crisis of corporate confidence!

Sometimes Bush and his staff find themselves defending against the absurd. Paul O'Neill was sharply criticized for going on a scheduled trip during the worst of the July 2002 stock-market dive. "I was only gone a few days," O'Neill said to NBC. "I'm interested that people don't somehow understand, with all the telecommunications capability that we've got now, it's possible to be constantly in touch." Even more ridiculously, this criticism came from the reporters who regularly work far from their company offices with laptops and cell phones—some have even done their jobs with bombs dropping around them![34]

Have Staff Coach Each Other

Gordon Johndroe, press assistant, materialized on the presidential campaign plane for the purpose of making the tiniest amendment to Karen Hughes's remarks to reporter Frank Bruni.[35] When a staff person makes an error that has to be corrected right away, other staff jump in, not Bush himself. Did Bush tell his staff that that's part of the system? No. So what makes them do it? Bush told them to seek each other's advice. Leave-'em-alone people also tend to be all-for-one, one-for-all people. It's an easy next step from "seek" to "give if it's needed, even if it's not sought." In police shows, partners say to each other, "I'll cover your back." Other leaders hire smart individuals. Bush hires a carefully constructed *team* of smart people.

Karen Hughes warned that vetoing a popular health maintenance organization (HMO) bill was sure to be a disaster. Other advisors disagreed with her, and the president ended up vetoing it. That evening Karen got a call from her deputy, Dan Bartlett. "Just like we predicted," he said, "we got killed tonight," sighing after surveying the networks' coverage of Bush's veto. It was seen as yet another example of a president working on behalf of corporations instead of the average American. Bush and his staff had been fighting this battle since the presidential campaign. "We can't just be against something. We have to be for something," Hughes coached colleagues in a White House meeting. Passage of some type of patients' rights bill was inevitable. Hughes helped her colleagues to agree to advise Bush to throw his support behind a House alternative that gave patients a limited right to sue HMOs in state court—something he had long opposed.[36]

Leave-'em-alone teams will disagree with each other and with their leader. Disagreement leads to discussion that leads to better ideas. Aides insist that the emphasis on collegiality does not shield Bush from real debate, although they can cite few instances in which Bush was forced to make a difficult policy decision in the face of disagreement among team members. "You work it out," Bush will often say to his advisors when there is a lingering dispute. Bush has been repeatedly criticized by the news media for allowing

> ## "Leave 'Em Alone" Makes People Incredibly Loyal to Bush
> "Bush was surrounded by a bevy of loyalists," Frank Bruni wrote. (Well, of course! Would you purposely have staff who *weren't* loyal to you?) "His aids," Bruni went on to say, "insist that in private they are free to disagree with him but in public gave no hint of this. They say 'the Governor believes . . . .'" (Bruni, *Ambling into History*, 71). Again, of course! That's how people who are the right people, loyal and left alone to do their jobs, behave when they're on a team.

his team to disagree. We read, in October of 2001, that his staff's indecision about how and when to strike Afghanistan would cause a problem. When their deliberations (disagreements) were finished and the outcome was positive, the team members were heralded as geniuses. We read, during the spring and summer of 2002, that Bush's "economic team have often bickered so openly that aides have found themselves struggling to suppress snickers." In 2003, the administration may take a big swipe at fixing the economy with a complete overhaul of the tax code,[37] and again the staff will be geniuses. We read, during the summer of 2002, that Bush's team disagreed with each other on how to handle Saddam Hussein, and that soon some of them would be leaving their posts. Then came the UN speech, which was a big hit, and what did we read? "For the first time in a while the Bush team is speaking with one voice"[38]—as though disagreement were bad.

Bush is in good company. President Dwight D. Eisenhower employed what has come to be called a "multiple advocacy" approach. "I have been forced to make decisions, many of them of a critical character, for a good many years," the former supreme commander once observed,

> and I know of only one way in which you can be sure you have done your best to make a wise decision. That is to get all of the [responsible policy makers] with their different viewpoints in front of you, and listen to them debate. I do not believe in bringing them in one at a time, and therefore being more impressed by the most recent one you hear than the earlier ones. You must get courageous men of strong views, and let them debate and argue with each other. You listen, and see if there's anything been brought up, any idea, that changes your own view, or enriches your view or adds to it. Then you start studying. Sometimes the case becomes so simple that you can make a

---

These are the things every leader wants to hear.

"But the only voice I really listen to is the voice of President George W. Bush. We've all known each other for many years. We get along fine. We have our little disagreements. Sometimes we have serious disagreements. I always find it much better to try to solve problems, not to create problems for your bosses," said Colin Powell (quoted in McGeary et al., "Odd Man Out," 24).

Bush called Defense Secretary Donald Rumsfeld on September 11, 2001. Rumsfeld refused to leave the burning Pentagon and Bush didn't order him to leave.

"We can make decisions based on his principles, which are very clear," says Vance McMahan, Bush's state policy director. "We don't have to run every decision up the flagpole" (quoted in Carney, "Why Bush Doesn't Like Homework," 46).

Governor Bush "really works from a big-picture angle," said Albert Hawkins, Texas budget director. "The governor is not totally hands-off, though. He stays engaged, but not at the detail level" (quoted in Tom Shoop, "How George Bush Would Govern," govexec.com; accessed January 14, 2000).

From the minute someone starts talking about an issue, Bush is itching for a recommendation. Albert Hawkins says, "If you're going on too long, he tells you so." (quoted in Carney, "Why Bush Doesn't Like Homework," 46).

"When you leave a meeting, you know what you are supposed to do," says a top aide (quoted in James Carney and John F. Dickerson, "Easy Does It," *Time,* March 19, 2001, 38).

Figure 5.1   What Bush's staff say about being left alone.

decision right then. Or you might wait if time is not of the essence. But you make it.[39]

Leaving staff alone to do their jobs is integrally linked with Bush's decision-making style. He makes decisions with his core values clearly in front of him. (These are core values that his staff share; in fact, they were carefully selected precisely because they shared those values.) Bush makes decisions with thoroughly researched information (from staff who were chosen because they were smarter than he in their specific jobs). His decisions are most often simply confirmations of the steps staff say (after thorough research, presented in an unvarnished way) are the best ones to implement Bush's vision. Figure 5.1 gives some examples of how Bush's staff people feel about his approach.

LEAVING 'EM ALONE: A TIMELESS PRINCIPLE OF LEADERSHIP

Is this leave-'em-alone practice dangerous? The experts aren't in agreement. Some say that it is very dangerous indeed:

- Bush speaks convincingly about how important it is for a leader to assemble a trustworthy cadre of advisors. He argues that there is no percentage, as governor or as president, in trying to master every subject or micromanage every decision. As to this stance, Bruce Buchanan, a political scientist at the University of Texas in Austin, says, "Bush is trying to turn his weakness into a virtue. He's not a policy wonk, so he has to rely on people who are." There is a risk to that approach, adds Buchanan, who is a Bush admirer: "Bush's biggest weakness is that he might not be in a position to discern the credibility of the options his advisers lay out for him."[40]
- Dr. Howard Gardner, a Harvard professor and renowned expert in cognition and education, concluded, "[T]here's no evidence in any of the [presidential primary] debates that he's di-

THE EXPERTS SAY

What the Experts Say

Hire good people and get out of their way. Trust your employees to use their judgment.

Leslie Yerkes[41]

Zapped!—the giving of power. When you have been Zapped, you feel like:

your job belongs to you
you are responsible
your job counts for something
you know where you stand
you have some say in how things are done
your job is part of who you are
you have some control over your work

William C. Byham, Ph.D.[42]

What the Leaders Say

The best coach I ever had asked, "How is such and such going?" I left those little meetings believing I'd come up with the answers. Only later did I realize that he directed my attention with those questions of his. He never came out and told me what to do; he led me there. He was never impatient or too busy to listen.

Former IBM staff person about his boss[43]

I am most effective as a manager when I think of myself as the sixth man on a basketball team. When they want to call me into the game, I am happy to play, but if they don't need me, I am also happy to stay on the sidelines and cheer.

Dan Ferguson, chairman of the board of the Newell Company[44] gested ideas, made them his own and is able to draw on them thoughtfully on his own."[45]

- Paul Begala, political strategist, says, "Bush has convinced himself that he can make good decisions based on the opinions and information he receives from those around him. That's dangerous for any leader; disastrous for a President. Such intellectual passivity would allow staff, the bureaucracy and the lobbyist to shape all W.'s decisions by controlling the information and the options that are presented to him. W. would be a helpless, hapless victim of those who work harder, read more, and think creatively regardless of their agenda."[46]

- One critic, Frank Bruni, who watched Bush's leave-'em-alone approach in action, reconsidered. In *Ambling into History,* he says that "leave 'em alone" is sometimes dangerous. "He and his advisors were right to say that a president depended on the expertise of the advisors and cabinet officials he had gathered around him. And that choosing them well and using their counsel wisely were as important as an encyclopedic familiarity with all the facts under discussion. Presidents before Bush had proved that an excessive attention to detail and temptation to micromanage the affairs of government did not always work. But there were bound to be situations in which he would field warring counsel, have to look to his own judgment and be served best, not simply by his gut instincts and overarching political philosophy, but also by information and a strong command of it."[47]

  "As his first year as President came to a close, the country's problems were undeniably too complicated for one man and Bush had indeed surrounded himself with seasoned players who at times provided reason for confidence in their abilities."[48]

Other experts say that "leave 'em alone" is the best practice:

- Benjamin Disraeli, a former prime minister of England, said, "To be conscious that you are ignorant is a great step to knowledge."[49]

- Amy Edmondson, associate professor at HBS and co-author of the *Teamwork Report,* says, "Team leaders need to design teams and create a safe environment that encourages everyone to participate and offer innovative ideas. Each team member is selected for their abilities, aptitude for working with others and ability to chip in when they had a strength that the leader didn't (based on the leader pointing out his/her own imperfections)." This study was done by Harvard on highly successful operating room teams. The researchers discovered that the more often leaders were ready to acknowledge their own shortcomings, the more likely the team members were to chip in. This forthrightness about their own weaknesses made the leaders more approachable and furthered the creation of a safe environment for trial and error. It was seen as inevitable that all team members would make mistakes along the way.[50]
- "Giants give others the gift of space, space in both the personal and the corporate sense, space to be what one can be," says Max DePree in *The Art of Leadership.*[51]

According to Carly Fiorina, CEO of Hewlett Packard:

Leadership is no longer about command and control, hierarchy title or status. Leadership is about making a difference. Creating positive change. It's about getting things done and getting rid of everything else that doesn't contribute. It's about encouraging, enabling and empowering every employee. It's about reinforcing core values, articulating a vision and then setting people free. Leadership is about trust and giving authority back where it belongs.[52]

HOW TO LEAVE 'EM ALONE

Scared? There's no need to be as long as you bring in the right people—leave-'em-alone people. Ahhhh, that's what you're scared about. You already have people you didn't hire and you don't think they're the leave-'em-alone kind. *You might be surprised!* Allow yourself to be open to the possibility that more of them are the leave-'em-alone kind than you'd imagined. Some of them, with the new environment you'll create, can transform themselves. And, yes, the people who can't change will have to go if you're really committed to the successes that are possible only in the leave-'em-alone environment. Keep the environment that Bush creates firmly in mind as you proceed. When you leave people alone, they can do their jobs and you can do yours. If you don't (and you know this all too well), you're doing their jobs and not yours. The consequence is that your ability to do *your* job suffers.

While his heavy hitters (Vice President Dick Cheney, Treasury Secretary Paul O'Neill, Chief of Staff Andy Card, Defense Secretary Donald Rumsfeld, Secretary of State Colin Powell, and National Security Advisor Condoleezza Rice) plotted big initiatives and thought big ideas, Bush floated both above and below them. He invited members of the Kennedy family over to watch *13 Days* and eat hot dogs. He fretted over the transition of Spot and Barney to life in the White House.[53] This is what leaders are supposed to do. We're so used to them plotting initiatives to fulfill their vision that we don't recognize their actions and influence when they're the alliance builders, ambassadors, visionaries, guides, and coaches.

You Can Leave 'Em Alone if They're the Right People

First, choose wisely. Reread Chapter 4 on hiring people who are smarter than you.

If they've already been hired, assess current staff for leave-'em-alone qualities. You know what to do to be sure you bring in the right people. Now let's figure out how to assess your current staff. Basically, you're trying to discover who can transform themselves to operate well in a leave-'em-alone mode if you create an environment that expects them to do so and supports them when they do.

The signs of outstanding leadership appear primarily among followers: Are the followers reaching their potential? Are they learning? Are they serving? Do they achieve the required results? Do they change with grace? Do they manage conflict appropriately? The measure of leadership is not the quality of the head but the tone of the body.[54] If they're not, it's you.

Hold on before you jump all over us, telling about your staff who are idiots. We'd rather have it be "us" than "them" because "us" we can do something about. Ask yourself (or be even braver and ask them) what you're doing that's keeping them from reaching their potential. (Use the list in Figure 5.2 as a starting point.) And what is their potential, by the way? Probably not what you thought, if you think the problems are theirs rather than yours. What are you doing that's keeping your staff from learning, serving, achieving required results, changing with grace, and managing conflict? Tone the body by changing the head.

"The free market frees individuals to make distinct choices and independent decisions," said George W. Bush.[55] He was talking about the economic free market and how central planning restricts local choice, but he could just as well have been describing his beliefs about

---

Write the answers yourself and/or have the staff person write the answers:

What is _____'s potential?

What are you doing that's keeping _____ from learning?

What are you doing that's keeping _____ from serving?

What are you doing that's keeping _____ from achieving required results?

What are you doing that's keeping _____ from changing with grace?

What are you doing that's keeping _____ from managing conflict?

Then set a plan of action for the changes you'll make. If you develop the plan in conjunction with your staff person, he or she will help you and will actually come up with ideas for his or her own transformation. Two birds with one stone!

Figure 5.2   Questions to "change the head."

freedom for staff. If you're not operating a free-market staff economy, that may be why your people can't be left alone. Those same people, who appear to need you to make all their plans and decisions, can juggle the most overwhelming Saturday schedule—three kids to three different parks for three different games, and see them all. They can manage their money. They develop action plans for committees in their church. They can do it—you just have to expect that they can and then let them do it. Oh, yes, and if they screw up you have to let them fix it.

Re-interview everyone as though they were potential hires. Use Bush's techniques (described in Chapter 4). Remember that Bush does the majority of the assessment for potential staff fit with the job, the organization, and the boss before the interview. This allows him to use interview time to learn about personality fit and sell himself. Bush used his interview with Vance McMahan, for the policy director slot in Texas, to say, "I'm not interested in the status quo. I'm interested in different ideas. I want you to think outside the box and find and develop innovative solutions to our state's problems."[56]

But you didn't get to tell staff people that you expect leave-'em-alone work, because you either (1) weren't the interviewer, or (2) are just now creating the leave-'em-alone environment. Assessing people's potential to be leave-'em-alone staff, given the right environment, is the first step. Telling them what you expect is the next. Doing it in a Bush-style re-interview gives you more information about their potential fit. They now know what you expect and what it's going to be like from here on out—and if they're going to have trouble transforming you'll surely hear it and/or see it from their reactions.

"I assured him that not only would he have the freedom to run the Governor's budget divisions, but that he'd be part of the decision making process on every major issue in the Governor's office."[57] Telling people that they'll be left alone helps Bush hire the right people. It helped him hire Albert Hawkins. (You read about him in Chapter 4—the crackerjack budget guy who only came to the interview out of courtesy, planned to say no to the job offer, and then took the position.) It will help you get the leave-'em-alone process started with current staff. It'll help you in the assessment process, winnowing out those who can transform themselves if you create the right environment from those who need to go.

You Have to Actually Create the Leave-'Em-Alone Environment

To create a leave-'em-alone environment, first use Bush's techniques (described earlier in this chapter). Then set expectations and measure results.

If you've ever had the pleasure of being in Chicago's O'Hare International Airport at midnight on a long snowy day (and your flight was scheduled to leave at 10:00 A.M.), you've heard our all-time favorite public-address announcement. When they finally give up and admit that no flights will be leaving, an amazingly (for the time of day) cheery voice comes on the public-address system and says, "For those of you who will be staying with us tonight, we have blankets and pillows available at the podium." When you have identified your leave-'em-alone staff, you need to make an announcement about the new environment. Yes, you did tell them in the re-interview (or for new staff, the interview), but you'll need to do it again and again. It's part of the leave-'em-alone environment: telling and reinforcing what you told. Even if you're still scared, you need to sound amazingly cheery. You will be able to get your work done. Staff members will feel great about their autonomy and accomplishments, and will further develop their skills and worth to the organization. Just keep your eye on the prize and you'll be motivated to keep going.

All organizations need to align authority and responsibility. Bush

> **A Clear, Uncomplicated Message**
> *Zapp! The Lightning of Empowerment* (Byham, at 137) tells us that for "leave 'em alone" to work, people need:
>
> Direction—key result areas and measurements
> Knowledge/Skills—technical, people, company, industry
> Resources—tools, time, money
> Support—approval, coaching, feedback, reinforcement, recognition

tells us it's a fundamental management principle.[58] Let your staff know that they will have authority, and remind them that with authority comes responsibility.

The skill of setting expectations and measuring is nothing more than the skill of delegating. Bush delegates to the person who has been hired because he or she is the smartest in his or her area. Bush sets the vision and hands the implementation tasks over to his hand-picked team of hands-on deputies. When delegating, your greatest success comes when the persons to whom you delegate have exactly the picture of the results that you meant them to and they feel confident they can achieve the results. To make this happen, complete each of the following steps, in this order:

1. Tell why the result is important and what skills they possess that will make them successful.
2. Define the specific result(s) you want.
3. Tell them why you're delegating this.
4. Agree on a deadline.
5. Ask for feedback. What barriers do they foresee? Be sure they have the same picture of the result as you do. Let them give you an idea of how they'll implement the tasks. (This is, of course, their job, but a short description will help you be sure you've defined the desired result clearly and accurately.)
6. Set up the measure of results and the measurement methods in consultation with the staff to whom you've just delegated.

Guidance, Support, and Coaching—Not Interference

"Bush will give his Cabinet officers and agency heads 'a lot of leeway' to figure out how to get the job done, once major decisions about basic goals are made," predicted Laurence Lindsey (who worked with G.W. in Bush Sr.'s administration). "He would not just delegate responsibility," Lindsey said, "he would also delegate power. If he thinks something is worth doing, he'll make sure that he puts a person in charge who can get it done."[59]

"Leave 'em alone" is the only successful way to run an organization. With an ever-growing workload, you just can't expect to be successful doing it all. The power that goes to staff in the leave-'em-alone organization will spawn some mistakes and missteps—but so will keeping all the power to yourself, because you'll be utterly buried under the work. We vote for the mistakes that happen because people are getting their jobs done. Help them by guiding, supporting, and coaching.

> While one person hesitates because he feels inferior, the other is busy making mistakes and becoming superior.
>
> If you're not making mistakes, you're not trying hard enough.
>
> He who makes no mistakes does not usually make anything.
>
> The greatest mistake a person can make is to be afraid of making one.

Guide

Guidance includes initial training on how to do specific parts of a job. It may consist of you helping a staff person learn, or it may be you suggesting resources for them to learn from (books, tapes, courses, other employees). This is the easy part. The harder part of guiding is the always-open door. Bush carefully constructed an organizational structure that gives everyone access to him.

You may think the hard part is obvious: Where do you get the time to talk with all these people and still get your work done? First of all, it *is* your work to talk with them (to guide, support, and coach). Second, if you create a leave-'em-alone environment and stick to it, they'll be doing their jobs instead of you doing their jobs. With leave-'em-alone staff, you can now do your job of guiding, supporting, and coaching people to fulfill the corporate vision.

The truly hard part is *only* giving guidance when your door is always open and staff come in for guidance. How many times do leaders give a know-it-all lecture instead of guiding ("This is how I do it . . . " or "This is what I'd do . . . " or "Do it this way . . . ")? Your number-one weapon in the fight against know-it-all lectures is—you guessed it—hire people smarter than you. If they know more than you about the topic, you can't give them the answers. They'll come to you for ideas or just to air their own ideas. You're great at drawing those out (trust). You're great at helping staff see what they're judging their decisions against (core values and big picture).

If you do happen to know a thing or two about the topic they want your guidance on, stick to the following kinds of statements. They help guide staff to make their own decisions:

- "If you got the result you needed, what would it look like?" (This helps you understand the result the same way they do.)
- "Describe the options you're considering."
- "What are the obstacles to implementing each of these options?"
- "What will happen if you don't take any action?"
- "Which other staff or sources have the expertise to get you the information you need?" (Tell them the ones you know of.)

If someone point-blank asks you, "What should I do?," ask those questions (or variations on them) again. The leave-'em-alone environment means that you set the vision and that they implement it; this requires a lot of decision making by staff. The decisions they make may be on what proposals to bring to you, so that you can make a final decision, but many preliminary and interim decisions are their responsibility. If they ask you to decide (to do their jobs) and you do, you will undermine the leave-'em-alone environment.

Support

Use Bush's techniques as described earlier in this chapter: Publicly defend and privately coach.

Coach

Successful coaches are able to help their staff improve by being extremely specific. Use constructive feedback (rather than opinion-based criticism) to describe factually what the person actually did, to plan what he or she needs to do in the future, and to facilitate discussion of how the person intends to get there.

Plan ahead for your constructive feedback conversation:

- Get the facts. What did the person do or say? Who else was involved?
- What do you want the person to do?
- How will changing benefit the person?
- Using the information you gained, write the first words you'll say—a factual description of what the person did or didn't do (and when it happened). Then write an equally specific statement of what the person should do instead (and include a deadline for making the behavior change). Finally, write how making this change will benefit the person.
- Rehearse the words while using assertive body language (calm gestures, maintained eye contact) and voice (low pitch, even tone, even volume). This is crucial. Even the most perfect factual words will still instantly raise a wall of defensiveness if you say them loudly or while shaking a finger in the person's face. Rehearse the words so that you can say them from your brain and heart instead of reading from a paper. Looking at the paper to get started is great. Reading through the whole discussion is not.

Conduct the constructive feedback conversation:

- Say your first words, the ones you planned in the preceding step. Avoid introducing them with something like, "You know, Brian, most of the time you do just fine, but yesterday . . . ." You can say hello, but then just say the first words you wrote. This lets the person know immediately what he or she did (factually). It allows him to see himself doing the behavior. If you beat around the bush, he has time to think "I wonder what she's going to say to me? Wonder what I'm going to be asked to do?," and you will hit a wall of defensiveness so high and so thick that nothing will get through.

    Likewise, if you get right to the point, but don't use words that are factual and specific enough for the person to see the same picture you do, he'll say, "No, I didn't." Then you'll say, "But yesterday you said . . . to Mrs. Jones," and finally he'll see it. But it will be too late: The person has already posted a denial and built a defensive wall.

You wrote the words, so just say them.

- Allow a moment's pause. If you didn't have the real facts, the person can say so now. However, just a moment is all that's needed; any longer and the person's brain will jump to "Wonder what she's going to ask me to do" mode.
- Say the words you wrote about how the change that you're going to ask for will benefit the person.
- Say the words you wrote about what the person should do and by when.
- Look for facial expressions, body language, and words indicating that the person will do what was requested. If you don't see acceptance, point out what you see and reiterate that the person needs to do whatever it is. Tell him why. Facilitate his planning for the steps he'll take to make this change. Many times the reason you see what looks like "Not today, not ever" coming back at you is simply because the person needs you to facilitate her thinking about how to make the change. Facilitate rather than telling her how.
- Let your words sink in. Wait a moment before leaving or moving on to other subjects, in case the person has anything else to say.
- Monitor and measure. When the change is made, make sure the person knows that you noticed and that you appreciate it.

Not Interfere

Most of us interfere without knowing that we're doing it. We call it guiding, supporting, or coaching. Leave-'em-alone staff call it interfering, taking over, micromanaging, or stepping on their toes. It's an uncomfortable situation when you think you're coaching and the staff person thinks you're interfering.

Perception = Reality

If staff think you're interfering, they'll have difficulty believing you when you say that this is a leave-'em-alone company. Often getting our staff to believe that we're for real about this is an uphill battle anyway, so avoid making it worse by doing something they perceive as interference. (Obviously, what constitutes interference will be different for different people and at different times.)

- Ask staff to give you examples of what would feel like interference to them.
- Write their answers down.
- If you agree, just keep that list handy when you're coaching them so you can avoid those behaviors.

If you really feel that the things they're describing are coaching, as opposed to interfering, explain why this feels like coaching to you. When you've come to some agreement, then write down the behaviors or actions that you'll be avoiding.

Recognition/Praise

Your job is to rally the troops. *Every* study on what employees want from their managers places "Recognition when I achieve results" at the top or near the top of the list (right after "Honest feedback and coaching on my performance").

Bush says that people "must know they have an equal chance to succeed. It doesn't happen by telling them they are victims at the mercy of outside forces; it happens when they realize they have a worth, a dignity and a free will given by God."[60] Bush was able to boost the morale of state workers by conveying his appreciation of their values and dedication. "You don't come into the public service expecting to get any stock options," Albert Hawkins says. He noted that Bush understands and respects employees who seek the less tangible rewards that come from helping others. Bush initiated a "Texas Stars" award to give recognition to employees of programs that excel in meeting targets set under the state's performance-based budgeting system.

In the view of Hawkins and former Texas Rangers partner Schieffer, much of Bush's success has come from his skill at making people feel good about working for him. Schieffer remarked on Bush's popularity with everyone connected with the baseball club, from ticket takers to superstars: "He has such a good spirit about him, and he is interested in people."[61]

People feel recognized and praised because Bush notices what they're doing and comments on it. They feel recognized and praised because he gives them responsibility in the first place. Responsibility with accountability—when people know they'll be held accountable, they realize that their work is important. They feel recognized and praised because, in addition to sincere thanks and commendation, sometimes they receive tangible awards like the "Texas Stars" and t-shirts:

"It started," George said,

> during the campaign. It was August and well over 100 degrees. We landed in Crawford and I said that I had to go for a run. I knew if I didn't get it in then, I'd never do it. So as I recall there was a change of shift of the Secret Service agents. And I just told them that we should all go for a run right then. So both shifts of agents went right with me in the heat. And afterward, I had 100-degree club T-shirts and certificates printed up and gave 'em away to everybody who went with me.[62]

You just can't beat spur-of-the-moment recognition. A client of ours calls it "Off the Cuff." This client wanted to continue to inspire busy physicians and other healthcare professionals to meet or exceed the company's stated core values. To achieve this, we held many interviews within their company with people from all areas (from physicians to accountants). We discovered that the staff felt most rewarded—

and therefore motivated to keep practicing the core values—when their department head or chief gave them something "off the cuff," with no apparent preparation or planning. It felt like you just did this good thing and you got a thank-you or some material reward pretty close to the time you did it.

The busy department heads said, "Oh, great. When we did this before, it was just luck. We just happened into these situations. We have no time for ordering things, planning things," and so on in this vein. To make it easy for the department heads, we made a little booklet that listed a variety of things to give or things to do (with phone numbers). The possibilities ranged from a limo ride, to tickets to a local basketball game, to a gift basket, to a simple thank-you note. Stocks of things that everybody would need (such as thank-you cards, lottery tickets, and so on) were developed so that it would be easy for department heads both to recognize and give immediate praise for practicing the core values.

Do employees know that their bosses have easy access to this stuff? Yes. It wasn't the dollar value of the gift or award, or the time someone spent getting this thing, that was meaningful and motivating to the staff. It was being recognized specifically for what they did ("you did X for our patients" as opposed to "good job"). It was also being recognized immediately—not at a performance review four months down the road—that really turned these staff people on.

The translation of goals into practice depends not so much on the mobilization of millions as on the detailed staff work of a few score. Bush's world begins with his closest advisors, extends to Cabinet officers and military commanders, and then reaches his friends and allies in other countries. All must be engaged, all must do their part.[63]

CHAPTER 6

Encourage Collaboration

Build Alliances

I am a uniter, not a divider.

George W. Bush[1]

Supporters and critics alike praise Bush for his skill at building alliances and rallying the troops. From his days as class president and high commissioner of stickball at Andover, through his days of cheerleading at Yale, Bush knew how to influence people and work a room. He has a photographic memory and is a master at memorizing names. During the hazing process at his Yale fraternity, DKE, all the initiates were asked impromptu to name the other pledges in the room. Several initiates were called on, struggled to remember three or four names, then stalled out. When Bush was put on the spot, it was a different story. He slowly and accurately named all 54 people in the room, to the astonishment of everyone present. Not only does he remember everyone's name, but eventually he nicknames them as well. Karen Hughes is the "High Prophet," Joe Allbaugh is "Big Country," Karl Rove is . . . "Turd Blossom."

All of Bush's biographers note his skill with people. Minutaglio, in *First Son*, says that Bush has been a master at building alliances "since

149

George Walker Bush . . . set foot on the campus of Andover, moved to Yale, to the National Guard, to the oil patch, to baseball. He was still the head cheerleader, still the willing salesman of everything from oilfields to baseball tickets."[2] He instinctively knows how to bridge and bring together people with different views. One classmate compared Bush to Tom Sawyer, the literary character who not only got his friends to whitewash a fence for him, but also made them feel lucky for getting to do it. Bush generates that kind of enthusiasm.

Colleagues and staff members agree that he is a charmer. Aubrey Immelman, an expert on the psychology of presidents, wrote:

> Political acumen may well turn out to be the defining feature of the Bush presidency. Bush's primary personality strengths are "people" skills. His outgoing orientation will be instrumental in rallying, energizing, and motivating others. It also will help in building the necessary public and political support for implementing his policy initiatives.
>
> Bush's campaign slogan, "I'm a uniter, not a divider," is more than just platitude; it's firmly rooted in the essence of his character."[3]

In college, Bush became famous for getting his friends to pull pranks despite their initial reluctance. Even when he was a teenager, it was evident that Bush had "inherited some extraordinary political skills," says Bill Semple, a classmate of Bush's at Andover.[4] When Bush was granted a release from the National Guard to attend Harvard Business School, his military file emphasized the same point: "Lt. Bush's major strength is his ability to work with others."[5]

Even critics who despise Bush's policy positions admit that he is hard to dislike. Molly Ivins says, "One reason that Bush is good at politics is because he's a likeable guy; you'd have to work at it to dislike him. He is far more culturally a Texan than his father, at ease with the kind of locker-room bull, rough language, and physical contact characteristic of Texas politicians."[6] Elliott Naishtat, chairman of the House Human Services Committee in Texas, once found himself in a Bush bearhug on the capitol steps. Still holding Naishtat in his arms, Bush said, "Elliott, I understand we are having some problems with the welfare bill. You're going to give us something we can work with, right? I'm counting on you."[7] Midway into Bush's first legislative session, he met personally with all but 6 of the 150 state representatives and 31 senators. Despite all the jokes about Bush's naps and his relaxed style, he has an energy that requires him to be with people—meeting them, cajoling them, joking with them, sizing them up.

BUSH BEFRIENDS BULLOCK

Bush's highest alliance-building achievement is, without doubt, his relationship with Bob Bullock, the legendary lieutenant governor of Texas. Bullock was the single most feared Democrat in Texas, the Boss Daley of Texas politics. He was famous for castigating staff, lawmakers, and lobbyists alike in what were referred to as "drive-by ass-chewings."[8] Despite his actual position as lieutenant governor, most people simply called Bullock "Governor." He had previously served as state legislator, secretary of state, and assistant attorney general, and understood Texas politics as well as anybody in the state. In one celebrated incident, Bullock shoved cow manure into a box and mailed it to a newspaper columnist with a note that said, "This is bullshit and so is your column."[9] George Bush knew that if he wanted to succeed as governor of Texas—a notoriously weak office as state governorships go—he was going to need the support of Bob Bullock. So, true to his excellent instincts as to alliances and collaboration, Bush started in on the project of winning Bullock over.

Several weeks before the election, Bush paid a secret visit to Bullock, who was recovering from open-heart surgery.

I knew that if I became the Governor of Texas, somehow, I would have to get along with him. Visiting his home during the final weeks of the 1994 campaign was the first step . . . . Mostly, I listened, and he talked. Conversations with Bullock were often a monologue. But by the time I left, I felt confident that we could work together. After I won the election, I continued my outreach . . . . I knew that only by working together could we all be successful . . . . We differed on key issues, including school choice, home equity lending, and some tort reforms, but we respected our differences and became friends.[10]

Bush handled a number of things well in building his relationship with Bullock. First, he made a point of listening. The most basic sales training course emphasizes the importance of listening, and yet many of us still don't get it. Bush does. Second, Bush found mutual areas of agreement. Expert mediators will tell you that the best way to move a negotiation forward is to find common ground. Bush thinks in terms of win-win solutions: what's in it for me, what's in it for them. Third, Bush kept their confidences and his commitments. Finally, despite their frequent disagreements, Bush persisted. The two continued to meet and talk, keeping the lines of communication open. In this way, Bush says, "gradually we built trust and friendship."[11]

The alliance with Bullock was testimony to Bush's skill as a uniter, not a divider. Bullock's endorsement of Bush in his reelection campaign was an enormous tribute to Bush's political skill. Bullock, who was the godfather to Bush's opponent's (Garry Mauro's) daughter, knew exactly what it would mean when he wrote a campaign contribution check to George W. Bush. Here was the Boss of Texas saying and showing, explicitly, that he supported a Republican governor. Bullock's endorsement didn't just shout; it screamed: *Bush is good for Texas!* It was proof positive for Texas voters that Bush had bipartisan appeal. G.W. had the political skills to collaborate with both parties and form a productive alliance.

The final, and huge, shock to the Democratic party came when Bullock endorsed Bush for president. This "betrayal," said Bill Minutaglio, "was so wholesale, so fraught with national implications, that liberal Democrats in Austin were rendered almost senseless and reduced to suggesting that Bullock really, finally, had lost his mind."[12] Bush's ability to turn a lifelong Democrat completely around—to the point where Bullock not only tolerated the idea of a Republican president but actually supported it—in the face of open hostility from Democratic colleagues, is nothing short of amazing. It explains why so many critics of Bush caution, "Don't underestimate him." Bush is a master at building trust and alliances.

What's most impressive, according to Republican David Sibley of Texas, is Bush's ease at working alliances. "He's like the guy at the pool party who sort of walks up to the diving board and does a double twist with a flip. He made it look easy."[13] Aides in the White House share this view: "His charm and people skills were supposed to survive the trip North, bust gridlock, untie policy knots like Social Security reform. His aides are still besotted. 'I just wish you could watch him,'" one of them gushed about Bush's collaborative abilities.[14]

ALLIANCES AGAINST TERRORISM

The terrorist attacks of 9/11 tested Bush's ability to build alliances. He and his top advisors saw clearly, from the start, that the United States could not respond alone to the attacks. As one top official said, even before 9/11, "There's no serious unilateral option. You've got to involve others."[15]

Bush had to build an international coalition and do it quickly. Fortunately for both Bush and America, he had learned the importance of developing good relationships: "I learned the value of personal diplomacy as I watched my dad build friendships and relationships with foreign leaders that helped improve America's stature in the world."[16]

Therefore, Bush and his senior staff rolled up their sleeves and did what Bush did so well as an oilman looking for backers, a baseball owner looking for partners, and a candidate looking for supporters: They hit the phones. Bush called leaders around the world, in Russia, France, and Italy. Russia's Foreign Minister Igor Ivanov stated that "Russia and the U.S. have agreed to closely coordinate their actions."[17] Powell and Rumsfeld handled some of the trickier negotiations, such as requesting the use of Pakistani ports for military actions. Asked how he knew he could count on support from General Musharraf in Pakistan, Bush said, "Because I trust Colin Powell and Don Rumsfeld."[18]

How successful was Bush in building a coalition? Russia joined forces completely:

Perhaps more important, Russia's President, Vladimir Putin, has thrown in his lot with Washington and London. (When Bush called the Russian President to commiserate on the crash of an airliner over the Black Sea, Blair was eating in Putin's quarters. The British leader had a chat with Bush too, signing off with "I'll give you back Vladimir.") Not only has Russia withdrawn its old objections to American military operations from former Soviet lands like Uzbekistan, but Putin has also signaled that he is prepared to reconsider his root-and-branch opposition to the expansion of NATO. For now he wants to be one of us.[19]

One observer who watched Bush build the coalition simply remarked, "When he's on, he's on."[20]

Bush excels at using a *both/and* mentality rather than an *either/or* approach. The former is inclusive, finding common ground and building alliances. The latter emphasizes differences and builds walls. For example, Bush made it clear that the U.S. military was attacking the government of Afghanistan but not its people. In fact, America dropped food and medicine—$320 million worth—for the benefit of the Afghan people, while simultaneously sending war planes to drop bombs on terrorist targets. "This is our way of saying that while we firmly and strongly oppose the Taliban regime, we are friends of the Afghan people,"[21] said Bush.

He used the same both/and tactic in explaining the war on terrorism to the Islamic people. He noted that their faith "brings comfort to a billion people around the world," and painted the terrorists as "traitors to their own faith."[22] The message was clear: The United States can be both in favor of the Islamic religion and against Islamic terrorists. Bush's skill in this area explains why he has had such success as a "uniter, not a divider."

ALLIANCES AND TRUST: TIMELESS PRINCIPLES OF LEADERSHIP

Only relatively recently have building alliances and fostering collaboration been recognized as skills of the extraordinary leader. Before the advent of the information age, it was possible for leaders to hire "bodies" to do the work in factories or on farms or on fields of battle.

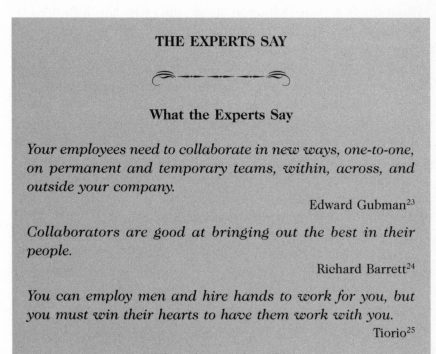

THE EXPERTS SAY

What the Experts Say

Your employees need to collaborate in new ways, one-to-one, on permanent and temporary teams, within, across, and outside your company.

Edward Gubman[23]

Collaborators are good at bringing out the best in their people.

Richard Barrett[24]

You can employ men and hire hands to work for you, but you must win their hearts to have them work with you.

Tiorio[25]

What the Leaders Say

The world must learn to work together, or finally it will not work at all.

Dwight W. Eisenhower[26]

Coming together is a beginning, keeping together is progress, working together is success.

Henry Ford[27]

Workers were mostly considered to operate as individuals, without the need to exchange information and ideas. Now, though, the information age has produced knowledge workers and workplaces where, in the words of Peter Drucker, "teams become the work unit rather than the individual himself."[28] This means that the command-and-control form of management, prevalent in industry and the military, is no longer adequate. Leaders must become excellent facilitators and negotiators to work successfully with teams.

Bush excels at these skills. For all the critics who knock Bush's IQ, few criticize his EQ, the Emotional Quotient. As Daniel Goleman, author of *Emotional Intelligence*, writes, "The single most important element in group intelligence, it turns out, is not the average IQ in the academic sense, but rather in terms of emotional intelligence. The key to a high group IQ is social harmony."[29]

Great leaders today know how to work with people. Although there may be times when reaching for consensus is not appropriate, such as during an emergency, that situation is the exception rather than the rule. Highly effective leaders know when it is appropriate to seek input from others, and to build coalitions, and when a simple declaration without consultation is more effective. Developing people skills and decision-making processes is what Goleman calls *emotional intelligence*, and it explains the tremendous growth of the executive coaching industry. Executive coaching, in this sense, is really emotional intelligence training. We know of one executive who was promoted to chief investment officer within a huge global investment firm; his first phone call thereafter was to hire an executive coach. When we asked about this move, he said, "I knew I was going to need help managing this organization. My background is numbers and theories, not people."[30]

Richard Barrett, author of *Liberating the Corporate Soul*, has done some good thinking about different types of leaders and the skills they bring to their jobs. His theoretical framework posits seven levels of leadership, all of them important but nevertheless hierarchically ranked. Barrett names psychologist Abraham Maslow's hierarchy-of-needs theory as the inspiration for his own model.

Maslow theorized that human needs are hierarchical. Our base need

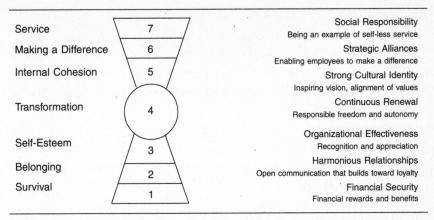

Source: Richard Barrett and Associates; www.corptools.com. Reproduced with permission.

Figure 6.1   Levels of leadership.

is survival: We need oxygen, food, water, and shelter. Once those needs are taken care of, we sense our emotional needs: to be loved and valued. Moving higher still, we have intellectual needs such as curiosity and learning. Eventually, when we have satisfied all the lower needs, we become free to self-actualize. When we reach this state, we have what Maslow called "peak experiences," moments of joy and wholeness.

Barrett's levels of leadership, shown in Figure 6.1, are ranked in a similar hierarchy. The skills required at each level are as follows, starting with the lowest level and working to the highest:

1. **Authoritarian**
   Good crisis director. Willing to take charge. Directive.
   Possible negative: Over long term, can be dictatorial, controlling, and exploitative.

2. **Paternalist**
   Promotes and develops positive healthy relationships internally and externally.
   Possible negative: May be emotionally insecure with a need to be liked. Can be manipulative and pretentious.

3. **Manager**

Regards management as a science. Efficient. Ambitious. Productive. Prefers hierarchical structures.

Possible negative: May be status-seeking. Possible problems with work/home balance and people skills. Tendency to be bureaucratic.

4. **Facilitator**

An enabler of human interactions. Invites participation. Team member and builder. Empowers others. Promotes knowledge and innovation.

5. **Coach**

Develops employees. Creates cohesion and community spirit. Values-driven. Displays integrity and emotional intelligence.

6. **Servant/Partner**

Mentor. Systems perspective. Responsive member of the local community. Strategic alliances and partnerships with customers and suppliers.

7. **Wisdom**

Wants to be of service to the world. Global vision. Long-term perspective. At ease with uncertainty and comfortable with solitude. Concern for justice and future generations.

Notice that the first three levels of leadership are double-edged swords, containing both positive and negative attributes. In Barrett's theory, the top half of the model consists of leadership traits that are self-less and therefore not prone to the excesses of ego.

The consummate leader is able to draw from each of these levels as the situation demands. For example, in the days following 9/11, Bush became much more Authoritarian, which was appropriate given the crisis that America faced. All American presidents have had similar reactions during times of war. It's necessary for the leader to bring order in times of chaos. In the archetypal sense, the leader—the king or queen—was the person who imposed order in the kingdom.

Mostly, though, Bush operates in the higher levels of the model, as Facilitator, Coach, and Partner. In this way, Bush displays a high level of emotional intelligence. In fact, Barrett says that the lower three levels of his model are more about intellectual abilities, whereas the upper levels require emotional intelligence. Barrett also characterizes the split between the lower and upper levels as manager versus leader. Given that Bush has displayed ingenious people skills, he truly fits the description of a leader much more than that of manager. Bush is the one who "plans the work" (i.e., leader) rather than the one who "works the plan" (i.e., manager).

The information age has made collaborative skills imperative. The direction in which we seem to be heading indicates that extraordinary leaders "will not be primarily players, or even coaches, but will be designers of the game who bring out the best in others. And when they do their job of indirect leadership well, the people will say, 'We did it ourselves.'"[31] Our sources on Bush agree with this statement. Working with him is empowering because he plans the work, delegates it, and then lets staff members feel that they accomplished it on their own.

HOW TO ENCOURAGE COLLABORATION AND BUILD ALLIANCES

Some of the skills needed to encourage collaboration and build alliances are discussed in the other chapters of this book. Building trust, for example, is a key skill in forming alliances. It encompasses the abilities to get results, to maintain personal integrity (be consistent), and to show empathy for others.

A second tool for building alliances is communication, and we cover that in Chapter 7. Communication includes skills such as listening, talking straight, providing appropriate feedback, and using language that inspires and unites rather than deflates and divides. For example, we facilitated a meeting in which one senior team member was having difficulty getting on board with the organization's vision. She didn't really see the importance of her role. After some further discussion, she suddenly lit up and exclaimed, "Now I see how I fit in and why I'm needed!" She added that in all her years of employment, she had never had this powerful insight. She beamed for a few moments and then the boss, next to her, looked directly at her and said, "I don't see it that way at all." The excitement went out of the executive like air out of a pricked balloon. We could not believe the tactlessness of the leader's comment. A valuable team member had finally caught fire and was excited about her role, and within minutes the boss had completely doused the flame.

Intuition, covered in Chapter 9, is yet another important collaborative skill. Bush's ability to read people and work a room, based on his intuition, has won praise from supporters and critics alike.

Executive coaches around the country teach these collaborative skills to corporate clients: How to give performance reviews. How to handle conflict. How to motivate employees. Earlier we mentioned Dan Goleman, who has become hugely successful by packaging these skills under the rubric of "Emotional Intelligence." He argues that leaders need the so-called soft skills even more than they need high IQs.

Collaboration and alliances require you, as leader, to choose the scope and involvement of your team. Who gets included, who is left out? How do you determine the appropriate level of involvement? How do you share responsibility without losing control? In simpler times, the military model worked. Leaders didn't share authority. They thought through the issue, made a decision, announced the results, and gave the orders. The military model assumes that the people at the top have the necessary information and are best suited to make the decisions. Participation by other stakeholders was not crucial to success and nobody talked about buy-in.

The world has changed. There is simply too much information out there, and too much *necessary* information, to assume that you can make good decisions by yourself. After 9/11, Bush knew that he would have to make decisions in concert with other nations. He knew that it would be hazardous to use military alternatives without support from other key allies. He also knew that he wouldn't make good decisions without input from sources around the world.

You now face a dilemma. You are reading this and agreeing that the world has changed. You agree that better decisions involve more people. The benefits of more participation are clear: a diversity of ideas, more creativity, greater buy-in for the final decision. Sounds good.

So what's the problem? Well, first of all, involving more people means giving up some control. This may not sound like a big deal on paper, but we've seen leaders hyperventilate when we suggest a planning process called "Open Space" (developed by Harrison Owen).[32] This process requires the leader to turn over the planning and decision making to the team. The leader decides on the topic to be brainstormed and then sends out invitations to all relevant participants. (For example, Coca-Cola used this process to design its booth for the Olympic Games in Atlanta. The project was completed ahead of schedule and under budget.) Participants determine what subtopics will be explored and then lead the discussions. All the attendees are considered equal; no one is allowed to pull rank. At each "Open Space" session we've conducted, we've made two identical observations:

1. The leader always feels nervous (sometimes even panicky) when we describe the process. As one said, it looks like the "inmates will be running the prison."
2. The results always exceed the leader's expectations. (Not surprising when you consider the first observation!)

Open Space is an extreme example of stakeholder involvement, and we discuss it for that reason—to make the point. The leadership dilemma is real. You can make all the decisions yourself, without the benefit of the wisdom and talent of others; or you can fully involve others and risk losing control of the process. Given these two extremes, how do you make intelligent choices about how many people to involve?

Interaction Associates has been advising leaders for 30 years on how best to make facilitated decisions. We are borrowing from our experience with them in this capacity.[33]

When the leader faces a decision that will involve other stakeholders, she must first decide who the relevant stakeholders are. The word *stakeholder* is defined as any person (or group of people) who:

- Is responsible for the final decision.
- Is in a position to implement the decision.

- Can block the decision or its implementation.
- Is affected by the outcome of the decision.
- Has information or expertise.

Given this definition of *stakeholder*, it's easy to see why Bush's decisions after 9/11 were so staggeringly profound. The fourth bullet point—"affected by the outcome"— includes nearly every person on the planet. Even if one could eliminate or ignore this point, the decisions still involved a huge number of people. A sizeable portion of the U.S. military was going to be part of the implementation team, so the military had to be involved. So did leaders of countries that were going to help the United States with the implementation: Pakistan, Saudi Arabia, Britain, Russia, and a host of others. All the leaders of Muslim countries that might try to block the military response could be considered stakeholders according to our preceding definition. Hundreds of experts who had specific knowledge relating to terrorism and al-Qaeda were also stakeholders.

You need to perform a stakeholder analysis if you are to intelligently organize and decide on key issues (see Table 6.1). List all the key stakeholders and their roles on the left half of a piece of paper. Then write the benefit to each stakeholder, from the stakeholder's point of view, on the right.

As shown in the example, Bush might have listed Pakistan's leadership on the left, because of Pakistan's role as a military base provider for the attacks on Afghanistan. On the right, he could have listed, as a "win" or benefit for Pakistan, U.S. economic aid and military support against India. If you're smart, you will consider all the key stake-

Table 6.1   Stakeholder Analysis Example

Analysis of 9/11 Coalition	
Stakeholder/Role	*Benefit to This Person/Group*
Pakistan's leadership	U.S. economic aid; support against India
[List other major nations here]	[List the benefit to those nations of joining the coalition]

holders and the "wins" for each of them before assembling a team. Typically, we see things only from our own point of view. You will benefit from performing a stakeholder analysis because it forces you to see things from another's perspectives. Abraham Maslow summarized this phenomenon well using an old saying: "To a hammer, everything looks like a nail." If you don't go through this exercise, you will tend to become a hammer, viewing the meeting only from your perspective.

Listing the stakeholders and the benefits they could receive helps you decide who should be involved in the decision-making process. However, several questions are still open: How will the decision ultimately be made? Will it be unilateral? (The leader simply announces what he wants to do and that's it?) Will it be a consensus? (Like a courtroom jury that stays in the same small room for days until all 12 jurors agree unanimously on the verdict?) What is the right way to decide? What is the range of options?

The following model, which is used by Interaction Associates in their work with leaders, moves from unilateral decisions (all leader) all the way to completely delegated decisions (all stakeholder). This model helps you think through how to involve the right people in the process and how to make decisions with them. When John Ward took over the reins as CEO of ServiceMaster, we facilitated his first offsite retreat with his senior executive team. On the way to the first strategic planning session, we pulled John aside and asked what decision process he wanted to use. John is a collaborative leader, so he answered, "Consensus." After some discussion of the ideas we've covered here, John agreed that consensus might not be appropriate for all decisions. Here are the range of options for collaborative decision making.

1. Decide and Announce. You are facing an urgent decision, perhaps a crisis. You take into account what you think are relevant options, make the decision, and then announce it. This option allows you to make a decision with little or no input. (See Table 6.2.)

Though Decide and Announce has gotten kind of a bad rap in our more "enlightened" society, keep it in your tool kit. You will need it,

Table 6.2   Decide and Announce

Benefits of Decide and Announce	Weaknesses of Decide and Announce
Rapid decision	Perhaps not well-informed
Leader remains in control	May not achieve buy-in
Can start implementation soon	Creates resentment about noninvolvement

especially for crises. The movie *U571*, which includes a lot of great material about leadership, makes this point forcefully. The second officer of a submarine has just replaced the dead captain as the new leader. His men are panicking. He asks them for suggestions as to how to proceed. One crewman says they should hightail it home. A second gives the opposite suggestion, arguing that they should head for closer safe harbors. Chaos ensues as the new captain tries to decide on the next move, admitting that he "doesn't have the answers." The next scene in the movie is especially interesting in light of our discussion on Decide and Announce: The new number-two officer pulls the inexperienced captain aside and tells him privately, "Don't *ever* do that again!" He explains that the crew needs to feed off the captain's confidence. The captain needs to be decisive and appear confident, regardless of what he actually feels. The scene is a great defense of Decide and Announce. It really makes the case that there are times when it is the height of folly to go for consensus.

Such was the case for Bush immediately after the terrorist attacks of 9/11. He needed to take charge and be decisive. He needed to reassure the public that he was in control. When the Air Force asked if they should shoot down commercial aircraft flying over Washington, D.C., Bush did not have the luxury of time for lengthy dialogues with key staff members, military and intelligence experts, and the like. He simply gave the order to do whatever was necessary to protect the airspace. When was the last time you used Decide and Announce? Was it appropriate?

The key to making this approach successful lies in the context in which it is used. Often an emergency requires this form of decision making. When you have to use Decide and Announce, you can maintain good rapport with people if you explain the reason for taking this type of action. If you decide to take your staff to a restaurant, for example, you won't ruffle too many feathers if you tell them, "I didn't want to waste any of your time, so I chose it myself. I picked a fairly popular place with a wide variety." Most of your staff will thank you for taking charge.

2. Gather Some Input, Then Decide.   You are facing a decision, but this time you check in privately with a few key stakeholders and get their input (see Table 6.3). Then you use Decide and Announce. Bush often uses this form of collaborative decision making. He has a group of advisors—Rove, Hughes, Cheney, and others—whose opinions he values highly. Rather than go to *all* relevant stakeholders, Bush will ask one or two members of his senior staff and then decide.

To use this approach successfully, you have to be prepared to explain why you included some people and not others. Consider what criteria you are using in the decision and therefore what input will be necessary. The Karla Faye Tucker decision, discussed in Chapter 3, is an example of Bush using this form of decision making. He conferred with several trusted advisors and then decided that the law was clear: Karla Faye Tucker, despite her religious conversion, would have to face her sentence of death.

When was the last time you made a decision using Gather Some Input and Decide? Do you think it was the right choice, given this new perspective?

Table 6.3   Gathering Some Input

Benefits of Gathering Some Input	Weaknesses of Gathering Some Input
More information for decision	Some may feel excluded
Faster decision time	If decision conflicts with input, may create morale issues
Doesn't require all players	May miss important information

3. Gather Input from the Team and Then Decide.   In this form
of decision making, you assemble the team, get input from all of them,
and then make your decision (see Table 6.4). Because of the magnitude of many of the decisions made in the days following 9/11, Bush
used this approach often. He met with his Cabinet and key military
personnel and advisors, discussed key decisions, got input from all
present, and then decided. Because of his preference for being a
"uniter," Bush often likes to reach consensus on proposals; he likes
to have all stakeholders on board, with no abstainers. This time,
though, the urgency of 9/11 forced him to use this more efficient
approach.

For this form of decision making to be successful, you must assess
how heavily you are invested in a particular outcome. If you are really
neutral toward the outcome, then you can facilitate the discussion.
Many times, however, you are not neutral. Be honest here. Think of
a recent decision that your team made. Was it appropriate for you to
run the meeting, or should you have asked a more neutral person to
do it? (Henry Ford once announced that consumers could buy any
color Ford car they wanted, as long as it was black. Do you think he
would facilitate a fair discussion about colors of Ford cars?) Neutral
facilitation is key, because otherwise the discussion can:

- Get way off track and waste time. (If this occurs, expert facilitation can save the day. Setting out typical guidelines for a meeting, such as ground rules, roles, intended outcomes, type of input
  desired, and time limits, is also helpful.)

Table 6.4   Gather Input from the Team

Benefits of Gathering Input from Team	Weaknesses of Gathering Input from Team
Synergy of group working together	Takes more time
Better informed decision	May get sidetracked
More buy-in for implementation	If decision conflicts with input, may create morale issues

- Be unfairly guided toward the biased facilitator's point of view. (To avoid this, neutrality is crucial. Professional mediators, for example, make a point of telling both parties that they have no interest in the outcome either way.)

When was the last time your team gathered to make a key decision? Who facilitated the discussion? Was it you? Were you neutral as to the outcome? (Really?)

4. Consensus.   The term *consensus* is commonly misused. People employ it to mean "majority vote" and "unanimous decision," when in fact it means neither. *Consensus* means that every member of your team is willing to support the decision and help implement it. It does *not* mean that each member is wildly enthusiastic about the outcome, as the phrase *unanimous decision* implies. It does mean that all your team members are willing to move forward with that decision. Consensus decisions require skilled participants. The individuals in these groups must be able to put aside their egos and think, "What is good for the group?" In this sense, consensus decision making is very different from normal thinking, which is usually based on "What's best for me?"

Big decisions that aren't emergencies often require consensus. Bush did not want to launch a military offensive unless he had consensus from his staff, Congress, and the military. A scene in the movie *13 Days* very closely parallels Bush's situation after 9/11. The context is the Cuban missile crisis. Kennedy must decide whether to take military action against Russian navy ships in the Caribbean. He has already made several key decisions without support from his entire staff, but for this decision he says specifically that he must have consensus. Everyone must be on board. Despite enormous pressure as international tension mounts, Kennedy waits until the group decides.

Consensus often takes considerable time and discussion (see Table 6.5). The process may seem agonizingly slow, but another war in another time—Vietnam—taught U.S. leaders the perils of moving forward without consensus.

For consensus to work, your team members must understand the concept of the greater good. They must be able to identify the larger

Table 6.5   Consensus

Benefits of Consensus	Weaknesses of Consensus
Active participation	Time-consuming
High support for implementation	Collaborative skills needed by team
Quick implementation because	members
team is informed and on board	Some see consensus as stemming
	from leader's lack of decisiveness

goal of the group and then decide, regardless of their personal positions, what would be best for the group. Team members must understand how to negotiate skillfully, how to listen openly to different opinions, and how to differentiate between positions and underlying needs and interests. They must understand what it means to reach common ground. They must think creatively to find solutions that satisfy the needs and interests of all parties. For example, residents of a private street may all agree that children's safety is important. They may also agree that traffic on the street is the most serious threat. But they may differ widely on solutions, which could range from speed bumps, to signage, to closing off one end of the street. It would require skillful facilitation to gain consensus on which solution to choose.

If team members are used to black-and-white thinking, they will have difficulty with the sophistication required in deciding for the good of the whole. You will have to explain why you have chosen consensus as a means of decision making and what the constraints are, for both time and financial limitations. Importantly, before the discussion begins, you must specify a fallback plan (such as majority vote or a decision by you) in case the group cannot reach a consensus. The worst-case scenario is when you promise consensus and then, due to an impasse, pull the rug out from under the group and make the decision yourself. You may never get them to participate fully again. They will remember and think, "She's just going to decide anyway, so why bother?"

5. Delegate with Constraints.   This form of decision making is also common to Bush. He prides himself on not micromanaging, and delegating represents the ultimate in hands-off management (see Table

6.6). When Bush ran the Texas Rangers, he delegated all the day-to-day operations and baseball decisions to the general manager. Bush and his partners were well aware that they did not have the expertise to make baseball decisions. Instead, they trusted the baseball people with those decisions and held them accountable for the results.

The keys to delegating are providing sufficient guidance and being willing to accept the decisions. (Chapter 5 gave detailed suggestions on how to delegate.) You need to think through this aspect of the process carefully. A worst-case scenario is that your team makes a decision and then, because you (or they) overlooked some aspect of the problem, you have to veto that decision. Rebuilding their trust after that will take a long, *long* time.

In the case of the Texas Rangers, the goal was simple: to win baseball games. When the team had lost too many games, Bush exercised his authority and fired the general manager (there's the accountability factor kicking in). Despite the fact that they have delegated a decision, good leaders remain accessible to answer questions and provide support.

Leaders can choose from any of these five different methods, depending on how much team involvement is appropriate. There is no correct answer, but do consider the following factors when deciding which of the processes to use:

Table 6.6   Delegating with Constraints

Benefits of Delegating with Constraints	Weaknesses of Delegating with Constraints
Frees up time for the leader	Staff or other delegates may not have the skills or experience required to make a good decision
Best method to get buy-in	
Develops leadership ability in others	
	Time-intensive
	Team may take on issues outside the bounds of the assignment

- *Stakeholder buy-in.* How much should key stakeholders be involved, so that they feel compelled to support and implement the decision?
- *Time available.* How much time can be used? Is the situation an emergency? Can it wait for the whole group to meet and discuss?
- *Importance of the issue.* How critical is the issue to be decided? Is it life and death? Is it relatively insignificant?
- *Information requirements.* What stakeholders have key information? Which decision process will adequately allow them to share important data?
- *Skill of participants.* If the team members are new and inexperienced, can they handle a sophisticated decision-making process?
- *Team bonding.* Sometimes using a more elaborate decision-making method is also a good exercise for new members, to promote learning about and connection with existing members.

This short checklist helps you choose the right level of involvement for your team's decisions. The simple rule of thumb, when stuck between two alternatives, is to use the process that allows more team involvement. Rarely will you be criticized for sharing authority with the team. The typical complaint is the opposite: not enough say in the decision making.

Using these methods, you can be confident that you are striking a good balance between control and participation. The efficiency and simplicity of "Decide and Announce" maintains your control, whereas "Consensus" and "Delegate with Constraints" reach for the ultimate in involvement and buy-in. Bush uses the entire range of options in his efforts to build alliances and be a "uniter, not a divider."

CHAPTER 7

Give It to 'Em Straight

Communicate

⌘

There is brashness, an honest directness in Texans that is sometimes viewed as too direct. I can be blunt, probably sometimes too blunt for my own good.

George W. Bush[1]

"George W. knows what he thinks and is willing to tell you," said Yale friend Robert McCallum. "He teases you, teases himself. He teased me about being a southerner. He teased me about being too serious. He teased me about screwing up on the basketball court— you know, like 'That was a good pass you made . . . right to the other team.'"[2]

Bush's teasing is clever and pointed and has just the right touch. Bush once proudly told reporters on his campaign plane, "I don't read half of what you write."

They shot back, "We don't listen to half of what you say," thinking they'd have the last word.

But Bush stole it: "This habit of reporters is abundantly apparent in the half of their coverage I do indeed read."[3]

171

Bush was nicknamed "Lip" at Phillips in Andover. Friend Donald Vermeil roomed with George for their junior year and said it was "probably the funniest year of my life. George had a way of keeping everything light and entertaining without offending people or getting out of line."[4]

The straight talk, the brashness, is many times said with humor. It makes him likable. It makes him real.

> The Governor comes right up to you, squints hard, almost as if he's trying to scare you. Then smiles, gets too close, closer than the permissible 18 inches, touches you and gives you a nickname. If that hasn't won you over completely, he moves on to someone else, and you go down on his Suspicious Characters List.
>
> On the other hand, Republicans cling to the notion that W. is tougher, and tougher-minded, than his dad. That he is steelier, a realist who isn't afraid of Democrats, reporters, anyone. It is said so often and by so many people that it's easy to forget his dad could be tough too. The difference is that his dad thought twice about letting you know. W. never tires of it.[5]

"One of the things in the public arena, a lot of people take themselves so seriously. And they've got this sullenness. And everything is so heavy. And humor, I think, is such a key ingredient in life" (Bush, quoted in Miller, *The Bush Dyslexicon* [New York: W. W. Norton, 2001], 120).

Bush is still real. He's still straight-talking; this example is just less humorous. It does, however, still make him likeable. People value the truth and that's what "giving it to 'em straight" is—truth. Some people may not like it at the moment, but if they do value the truth, their attitude later (when they're not livid anymore) turns into liking, or at least respect.

Doug Wead, a former Bush campaign staffer, noted, "Junior particularly enjoyed putting people who thought they were big shots in their place . . . harassing them with wisecracks and booming it out so everyone could hear it." Bush responded, "I was a pretty straightforward person." In his own defense, he noted, "Maybe people in Washington are used to double-talk."[6]

Straightforward goes with the territory. It wasn't just then. It wasn't just at Yale. It wasn't just at Phillips. It wasn't just while he served as his father's "loyalty thermometer" when the elder Bush was vice president. It wasn't just as governor of Texas. It wasn't just on the presidential campaign trail. G.W. was and is straightforward—always. After all, his mother is the famous "tell it like it is" Barbara Bush (and you were wondering where he gets this from?).

This president makes pronouncements unlike those of any other. Before 9/11, the American people didn't know quite what to make of him, but they sure weren't dismissing him either: Bush's Gallup presidential approval poll in the first 100 days was 55 percent. After 9/11, his approval rating shot up to 90 percent. Through it all, his humor, teasing, nicknaming, bluntness—in short, his "give it to 'em straight" communication—didn't change one iota.

GEORGE SAYS IT STRAIGHT

G.W.'s give-it-to-'em-straight messages have impact. They're easy to visualize; your mind paints an immediate picture of the situation. For instance, when we quote Bush as saying, "Are Security Council resolutions to be honored and enforced or cast aside without consequence?,"[7] you don't need the context of the message—you can visualize it. You get a vivid picture of resolutions being tossed aside without a second thought by someone who cares nothing for others. Here are a few more examples of Bush's straight, forceful messages:

- "We're not going to forget what happened on September the 11th. We've learned more about the enemy. We learned a good lesson: that two oceans can no longer protect us; that because we're an open society, we're a vulnerable society. But we're not going to allow our openness and our love for freedom to go away. I mean, one of the things the enemy wants to do is to say, you know, since you love freedom, you're under attack. And I guess the corollary is, is that, get rid of your freedoms. But that's not the way we think in America. When it comes to defense of our country, when it comes to our defense and defending our values, we're plenty tough. And that's the way it's going to be."

- "This war will not be easy or satisfyingly dramatic and might yield only incremental victories."
- "Suspicions and insights of some of our front-line agents did not get enough attention."
- "Either you are with us or you are with the terrorists."
- "We'll get him—dead or alive."
- "The deliberate and deadly attacks that were carried out against our country were more than acts of terror. They were acts of war."
- "Don't take out your anger by picking on someone who doesn't look like you."
- "The terrorists misunderestimated America and its leader."
- "I would never have sat idly by if I had known. Had I known about the plot, I would have used the whole force and fury of the United States to stop them!"
- "The nation's economy is bumping along."
- "You'll hear people say it's racist to test. Folks, it's racist not to test."[8]
- "I have a confession to make. I am a Killdee killer."[9]
- "When I take action, I'm not going to fire a $2 million missile at a $10 empty tent and hit a camel in the butt. It's going to be decisive."[10]
- "Some say it is unfair to hold disadvantaged children to rigorous standards. I say it is discrimination to require anything less."[11]
- "And so we've put the death tax on its way to extinction. However, as a result of a quirk in the law, it arises again 10 years from now. That's a hard one to explain. But, nevertheless, it does."[12]
- "I was dead tired."[13]
- "Late is rude."[14]

- "Do you like having your name yelled out loud in public in a derogatory way? Neither do I."[15]
- "I know people don't like it when I say there's evil, this is evil versus good. But that's not going to stop me from saying what I think is right."[16]
- "Make no mistake," Bush said, stabbing his finger on the table. "Understand my resolve, and all your people need to understand it."[17]
- "I sniff some politics in the air."[18]
- "This is better than a press conference."[19]
- "I mean it. I'll veto it."[20]
- "I've always said it was a vocational training exercise in capitalism."[21]
- "I want you to know I resent what you all said about my dad."[22]
- "What's the protocol here?" They laugh.[23]
- "How do we know we can trust you?"[24]
- "No, I was not born in Texas. Because I wanted to be close to my mother that day."[25]
- "Reading is to the mind what food is to the body."[26]
- "Am I going to benefit off it financially? I hope so."[27]
- "Seriously, I would respect that. I'm not going to like it. But this is a democracy. I love the system and I love the country."[28]

Sometimes saying it straight doesn't even need words:

Reporters were waiting to talk with [Bush] as he went into the Shoreline Grill with his family on election night after hearing he'd lost two pivotal battlegrounds to Gore—Michigan and Pennsylvania. As he went in, reporters shouted questions. He didn't use any words, a smile or waves. He scooted out of the public eye and into the restaurant as fast as he could. Disappointment was in his gait.[29]

During the presidential election recount, Jeanne Meserve of CNN was asked what the Bush camp was doing and how it was feeling. She held up her cell phone to the camera and said she was waiting for it to ring.[30]

Bush attended church in Jarrell, Texas, the Sunday after the devastating tornado there. He didn't speak; he simply attended the service to lend his prayers and comfort. Likewise, after a horrible shooting at a church in Fort Worth, Governor Bush attended a community memorial service. He didn't speak or sit on the stage; he sat with the crowd.[31]

George gave Laura a Christmas present. He gave the "Laura Bush Promenade" in her name to her alma mater, Southern Methodist University. It's a beautiful and restful tree-lined passageway leading to the campus library. "This promenade reflects a lot," he said to the audience gathered that day. "It reflects a visionary, a decent soul, and one who loves literacy. And it reflects my love for Laura." Tears prevented him from speaking and Laura came to the podium, hugged him, and led him back to his seat.[32]

Bush touches most people when he's interacting with them. Frank Bruni, after being with Bush for most of the presidential campaign, said, "What we saw was campaigning as facial calisthenics and Bush was its Jack LaLanne."[33]

WHAT HAPPENS WHEN BUSH SAYS IT STRAIGHT

"It was the best of times, it was the worst of times, it was the age of wisdom, it was the age of foolishness, . . . it was the spring of hope, it was the winter of despair . . . " How could Charles Dickens, writing in 1859 about the England and France of 1775, capture the late twentieth and early twenty-first centuries so exactly?

When it's the best of times, Bush's plainspoken style makes us feel confident, because he is. When he tells people, "I'm going to win the nomination and I believe I'm going to win the presidency,"[34] we believe it too. His brief (for a political figure) speeches, lasting less than 15 minutes, give us what we need to know without a lot of rhetoric. His repetition of his agenda, using the same words again and again, leads us to believe that he's telling the truth. Repetition without variation (*message discipline*) preserves the clarity of the message. This message discipline also helps Bush actually achieve his goals, because the more you say something, the more committed to it you and all those around you become. It becomes a part of you. When Bush says something, it becomes a part of us all.

When it's the worst of times, Bush's plainspoken style comforts us. "Well, I don't think about myself right now," President Bush said when answering questions about a possible assassination plot connected with 9/11. "I think about the families, the children." Tears welled up in his eyes. His tears made you feel he was compassionate, not weak. He'd never been much of an actor. The expressions that flashed across his face could be trusted as accurate reflections of what he was really thinking and feeling.[35]

Whether it's the best of times or the worst of times, Bush's plain and simple speech lets people know what's in his heart. The combination of just-the-facts brevity, confident wording, message discipline, and compassionate emotion is well suited to a time of fear, grief, and rage. It's equally well suited to "the spring of hope." When you net it all out, people like someone who tells it like it is. Bush said to a British journalist, "My job isn't to try to nuance. My job is to tell people what I think."[36]

Laurence B. Lindsey, economic advisor in George H. W. Bush's White House (and in G.W.'s White House), says he knows from personal experience that Bush the Younger is not at all shy about rejecting advice he thinks is unsound, or about demanding more information. "He's very much a Texan, and I was once on the receiving end of a very straight-shooting response that one would not want to see printed," he recalls.[37]

Giving it to 'em straight also causes people to remember what you said. Remember when G.W. overheard a reporter questioning his father's choice of Dan Quayle as vice presidential running mate. George walked right up to the reporter and told him that he resented what the reporter had said. Ten years later, that same reporter interviewed George W., who by then was president himself. Bush introduced himself, and the reporter said, "We've met," reminding Bush of the "conversation" they'd had ten years before.[38]

Not so incidentally, that reporter, though he probably wasn't thrilled while that "conversation" was happening, didn't hold it against Bush. Remember, people value the truth; when they get over being livid or embarrassed, what's left is respect. People who say it straight often get under your skin. They are also likely to be outgoing, confident, dominant personalities. Dean Keith Simonton, a political psychologist, calls this the "charismatic" presidential style, and says that Bush displays it.[39] *Charisma*—defined as a rare personal quality attributed to those who arouse fervent popular devotion and enthusiasm—sure sounds like something we would want in a leader!

Bush's straight talk in his address to Congress after 9/11 aroused such fervent popular devotion that Esther Margolis, of the New Market Press, published the address quickly, titling it *Our Mission and Our Moment*. As to the reason for the printing, she said, "As publishers, we believed people might want to have this little book, as immediately as possible to put in their pockets or purse, to revisit the words that so strongly set our course as a nation in this crucial time."[40]

Time magazine predicted that Bush's gift for plain talk and simple formulations may someday earn him a place in *Bartlett's Familiar Quotations*.[41] Simple formulations may land you in *Bartlett's*, but not all the quotes in *Bartlett's* were easy for the formulators to utter. George's plain talk and simple wording now lead him to just say what everyone else is already thinking—even when it's the thing that no one else would say. "I have found that by directly confronting a slight or a hurt, you can minimize it," George says.[42] That's good advice, but we all know how hard it is to confront those slights and hurts. We want to be above it all. We don't want a confrontation. We wait so long that we begin to say, oh it's not that important—but it still bugs us. It wasn't always easy for Bush, plain talker that he is, to confront those slights either.

Bush tells a story about confrontation:

In late October, I was campaigning in Lamesa when a guy came running up to me as I was finishing a radio interview. "How dare you use alcohol to try to influence voters!" I didn't know what he was talking about.

He pulled a "Dear Fellow Christian" letter out of his pocket which alleged that I had tried to serve beer to influence the votes of college students. What had actually happened was that I had attended a Bush for Congress campaign reception near Texas Tech University at which beer was served. The letter was sent to Baptist and Church of Christ congregations throughout the district and it created quite a stir.

A number of my supporters urged me to condemn my opponent Kent Hance as a hypocrite. You see Kent was part owner of a piece of land that had leased space to a bar where Texas Tech University students drank.

I said no. I thought people would appreciate a campaign that stayed focused on the issues. I learned an important lesson. When someone attacks your integrity, you have to respond. I should have countered with an explanation that laid out the facts.

I don't engage in personal attacks but if someone attacks me, I will never again fail to speak up with the facts about me.[43]

Saying it straight may get Bush a few entries in *Bartlett's,* but how about the rest of us? Are you worried that saying it straight means being rude to someone? Again, follow Bush's lead. Bush says Texas politics is a contact sport but he didn't suit up for the game. In the preceding "beer for votes" incident, Kent Hance gave people misinformation about Bush's activities, so George needed to explain the facts—about the situation and about himself. In contrast, during Bush's first run for governor, incumbent Governor Ann Richards called him everything from "son of a Bush" to "some jerk." In this instance there was no misinformation, just an outright personal attack. Bush was determined not to respond in kind. He'd say it straight about Richards's policies, but never about her personally.[44]

Are you worried that saying it straight will cause people to think you're not a "people person"? Bush is described by many as a thoughtful person with a genuine and unique way of relating to people.

Maybe you're worried that clipped, short messages will make people feel that you don't have time for them? Karen Hughes points out,

I've seen Governor Bush stay for an hour after a graduation speech to shake the hand of every graduate. I have waited as he talked with every one of the hundreds of people who came up to see him in huge community receptions. I've walked through countless hotel kitchens and back door entrances to buildings with him; he always stops to talk with the people—the cooks, elevator operators, janitors—on his way through.[45]

In fact, far from making your worries come true, saying it straight encourages people around you to do so too.

It encouraged reporter Frank Bruni to admit that the presidential campaign reporters "were in essence . . . covering ourselves." In his book, Bruni notes that many news stories are reporters' assessments of events, but come off as objective realities. He said that what they wrote about the campaign was all "partly true and partly imagined, motivated by our desire to create and live in a political universe more interesting than the one that really existed."[46]

It encouraged Treasury Secretary Paul O'Neill to keep straight-talking right through the criticism. On several occasions, the White House has had to try to quash rumors that Treasury Secretary Paul O'Neill will soon get the boot. The rumored grounds for firing vary (he's out of touch with Wall Street; he's not paying attention to the economy because he's too busy traveling overseas), but mostly, it's that he's just too honest for the Beltway. When O'Neill is asked a question, brace yourself! He says what's on his mind, even if it contradicts the president or jostles the markets. "He's always called the 'blunt-spoken Paul O'Neill.' Sometimes I think Blunt Spoken is his first name," says a Treasury spokesperson. This administration likes to celebrate blunt talk, but O'Neill can be too blunt even for the president at times.[47] Straight talking can cause people to overstep their bounds; sometimes it seems that George created a monster. Still, Bush would much rather deal with someone who occasionally steps out of bounds than a long-winded, waffling, wimpy talker.

George's straight talk encouraged a tough juvenile delinquent to ask a pretty revealing question. The question came at the very end of a conversation Governor Bush was having with offenders in the juvenile jail in Marlin, Texas. Bush sat next to the kids while they talked. He looked in their eyes and asked them why they had ended up in jail. Then he listened. He asked them whether they belonged to gangs and listened intently as they eagerly told their experiences. Then the question—one young man, about 15 years old, raised his hand and quietly asked, "What do you think of me?"[48] Bush creates the kind of atmosphere that allows the toughest people to say it straight.

BUSH WANTS OTHERS TO SAY IT STRAIGHT

Saying it straight creates an environment that encourages others to say it straight. Bush wants others to say it straight, so he models it. He doesn't leave it at that, though. He also tells them straight out to do it. Bush always reviews the words that go out under his name, keeping a keen eye out for the pompous and the overwrought. When he spots a sentence that wouldn't make sense to the average person, Bush peers over his half-glasses and reads it back to his staff in a haughty, mock-intellectual voice.

> "I do like people to make their points and express their opinions directly and concisely" (Bush, *A Charge to Keep*, 103).

Staffers say, "He's always asking, 'How can we say it more directly?'"[49]

Michael Gerson wrote an elegant, ornate script for Bush's first address to Congress as president. Karen Hughes read it, marveled at its beauty, and then rewrote it in the plain language the president wanted. It was easily President Bush's best speech to that point.[50]

Bush wants more than just his own speeches and messages to be written straightforwardly and plainly. He demands it in the proposals, requests, descriptions of events, and other information that comes to him from staff. Larry Lindsey, Governor Bush's economic advisor, recalls that after he'd unloaded some superintellectual, professorial-type sentence in meetings, Bush would say, "Hey Lindsey, run that by me again in English."[51]

MORE OF WHAT HAPPENS WHEN
BUSH SAYS IT STRAIGHT

All right, now. We've been encouraged by Bush's example to give it to you straight, so we have to admit that giving it to 'em straight can get you into trouble. Bush has been saying it straight for a lot of years, and he's seldom at a loss for words. The sheer number of total communications means that some of them, inevitably, will cause trouble. The key when you're in trouble is to be able to get out with your integrity and self-esteem intact. Use Figure 7.1 to watch and learn.

There are numerous benefits to giving it to 'em straight: People feel that you're being honest, confident, and compassionate; they get the information they need quickly; they feel that they can open up to you. Bush doesn't let a few stumbles keep him from saying it straight,

> There are periods when to dare is the highest wisdom.
> **William Ellery Chaning**

and neither should you. Of course, if you're not ready to dare, the alternative is communication that's pompous, emotionless, eminently forgettable, content-obscuring . . . by now you surely can complete this list!

One warning, even if we've already sold you on the virtues and benefits of straight talk: There'll be plenty of critics. Remember, straight talk encourages straight talk.

DOES BUSH REALLY SAY IT STRAIGHT?

We constantly hear two themes from critics who think G.W. doesn't actually say it straight: "packaging" and language usage errors.

First let's look at the "packaging" criticism. In August 2002, Bush took a month-long working vacation at his Texas ranch. Americans tend to think of *vacation* in terms of "have a good time" and not calling in to the office. To give Americans an understanding of just how much work a president does while on "vacation," his ranch was

BUSH IN TROUBLE	BUSH OUT OF TROUBLE
Without a script in front of a group, without rehearsal, he can sound brash or even unprepared, leading some to think he's stupid.	With no script, the fast-thinking Bush can use spur-of-the-moment inspiration. On his first trip to Ground Zero in New York, Bush started to talk to the crowd. Someone yelled, "I can't hear you." Without missing a beat, Bush offered the perfect response. "I can hear you," he said. "I can hear you. The rest of the world can hear you. And the people who knocked these buildings down will hear all of us soon" (Bruni, *Ambling into History*, 10). So much for Bush sounding brash and stupid if he hasn't been rehearsed.
Answering questions is a problem for someone who needs a script to address a crowd. On the presidential campaign trail, Bush gave some long, rambling answers that led nowhere.	Bush ended his answers in the presidential debates many seconds before his allotted time was up. This created moments of silence and awkward pauses before the moderators realized he was done (Bruni, *Ambling into History*, 53). Well, the critics said his unscripted answers were way too long, so he fixed it.
Before the September 11 terrorist attacks, Bush did a lot of shuffling, stammering, and pausing.	He delivered his speech at the National Cathedral smoothly; he was in his element because he'd found his calling.
He was criticized for his mistakes (*Bushisms*), for his lack of eloquence, and for sounding like a broken record.	Bush said his job was not to dazzle. As he saw it, his job was to iterate and reiterate his priorities and convictions, without falling prey to the temptation for variation, until people began to hear, understand, believe, and agree with him (Bruni, *Ambling into History*, 45). This worked, by the way. We know you can repeat his four-point agenda by now.
After being told that airplanes had hit the World Trade Center towers, Bush retreated from the classroom. In a little more than 15 minutes, he re-emerged, with some words scribbled in black felt-tip marker on a yellow pad, to make his first public statement about the unthinkable events. He looked somewhat stricken. He sounded slightly shaky. His words were colloquial: "Hunt down and find those folks" (Bruni, *Ambling into History*, 2).	He prepared for the statement "in little more than 15 minutes." (You mean Americans wouldn't have minded if he had taken a day or so to have Michael Gerson write something for him to review?) "He looked somewhat stricken." (Big duhh!) "His words were colloquial." (In this emotionally charged situation, would it have been better if Bush had used big, pretentious words and made long, rambling statements that led nowhere?)
Straight talk is too blunt for some situations. In a getting-to-know-you session with German Chancellor Gerhard Schroeder, the subject of global warming came up. Schroeder made plain that his government objected to the U.S. lack of support for the Kyoto agreement on limiting greenhouse gases. Bush challenged Schroeder, saying, "Where are you going to get your energy in 20 years?" German embassy officials reported to other European governments that the exchange had been uncomfortably sharp.	Bush White House officials said that from their vantage point, the session had gone fine, with the president just speaking his mind directly (Charles Babington and Dana Milbank, "Bush Advisors Try to Limit Damage," Washingtonpost.com, April 29, 2001; accessed July 12, 2002). Chancellor Schroeder had made his views plain, so Bush was encouraged to "give it to him straight" by a fellow straight-talker.

Figure 7.1   Bush in and out of trouble.

dubbed the Western White House. Bush's critics called this *packaging* (or *spin*). The complaints went up: How can he go on vacation so much? How can he take off for so long? He needs to be working! We're in the middle of a crisis of corporate confidence and the war on terrorism, not to mention mid-term elections!

Hang on a minute. Do you have any idea how much work actually goes on during most presidents' vacations, and definitely during this particular president's? When Bush's critics go on vacation, maybe they do call in to the office a few times, but they know theirs aren't working vacations, so they figure his isn't either. In fact, during his August 2002 working "vacation," Bush spoke at fund-raising events all over the country. He toured a forest decimated by raging wildfires. He made his regular weekly radio address. He spoke at a back-to-school event. He made nine appointments to administration posts. He read numerous briefing papers. He had innumerable meetings and held multiple news conferences from his ranch (you could have watched them, so you know he did it). There's more—lots more—but you get the idea. Is this packaging, or just a working vacation? You be the judge.

Then there's a lot of carping about George W. Bush's frequent language usage errors. It's the wrong word or the wrong meaning; it's not the greatest grammar; it's a confusing progression of words. The question from the critics is why? Why does he do this? Does he make these language usage errors on purpose, in an effort to seem like a regular guy? Or is he just stupid or uneducated? (Well, he got through Phillips Academy, Yale, and Harvard, so it's not likely a lack of education.)

The flubs don't happen when he uses a teleprompter, so we know he can read. You couldn't make up some of the stuff he says, so it's apparently not that someone is planning this all out for him. Some have said that he's just not good in front of a crowd, although he's excellent in a small group—so is it nervousness?

"In many ways his mistakes are endearing. But every time he speaks these days," a Republican supporter said during the presidential campaign, "he's commanding the world stage. Everybody's looking at his leadership. Everybody's looking at his judgment."[52] Yes, it causes concern for some people about Bush's leadership. But mistakes do happen, and they happen to all of us. Maybe you won't make as many as Bush does. Maybe you won't be as visible as he is when you commit a language usage error. Maybe you'll make even more than he does. Who knows? Who cares? The genius of George W. Bush is what he does about these errors.

George calls attention to them. He uses them to poke fun at himself. He doesn't allow himself to be embarrassed by them (remember, he had said that "my job is not to dazzle . . . just to call ['em] as I see 'em"). Think of this the next time you can't come up with a word or you utter some absurdity. Stay calm, move on, laugh at it, and know you're destined for fame.

Yes, George pulls some bloopers. A whole website and two books are devoted to his bloopers. He's a "what you see is

Can You Top That?

Q: If you could live forever, would you?

A: I would not live forever, because we should not live forever, because if we were supposed to live forever, then we would live forever, but we cannot live forever, which is why I would not live forever.

> Miss Alabama in the 1994
> Miss USA contest

I never had major knee surgery on any other part of my body.

> University of Kentucky
> basketball forward

It isn't pollution that's harming the environment. It's the impurities in our air and water that are doing it.

> Albert Gore, Vice President

I love California. I practically grew up in Phoenix.

> Dan Quayle, Vice President

We've got to pause and ask ourselves: How much clean air do we need?
Lee Iacocca, former CEO of Chrysler

If we don't succeed, we run the risk of failure.

> Bill Clinton, President

I'm not going to have some reporters pawing through our papers. We are the president.
Hillary Rodham Clinton, First Lady

what you get" kind of guy, and when he's unrehearsed it happens. If it happens to you, and it gets a bunch of books written about you, at least you'll be in good company.

GIVE IT TO 'EM STRAIGHT: A TIMELESS PRINCIPLE OF LEADERSHIP

Communication performs two functions: to liberate and to inform. Of course, by informing we also liberate. It's easiest for people to understand what we mean (to learn, and therefore to become informed) when we speak or write simply and to the point. There are always people who want much more detail than your average give-it-to-'em-straight communicator gives, but even those detail-oriented people want to know the bottom line first.

To Liberate

Everyone has a right to receive, and an obligation to give, simple and clear communication. When we give it, as Bush has found, we are more likely to receive it. When we create an environment that allows others to give it to us straight, we're even more likely to receive it.

Listening is the clearest signal to others that you want them to give it to you straight. You're open. You really want to know what happened, no matter how hard it is to hear. After the British left Boston on March 18, 1776, General George Washington saw a man sitting in the doorway of the Old South Meeting Hall, where so much of the rebellion had begun. His head was down, his musket across his legs. General Washington simply sat down on the steps near the man, where they remained in silence for a long while. The man couldn't speak because of the abuses the British had inflicted on this stately building. It had been used as a horse barn; everything was broken; rude words were written on the walls. Finally, the man began to recount the things he'd heard Sam Adams, Dr. Warren, and others say in this building—the speeches that had engendered the feelings that made him want to lay down his life for the cause.

THE EXPERTS SAY

What the Experts Say

If it is clear to your staff that you are being straightforward with them, they will know that the best approach is to be straightforward with you.

Chris and Reina Komisarjevsky[53]

Successful managers have a genius for getting to the heart of information rapidly. They use key phrases and words that communicate their most important ideas with great precision.

John Grinder and Richard Bandler, researchers who studied successful people[54]

What the Leaders Say

Make a habit of eating breakfast at the same table in the company cafeteria about twice a week. Everyone knows you'll be there and it makes you look like they're welcome to come and sit down. Note that at first they didn't come. Then a few brave souls, who probably felt sorry for me, sat down.

President of Syntex Corporation[55]

In the following pages I offer nothing more than simple facts, plain arguments and common sense.

Thomas Paine, in the first words of *Common Sense*, 1776

Washington felt the man's grief deep inside, and fought his rising fury at the crass assumption of superiority that would cause people to desecrate an important place like this.[56] General Washington, an expert listener, created the perfect environment for this man to say it straight; the man knew by Washington's patient silence that he was ready to listen.

Bush also uses humor masterfully to create an environment that allows and encourages people to give it to 'em straight. Allan Cox, author of *Straight Talk for Monday Morning*, says, "People who form the interpersonal network known as the company must learn the technique for generating the best ideas from each other as well as pulling together rather than getting in each other's way. This requires bonding and bonding takes place in the presence of humor, real human comedy."[57]

To Inform

Only through communication can we convey and preserve a common corporate vision. Communication can sharpen, embody and help enact that vision. Plato says a society cultivates whatever is honored there. An increasingly large part that communication plays in expanding cultures is to pass along values to new members and reaffirm those values to old hands.[58]

Straight talk allows us to pass along values and a vision that people can understand. To live a vision and preserve it, you must understand it.

"'The Emperor is naked,' said the child.

"'Fool!' his father reprimanded, running after him. 'Don't talk nonsense!' Be prepared—the one who calls 'em like he sees 'em may be ignored or at least viewed as hopelessly naïve,"[59] warn Gloria Gilbert Mayer and Thomas Mayer, authors of *Goldilocks on Management*. Sometimes your straight talk is so plainspoken, so straightforward, that people can't believe that's all there is to it, so they discount what you've said. Repeat the straightforward statement, as Bush does with his message discipline. Avoid the temptation to overexplain. Just repeat it, they'll catch on.

Fred Greenstein, an authority on presidential leadership styles, notes:

The modern presidency places a premium on the teaching and preaching side of presidential leadership. Kennedy, Roosevelt,

Reagan and Clinton—all outgoing personalities. They were the best public communicators among post war presidents. Bush, though just as outgoing as they were, lacks their eloquence. Eloquence is partially a product of effort and experience. Bush will no doubt improve in time, just as he refined his debating skills in the presidential campaign.[60]

Certainly, there's hope for us all to improve!

HOW TO GIVE IT TO 'EM STRAIGHT

Identifying Your Core Values and Being Disciplined Make Saying It Straight Easier

George Bush has a novel approach to the Middle East; he tells the truth. Yesterday's statement wasn't filled with diplomatic jargon. It didn't try to reconcile six different policies through artful fudging. Instead the statement has the ring of honest conviction.

The major advantage—when Arab rulers come down to Crawford, there won't be any need to shade U.S. policy this way or that to meet the exigencies of the moment. The president will be able to point to his vision and say, this is what I believe.

This is yet another time President Bush has given us cause to be proud of him. He has spoken the truth in a straight and simple way. He has upheld our cherished national ideals.[61]

Bush has identified his core values: family, faith, integrity. He disciplines himself to tell the truth no matter what the consequences to him personally might be. Knowing his values makes decision making a breeze. He simply asks himself, "How will this decision affect family, faith, integrity?"

If you know what your values are and always tell the truth, you can say what you need to say straight. When it's clear to you, it's easier to make it clear to others. In addition (especially for those of us whose memory banks are aging rapidly), straight talk comes easier because we don't have to remember what untruths we told or what the value "flavor of the week" is.

Straight Talk

Whether writing or speaking, use:
Short sentences
Powerful words
Optimistic/positive words
Open body language and facial expressions
Tone, volume, pacing
Stories to paint pictures

Short Sentences

"We refuse to be discouraged."

Look for ways to use shorter words and sentences in your writing and speaking. There are sure to be 9-letter words for which you can substitute 5-letter words, and 15-word sentences that you can shorten to 10. Short, simple words and sentences make it easier for people to get your message more quickly. You can still say many things. Just do it in many short sentences instead of a few long ones.

Many short sentences are easier to understand because they draw listeners or readers in. Your audience can picture what's happening because they're understanding as they're reading or hearing. Long sentences require people to go back over the words to get the meaning and make the picture—and most of us don't bother. We just go on to the next sentence instead.

Powerful Words

"America must keep its pledges to defend friends from aggression."

Normally, the word *must* is on our "not today, not ever" list. It sounds overbearing and patronizing. (Think about it: Who in your life said, "You must . . . "? Your parents, your teachers . . . do you need more of that?) But coming out of Bush's mouth in the preceding example, *must* is a powerful word. That's because it's *America* (a vision, a concept) that "must" instead of *you*. When speaking about yourself, *must* is powerful as well—as in "I must commit myself to moving this organization ahead."

Table 7.1 gives you powerful words and powerful ways to use them.

Optimistic/Positive Words

"It was exciting the first time I flew."

Use words that make people feel your optimism. Bush uses the words *excite*, *excited*, and *exciting* frequently. It's important that you be sincerely excited, or your use of the word, instead of creating a feeling of optimism, will create a feeling of being lied to.

> **Just to see how it feels, for the next 24 hours refrain from criticizing anybody or anything.**

"a smart, talented lawyer"

Bush says good things about people and situations. In the famous words of Ena, Bambi's mother, "If you can't say something nice, say nothing at all." It's a goal worth working toward.

Finally, there's the obvious: Delete the negatives. Table 7.2 gives you some pointers on useful substitutes.

Table 7.1 Powerful Words and Phrases

Instead of	Say	Because
"You need to . . ." or "You must . . ."	"To achieve your goal, you need to . . ." "It's important that you . . ."	Many adults will respond to "you need to" by thinking (or even saying), "I don't need to do anything." Telling them why it's important for them to do something increases the likelihood that they will want to do it.
"Since you were late, fill out the form."	"Fill out the form, since you were late." (Move the verb to the beginning of the sentence.)	This active sentence encourages action.
may *maybe* *possibly* *possible*	*are* or *have*	These tentative words imply that you're unsure whether something will or won't happen. We use these words to protect ourselves because we're not in total control (for example, "You may find this helpful"). The person unconsciously feels less than confident that what you're suggesting will work for them. Stating what will happen as though it were a given creates confidence in the person. Another reason why we use these "waffle" words is to keep from sounding pushy or demanding (for example, "You will do . . . "). You can prevent listeners from feeling this way by using assertive body posture and tone when talking.
hopefully *hope* *should*	"I can achieve our sales goals." (Omit words such as *hopefully* and simply state what will happen.)	
could *perhaps*	"You will learn how to communicate powerfully." (Substitute the word *will*.)	
"try to do . . ."	"do . . ." (Omit the words "try to.")	

192

"I'm going to have you . . ." "I need you to . . ." "I want you to . . ." "I'd like you to . . ."	"Tell me how you plan to get cooperation from your staff." (Omit lead-in phrases such as "I'm going to . . .," and just say what you want or need the person to do.)	People are more motivated to do things when they hear *you* than when they hear *I*. They act faster, too (it's unconscious). In addition, you'll save words and time with your straight-to-the-point language.

Table 7.2 Getting Rid of Negatives

Instead of	Tell the Person	Because
shouldn't *didn't* *don't* *can't* *won't*	what to do what they can do what you can do what you will do	The brain only holds positives. If you use a negative when telling someone something, the listener's brain will drop it and actually think the opposite of what you said. For example, you say, "Don't use that key." The listener's brain drops the *don't* and she is left with a mental picture of "use that key." She then has to unconsciously reattach the *don't*, thereby erasing "use that key." But there's no instruction, either from your message or the listener's interior mental processing, on what to use instead of "that key." Just tell the person what key to use in the first place. We hear you skeptics. If you don't believe us, try this: "Don't think of a blue tree with pink leaves." What's the picture in your mind? Right. Now do you believe us?

Open Body Language and Facial Expressions

Look people in the eye. We all know we should do this, but are we doing it? Always? Even when we don't feel like listening to the other person? Even when we're busy and looking at a computer screen while we're talking with them?

Leave your arms at your sides, or at least uncrossed. You may cross your arms because you're cold (get a sweater) or because it's comfortable to you (get over it). Crossed body parts are perceived as defensive, aggressive, less than confident—in short, not straight-talking.

Stand up or sit up straight. You will be perceived as more confident and more honest. (As a big bonus, you'll also burn more calories.)

People perceive the one looking them in the eye, with arms uncrossed, standing or sitting straight, to be the straight talker. Are we wrong here? Just check your own reactions: Do you prefer to talk with someone who doesn't look at you? Who has his arms folded over his chest? Who is slouching?

Tone, Volume, Pacing

Did you ever hear someone give it to 'em straight in a shaky, inaudible voice? Use a firm tone of voice with an even, reasonable volume. People who talk louder than we're comfortable with are perceived as aggressive and/or insensitive. People who speak softly are perceived as passive or lacking in confidence. If you're concerned that your voice will shake—when you're nervous or angry, for instance—take a tip from the great public speakers. Consciously lower the pitch of your voice (speak in just a slightly deeper tone than usual) and speak more slowly. You'll only need to do this for a sentence or two. When you hear your own firm tone, you'll feel great about how you sound, gain confidence, and naturally go back to your regular pitch and speed. No one will know but you.

Straight-talk pacing covers more than whether you normally speak too fast or too slow. Speaking too fast for an extended period of time will make you sound nervous, although if your tone is firm, it may come across as merely excited. Speaking too slowly for a long period of time causes listeners' minds to wander. It's unlikely that anyone will see slow speech as straight talk, because they couldn't pay attention long enough to grasp your point. Unless, that is, you use faster-than-normal and slower-than-normal segments for emphasis—then you'll have people hanging on every word.

The modern master of this technique was John F. Kennedy. He did it by using pauses. JFK actually wrote pauses into his speeches, and noted the places where he wanted to say a sentence quickly or slowly. Listen to his speeches and imagine the change in meaning there would have been if he had paused in different places or emphasized different words. (The JFK Library has many of his speeches, in both written and audio forms, on its website: http://www.cs.umb.edu/jfklibrary.)

For instance, note the pauses in this famous line: "Ask not (pause) what your country can do for you—(pause) ask (pause) what you can do for your country."

Imagine if he'd said: "Ask (pause) not what (pause) your country can do for you—ask (pause) what (pause) you can do for your country." In this form, the actual meaning isn't changed, but the sentence certainly lacks the power and straightforwardness of the original. Lest you think this was any easier for JFK than for you, know that he tested plenty of other versions with pauses in different places before he decided on the one we actually heard. Consider the opening of his inaugural address. The opening is the most important part, so imagine how many ways he must have planned this before deciding which was best: "We observe today, (pause) not a victory of party, (pause) but a celebration of freedom."

And then there is Bush, who, up until his speech to the United Nations in September 2002, had only been described as severely lacking in oratorical skills. After the UN speech, he was described by *Newsweek* as "rapping out his lines like a prosecutor." The speech was called one of the most masterful coups of his presidency.[62] If you didn't get to hear that speech, you really should (www.whitehouse.gov). His pauses were huge, causing you to hang on his every word. Most of the pauses were accompanied by a nod or pursed lips or a furrowed brow. He said the longer sentences at a fairly rapid pace and the shorter sentences almost imperceptibly slower. Most of his sentences used fewer than 10 words. When they were longer, they were always followed by a two- or three-word sentence. His volume built toward the middle of the 25-minute speech and then got quieter at the close. How did he know when to use the pauses? How did he remember when to get louder or softer? Yes, he rehearsed. But the teleprompter and his paper notes acted as memory tools too. The pacing was *written in*.

Whether you're writing for later verbal use, as Bush was, or a piece to be read by another person, you need to pace the written word. Remember the section on "Short Sentences" a few pages ago? In addition to length of sentence, you can also control pace by using commas, exclamation marks, short paragraphs, and italic or bold type for certain words. These straight-talk pacing tools lead readers to read the piece as if you were speaking it. It allows them to understand it as you meant it. This is tone, volume, and pacing in the written word. Straight talkers use these tools, judiciously placed, to get their meaning across with complete clarity.

To test your work, have someone read aloud what you wrote. Is that how you meant it to sound? If not, grab your straight-talk pacing tools and rework it.

Stories to Paint Pictures

Everyone loves a good story. There are stories you make up to illustrate a point. There are stories that already exist that we use to illustrate a point. There are "stories" that tell the facts in story form. Why do straight talkers use any of these three? Because stories draw people in. Stories make the information easy to visualize. Your mind paints an immediate picture of the situation. Stories convey knowledge and procedures in a way that people will both understand and remember. "Storytelling is a fun, friendly form of communication," says David Armstrong, author of *How to Turn Your Company Parables into Profit*.[63]

Storytelling does much more than help listeners visualize. Tichy and Cohen's book, *The Leadership Engine*, advocates that the best tool in the leader's arsenal is storytelling. Stories carry lessons and send messages. At its simplest, storytelling has the ability to touch human emotion and move people.[64]

Bush's UN speech was in essence a story that moved a great many of America's allies to agree that the United Nations had to do something to force Iraq to comply with the UN's inspection and disarmament demands. These were the same allies who had spent the summer of 2002 unconvinced by Bush and the United States that Saddam Hussein posed an urgent danger. It moved them—for the first time all summer—because Bush's words and the way he delivered them painted a picture in their minds of a serious threat. Bush recited a litany of Security Council resolutions (16 in all) that Iraq had flouted.[65] Bush repeated phrases like "weapons of mass destruction" again and again. Read any children's story and you'll see great examples of repetition and listing.

Here are some additional tips for straight-talking storytellers:

- Keep stories short.
- When making up stories, think of ones that illustrate your core values, mission, and policies.
- When delivering your information in story form, turn flat how-to's into dialogue (for example, use "To do . . . , Mary says, 'I turn on the . . . '" instead of "To do . . . , Mary says you should turn on the . . . "). It's a small change that makes visualization much easier.
- When using existing stories, carefully choose ones that closely parallel the meaning you intend to communicate. Irrelevant stories will actually divert attention from the main thrust of your message.[66]
- Stories are also enhanced by visuals. Use hand gestures, or facial expressions, or (as the Bush team does for every speech) projected photos or words behind you (thank you, Karl Rove).

What if you already give it to 'em straight? (Or at least you do now that you've practiced the genius techniques in this chapter.) George W. Bush is a wonderful straight talker, as many of the rest of us are.

The key to becoming excellent is to constantly look for ways to improve. Be open to advice you get from experts—no matter who they are. Early in his presidency, Bush solicited pointers on speaking to large crowds from Bill Clinton. Clinton is a recognized expert and Bush knew that public speaking was one of his own weaker areas. Are you that open?

Saying It Straight in Times of Crisis

Bush said it straight during one of the most horrific events of the modern era. Your crisis will no doubt be smaller, but any crisis is still a crisis to the people you lead. Keep the list of hints on "How to Give It to 'Em Straight" (from the preceding section) handy; it's hard to remember everything during a crisis. In your communications, put extra emphasis on the reality of business conditions, how the situation developed, and how you plan to move forward. Then and only then can you leave 'em alone to do their jobs.

Tell the truth. Of course you will speak the truth, but also take the time to be sure your message was understood. A relationship is strengthened by your telling the truth only when the person receiving the message understood it to be the truth. "Make no mistake," Bush said, stabbing his finger on the table. "Understand my resolve, and all your people need to understand it." Then he paused, checking for comprehension.[67]

Ask for help. Lots of say-it-straight communicators say they want their staff to put forward ideas, but the staff people never do. Why? Because saying it straight can often be perceived as "already decided." This is a danger of saying it straight. You can minimize this risk

> **Candor**
> Candor by national leaders summons us to settle for nothing less than straightforward truth-telling. Align your words with your conscience. Relationships will be strengthened by the sincerity of your communication. This is always true but even more important in times of crisis.

and encourage more input by following G.W.'s methods for "leave 'em alone."

Explain your plan. Tell the outcome and how you'll measure success. Work with your staff, either individually or as a group (or both) to set up methods, timelines, and individual responsibilities.

Maintain your delegation and mediation practices. It's very tempting to just take over in a crisis. Your true role, though, is to describe the situation, tell your plan, ask for help, and then guide, support, coach, and reward. You can't do it all yourself, and even if you were a superhero you'd lose the input of others, now and after the crisis has been resolved. Bush's real leadership genius is that he consistently applies his 10 leadership actions, every day, in every situation, with every person.

Share the glory. Keep telling everyone how your whole group or organization is progressing toward the outcome. Tell all your staff specifically what they're doing that's great or good or excellent.

Create an Environment That Lets Others Say It Straight

If you want other people to "give it to you straight," you'll need to use these two tactics together.

Listening

I want members of my staff to know I think about what they say. It's important to listen and I often call to follow up or ask about something someone said in a conversation.[68]

To get straight talk from others, you have to show that you want it. People who believe that someone is actually listening to them will be able to get to the point faster and with more coherence. They'll also feel that they can tell the truth without fear of repercussions.

Hearing is distinctly different from listening. *Hearing* is the unconscious, physiological effect of sound waves resonating through the eardrum and other parts of the ear and brain. *Listening* is the conscious use of certain active behaviors. Because it consists of behaviors, active listening is something the other person can actually see (look at the descriptors in Figure 7.2).

Looking directly at the other person; maintaining an erect, open body posture; nodding; using facial expressions that are appropriate for what the other person is saying to you—these behaviors come more naturally to some of us than to others. In fact, you may be able to listen quite well without some of them. You may be one of those people who really can focus better if you're doodling.

You yourself may be able to focus and understand what a person is saying without using the active listening behaviors. Remember, though, that this list of behaviors comes from people who answered the question: "Think of someone you felt was really listening to you. What was he or she doing?" Other people—the ones you want to give it to you straight—need to feel that you're listening. It encourages them to say it straight. They need to see you actively listening in order to believe that you really *are* listening.

What happens when people don't think you're listening? They may go on and on because they didn't get a signal that you understood. They may also start giving very short answers or even stop giving information altogether (not very straight talk). You may be able to listen with your arms crossed or while looking out the window, but

---

- Look directly at the person who's communicating.
- Take notes.
- Sit straight in your chair or stand.
- Display open body language.
- Ask questions related to what the person just communicated.
- Paraphrase.
- Nod.
- Say "uh huh," "yes," or other forms of verbal nodding.
- Respond facially by using an expression that's appropriate to what the person is saying.

Figure 7.2   What does active listening look/sound like?

you won't get as much coherent or truthful information to listen to. The person speaking is diverting part of the thought process wondering why you're not listening to him. He then loses his ability to give it to you straight. Such a shame!—when you really want it and all you have to do is practice a few easy behaviors (and change a habit or two).

Modeling

"The role of the President, as far as I'm concerned, is to stand up and tell the truth."

Always model straight talk. Be disciplined enough to keep talking straight no matter what the situation. No matter who you're talking to. No matter what you're talking about.

Telling the truth is one important component of giving it to 'em straight. Short sentences, positive words, strategic pauses, and storytelling round out the straight talker's tool kit. Blunt, brash, or too direct? Not a chance.

CHAPTER 8

If It's Noon, I Must Be Jogging

Be Disciplined and Focus

I realized the stronger I was, the more resolute the country would be.

George W. Bush[1]

The report you just wrote has all the right information. You started and ended every appointment today on time. You found every file and piece of paper in the first place you looked. Your staff all met your expectations today because they knew just what you needed done . . . This could be you!

WHAT DOES BEING DISCIPLINED LOOK LIKE?

You've heard the criticism that George W. Bush's "discipline" is just a good spin on the fact that "he's overly cautious, lazy and needs the comfort of routine." And where did you hear it? From the media and the political pundits. They originated the notion that Bush's use of a planned schedule equals "needs the comfort of a routine"; that letting his staff do their jobs means he's "lazy"; that sticking to his original course of action is being "overly cautious."

You be the judge. Check each behavior on the following list that looks like "overly cautious," "lazy," or "needs the comfort of a routine."

- ☐ Frugal.
- ☐ Reads through the Bible every other year.
- ☐ Donated his share of proceeds from his book, *A Charge to Keep*, to charities.
- ☐ High ethical standards.
- ☐ Keeps environment as positive, happy, and festive as possible.
- ☐ Lives in the moment; seizes opportunities and makes the most of them.
- ☐ Keenly attuned to people's physical appearances.[2]
- ☐ Hard worker who catches a dream and refuses to let go.[3]
- ☐ Ability to memorize lots of names.[4]
- ☐ Decided to quit drinking and realized the enormity of that decision only after he followed through with it (he never took a drink again).
- ☐ Expects his appointees to abide by "clear principles."[5]
- ☐ Discipline is not necessarily formal; normally Bush is casual and often humorous.
- ☐ Thrives on methodical planning.
- ☐ Stickler for being on time.
- ☐ Runs three miles almost every day.
- ☐ Thick skin for criticism.
- ☐ Never one to stay up late.

How many did you check? None, you say? Could it be that these behaviors are really the behaviors of a very disciplined leader? Yes. And here's how he does it.

STICK TO A SCHEDULE

Bush likes to receive drafts of major speeches five to seven days in advance. The quest for order at the White House represents both the president's personal style and a political strategy designed to replicate the legislative successes Bush enjoyed during his first year as governor of Texas, which aides believe set the tone for the rest of his tenure.

Before his inauguration, Bush demanded a detailed script—which became a minute-by-minute schedule—outlining the opening weeks of his presidency in a way that highlighted his major initiatives and created the right first impressions. He also requested a longer-term plan, repeating all of his major campaign promises and setting out a strategy and timetable for turning them into reality.

Every day's schedule is designed around the priority of advancing that agenda.[6] Being disciplined about maintaining your schedule (see Figure 8.1) is for the purpose of getting the most important things done—like keeping your campaign promises. This is not an irrational obsession with a set schedule, it's about focusing your energy on what's important. It's about setting up a system that keeps you from getting drawn away from those important things. The more successful you are, the harder it is to stay focused. Everyone wants your advice. Everyone wants to meet with you. Everyone wants you to do something.

Scheduled appointments never lasted five minutes more than their designated allotment when Bush was governor of Texas. When the time was up, an aide knocked on the door. If George thought the subject was important, he'd wave the aide off. But when the knock came five minutes later, the visitor would be shunted out. That blunt style served Bush well in dealing with the complex Texas state bureaucracy,[7] and Bush maintained this practice as president.

"It requires a lot of discipline to not get sucked into [an unplanned] lunch or meeting or something," said Clay Johnson, "when you're working on sticking to your schedule." Johnson worked with Bush both in Texas and in the White House, so he knows. Some staffers, despite being carefully chosen for personality fit, had difficulty in the beginning of their time with Bush. At the end of a late night of celebrating his election as governor, Bush announced an 8:00 A.M. staff meeting. He remembered, "I was eager to begin."[8] You can imagine his staff members' enthusiasm at hearing this. They soon became converts, though, when they saw how easy it was to get their jobs done in a scheduled environment.

Governor Bush

Gets to office between 8:00 and 8:30 a.m. and leaves about 5:30 p.m. At the mid-point of each day, takes a break of 90 minutes to 2 hours, usually for exercise, but sometimes for quiet respite. This time is impregnable. Leaves office by 6:00 p.m.

Goes to bed at 10:00 p.m.

Presidential Candidate Bush

Adheres to a daily campaign schedule. It is different each day, out of necessity, but always includes time for exercise and/or quiet respite.

Goes to bed at 10:00 p.m.

President Bush pre-9/11/2001

Arrives at the Oval Office at almost precisely 7:20 a.m. each morning. For the first 40 minutes of the day, reviews paperwork organized by staff secretary Harriet Miers and reads briefing papers.

At 8:00 a.m., is joined by Cheney and receives his daily intelligence briefing. At 8:20 a.m., has his national security briefing from National Security Advisor Condoleezza Rice. Then spends 15 or 20 minutes with Chief of Staff Andy Card to review the day's activities.

On many days, will meet with a member of his Cabinet, usually for half an hour. Secretary of State Colin Powell, Secretary of Defense Donald Rumsfeld, and Treasury Secretary Paul O'Neill are regular visitors. Others in the Cabinet are scheduled less frequently. Cabinet Secretary Albert Hawkins sits in.

Also blocks out half-hour chunks, in most mornings, for a meeting with domestic policy advisors Margaret La Montagne and John Bridgeland, economic policy advisor Lindsey, or budget chief Daniels. Deputy Chief of Staff Josh Bolten often is the gatekeeper for these meetings (the man who decides when they are necessary and on what subject).

At noon or so, takes a break of 90 minutes to 2 hours for exercise. Leaves the office by 6:00 p.m.

Goes to bed at 10:00 p.m.

President Bush post-9/11/2001

Not much has changed, except that he gets to the office at 7:00 a.m. Still gets up at 5:30 a.m. Still takes time, at lunch or at 6:00 p.m. when he leaves the office for the day, to work out.

Still goes to bed between 9:30 and 10:00 p.m.

Still has friends to the White House for dinner on weeknights and friends to Camp David on weekends. Weekends at Camp David still start midway through Friday afternoon.

Figure 8.1   Daily schedule (a day in the life of G.W. Bush).

"When you leave a meeting, you know what you're supposed to do," says a top aide—and you leave on time. Bush runs meetings with precision. He starts by announcing the objective; listens; and then, at the end, recaps what has been decided. Aboard Air Force One one day, he appeared in the press section and bragged, "This is the On-Time Administration." Bush marks time so closely that a cult of punctuality has developed around him.[9]

"Late is rude," Bush declared.[10] Furthermore, being late for one thing makes you late for the next. A lot of us are in that cycle and we can't imagine how, when we're rushing to meet a deadline, we could possibly just go exercise in the middle of the day. Or leave the office every Friday afternoon at mid-afternoon. Or leave the office at 6:00 P.M. every day. Bush well knows his own needs for rest, family, and physical exercise. You don't get the Red Badge of Courage for working constantly. In fact, time and stress management experts have found that taking breaks every so often during the day actually allows you to work faster (and more accurately) when you return. A break refreshes you so you can focus and get more done more efficiently. We read it; it seems reasonable (the few times we've been forced to do it by exhaustion, we saw that it actually does work)—but in the heat of the moment we stay there pounding away at it. Not so with Bush. He read it, thought it was reasonable, saw that it really worked, and disciplined himself to stick to it.

> "The true baseball fan loves the dull spots in the game. They allow you to think and remember, to compare the present with the past" (Bush, *A Charge to Keep*, 207).

Runners World magazine asked Bush, "What role does running play in your mental and physical fitness?" Bush answered:

It's very important. That's why I try to run at least five times a week, sometimes six. Running does a lot of important things for me. One, it helps me sleep at night. Secondly, it keeps me disciplined. For example, I'm a person who believes in punctuality. That's a discipline. I expect the White House staff to be on time and sharp and to exercise. And in my case, running helps me keep that discipline.

Running also breaks up my day and allows me to recharge my batteries. Running also enables me to set goals and push myself toward those goals. In essence, it keeps me young. A good run adds a little bounce to my step. I get a certain amount of self-esteem from it. Plus, I just look and feel better.

Runners World: You must have the most stressful job in the world. Does running help you cope with that level of stress?

Bush: It does. Running has helped me in times of enormous stress. It's interesting that my times have become faster right after the war began. They were pretty fast all along, but since the war began, I have been running with a little more intensity. And I guess that's part of the stress relief I get from it. For me, the psychological benefit is enormous. You tend to forget everything that's going on in your mind and just concentrate on the time, distance or the sweat. It helps me to clear my mind.[11]

Bush has been criticized for taking too many vacations, but his vacations are working vacations. (When he's not doing his paid job on his ranch "vacation," he's cutting down trees and clearing brush.) These vacations give him a change of scenery and purposeful exercise. He has been criticized for taking breaks in the middle of the day. He unabashedly told the press corps one day that his afternoon back at the White House would include a little shut-eye.[12] He knows how much rest he needs to stay at his best.

> No one ever cried out on his deathbed, "I wish I had spent more time at the office!"

Another part of being disciplined is recognizing when you need to change your schedule. Bush can keep an intense schedule if it focuses on the agenda (his vision) and is the exception, not the norm. By election day for his second term as governor, he had done 23 press conferences in seven days—and he was still bantering, beaming, and full of nervous energy.[13] Not what you'd expect from a guy who needs his sleep. Why was he able to do this? All that intense activity advanced his agenda (getting elected), and it was for a short period of time. "The word lazy is used to describe him," says Molly Ivins (*not* one of Bush's biggest Texan fans). "I get no sense of laziness from watching him—if anything, he seems to have a rather short attention span and often seems impatient to move on to the next topic or project, leaving an impression of restless energy."[14]

Bush maintains his schedule and his "stick to it" beliefs through all the criticism. If you want to get the benefits of sticking to a schedule, you'll have to stick to the beliefs and the behavior as well, because you'll draw flak from a lot of naysayers (we think they're people who can't stick to a schedule like Bush does, so they believe it's impossible). When we first learned this about George, we said to each other, "I wish I had his schedule." But now we know it works—if you *really* stick to it. As soon as you allow yourself to stay later at the office one day, it quickly becomes two days and then "next week I'll get back to going home at six." Pretty soon you see the new time, 8:00 P.M., as your regular departure time. You know this at the beginning of the day, so it takes you until 8:00 P.M. to get the work done.

The same applies to getting enough sleep to function at your optimal level, and to scheduled exercise. An exercise schedule works great until you have that big proposal and you say, "Today I'll skip it because I have all this to do." Then the next day, you're not done with the proposal (shockingly, it took longer than you'd expected). Pretty soon you don't have time for exercise anymore. George says that you don't have time *not* to stick to a schedule.

Being disciplined means choosing the things to do that will advance your agenda and setting a schedule that fits you and your goals. We know, you just have to work all those hours to get the job done (still in the naysayer camp?). Consider, though: If your body, ugly as it will be with little sleep, shows up tomorrow but your brain is only half there, do you really believe that you'll get your work done as efficiently and effectively as Bush, who has one whole brain at work with him?

Being disciplined also means relentlessly saying no to everything that doesn't help you meet your goals. Stay the course on your disciplined schedule and "consider the source" when you hear criticism.

If the naysayers achieve all their goals and look years younger than their true ages, listen to them. If not, stay your course.

STAY THE COURSE

Bush won the governor's office in Texas in 1994, against a popular incumbent, largely because he was disciplined. Month after month during the campaign, he kept repeating his four-point agenda. Once in office, he took the same approach and applied it to governing. In each legislative session, he set a few policy goals, outlined the principles by which he would judge success, gave other people the power to work out the details, and stuck to his agenda with remarkable discipline.[15]

People need to hear the same thing again and again; consistency and "staying your course" are crucial for them to believe you mean it. Bush calls it *message discipline*. Of course, the broken-record approach can get boring. That four-point agenda became five in a "state of the state" address when Governor Bush said, "You're ready for number five. Here it is—Number five is to pass the first four!"[16]

He did the same thing as president when he got to Washington. He had a four-point agenda and hammered away at it point by point. The Washington crew knew that he'd been able to stay the course in Texas, but wondered if he would when the stakes were higher. When Representative Peter King challenged Bush's commitment to passing a patients' bill of rights, the president didn't waver. He wanted a bill he could sign, but vowed again to veto the Democratic version, because it would cause some serious problems for patients. "Many of us, when we heard the veto threat, weren't convinced he was serious, because from Day One he has been trying to get this off his plate (one of his four points). But I'm convinced now that there is a line in the sand," said Representative King. "I'm not sure where it is, but it's there."[17]

Bush holds off on using his clout until the facts are in and he can close the deal. Once a plan is in place, he doesn't tinker. He stays the course and resists changing that course until the last possible moment.

In some cases, he gets high marks for this: He didn't rush the bombing in Afghanistan and stayed the course when the battle plan stalled in October 2001. His military aides told him the United States had no good targets for a quick strike inside Afghanistan, so Bush wisely resisted the urge to launch an attack.[18]

In other instances, he gets criticized for staying the course. Some critics said that he was slow to develop a sense of urgency about corporate reform. What made them think this? They said he was consumed with the Middle East and neglected to deal with corporate confidence issues early, before they caused the stock markets to plummet.[19]

This is precisely what causes so many leaders to become ineffective. They change their course, their agenda, their goals—call it what you will—at the drop of a hat (or at least at noise from loud, squeaky wheels). If Bush hadn't kept his focus on the Middle East, there wouldn't be a United States in which to have corporation confidence issues.

It's not that Bush was focusing so much on wiping out terrorism that he had no idea there were corporate scandals—he was asked a few hundred questions about his own corporate work, as you may recall. It's that Bush's focus was on what he calls "the real economy," how businesses in general are doing. He sees a vast disconnect between the real economy and the stock markets. The real economy had hired small numbers of workers and unemployment was only 5.9 percent in June 2002 (still historically low). Home buying, appliance purchases, and furniture sales were strong. Low-interest loans and price discounts sustained auto sales, and June 2002 saw the sixth monthly rise in industrial production. Most economists in July 2002 said, "The real economy will prevail."[20] Bush was apparently slow to respond because in fact the real economy was doing well. The media called it "Bush Team's Inaction." (Of course, that's what they said after 9/11 about the lack of immediate bombing of Afghanistan. We now know that his "team's inaction" was invaluable in securing the alliances required for a plan that would work.)

As if 2001 and early 2002 weren't enough of a test of G.W.'s ability to stay the course, there's the summer of 2002. How do you take a country to war . . . a big, long war? If you're Saddam Hussein, you just call out the Republican Guard, invade your neighbor, and ignore the consequences, the way you did in August 1990. But if you're the president of the United States, you have to run the high hurdles. You have to talk to Congress. You have to listen to your generals. You have to build alliances. You had better measure the ability of your economy—especially if it's feeling weak—to go the distance. Above all, you have to get approval from your people, who might think you have enough on your plate already.

One man runs an iron dictatorship; the other has to wrestle with a real democracy. This is as good a reason as you'll find to explain why, even as the noise level on Iraq rose throughout the summer and fall of 2002, the signals from the Bush White House quietly flickered from green (go to war) to yellow (keep planning). A senior administration official informed a key lawmaker that Congress should not expect U.S. action before the November elections. Another pushed the timetable into 2003. "No decisions are going to be made on Iraq for the foreseeable future," the official said.

The president, whose near-obsession with extinguishing Saddam remains strong, was giving nothing away. When asked about Iraq in an Oval Office meeting with Jordan's King Abdullah II, Bush paused for a long time and then said, "Saddam Hussein is a man who poisons his own people, who threatens his neighbors, who develops weapons of mass destruction. And I assured His Majesty, like I have in the past; we're looking at all options. I'm a patient man. But I haven't changed my opinion since the last time he was in the Oval Office." Translation: I've changed my timing but not my goals. Bush's timetable was being revised by an economy that kept sputtering, continued violence in the other troubled areas of the Middle East (where Palestinian bombers claimed five Americans along with numerous Israeli lives), and new questions about his strategy from Capitol Hill.[21]

By the time of Bush's UN speech in September 2002, columnist Jim Hoagland was saying what was obvious to all of us: that Bush has what it takes to stay the course. "Nearly 20 months into his presidency, Bush has demonstrated an ability to tolerate evolving [i.e., messy] strategies and situations filled with inconsistencies that would unsettle more conventionally minded politicians. He does not resolve big strategic debates so much as push them forward."[22]

Because of the global and economic crises, Bush's August 2002 vacation plans drew heat from everyone. Democrats said he had no business taking a scheduled one-month vacation[23] at his ranch while the stock market plunged and foreign affairs were volatile. David Letterman said, "Unwind? When does this guy wind?" (Don't those guys read the papers? When presidents are on vacation, they work the whole time!) In Chapter 7, we saw just how much presidential work Bush does while on "vacation." In Chapter 5, we pointed out that it is possible, in the year 2002, to work while away from one's primary office (aside from late-night talk show hosts and members of Congress, most of us *do* work while we're on vacation). Bush did both presidential work and physical ranch labor for the vast majority of his vacation. But his ranch is his home base—a needed change of scenery—and he knows the benefits of respite to him as a leader and in staying the course.

He stays the course on exercise, too. Bush says that if he's in a place where he can't run, he uses an elliptical trainer machine, lifts weights, and stretches. "There's never a question in my mind that I'll exercise."[24] That's both the key to and the benefit of discipline. There is never a question in your mind about staying the course. The discipline of never questioning simply begets more discipline.

Bush is so sure. He has such clarity about his need to stay the course. This certainty itself is discipline, and it comes from the discipline that springs from knowing his core values. When you set your course (vision) on three core values, you can measure every action against that vision.

BUSH CAN CHANGE WHEN HE NEEDS TO

Discipline doesn't mean inflexibility and intractability. It does mean that the disciplined person, such as George W. Bush, doesn't change on a whim. He thinks hard and weighs the pros and cons. Sometimes that means staying the course even if it's not popular. For example, people became concerned that things weren't moving fast enough in the war on terrorism. "People started worrying that we were on the same track the Soviets had been on," says Rumsfeld, and "some people in the neighboring countries were characterizing [the war] as being bogged down." Behind locked doors, the president's top advisors were kicking around the idea of putting more troops on the ground. However, at a meeting in late October 2001, the president stopped the debate and said, "We did all agree on the plan, didn't we?" Everyone nodded. He turned to General Franks and asked, "Tommy, is this plan working?" Franks said simply, "Yes." Bush concluded, "I've made it clear to the American people. I've got confidence in this plan. We should all have confidence in this plan. Be patient, people. It's going to work."[25]

In other cases, you weigh the pros and cons and discover it's time to change.

> *Barbara Walters:* Do you ever take, like, a glass of wine at a wedding or something?
>
> *George W.:* No, I've had no alcohol since I decided to quit.
>
> *Barbara:* Are you afraid you're an alcoholic?
>
> *George W.:* No.
>
> *Barbara:* Then why wouldn't—couldn't you take, you know, I don't know, a "Happy New Year, here's a sip of champagne"?
>
> *George W.:* Because I just decided to quit.
>
> *Barbara:* Period.
>
> *George W.:* When I said I was quitting, I was quitting. And I think that speaks to my discipline and my focus.[26]

Sometimes the change is made over a period of time. Running for president can cause a person to reexamine his or her behavior. Frank Bruni called it "morphing." He said we were watching Bush grow before our eyes. He saw candidate Bush change some of his personal behaviors to become more serious. It wasn't a personality change; he wasn't transforming himself into some completely new kind of leader.

Instead, he was seeking to strike a kind of balance, to elevate his behavior and bearing without abandoning his humor, positive attitude, friendliness, and down-to-earth attitude. Those qualities were, after all, what had made so many people like him so much.[27]

The time period for a change may be as short as a campaign or as long as 15 years. In July 2002, the *Washington Post* and the *New York Times* ran front-page stories about the loans Bush had received from Harken Energy while on its board in the late 1980s. Both stories accused Bush of being hypocritical for cracking down on the corporate loans to CEOs and board members when he had benefited from this himself.

Being disciplined doesn't mean you cling to beliefs or behaviors once you have information proving that they aren't the best ones. Yes, Bush benefited from Harken corporate loans made to him as a board member in 1986 and 1988. Yes, in 2002 he called for corporate responsibility reforms that would outlaw corporate loans to board members. Bush weighed the pros and cons. He saw what a large number of those loans had done to many companies' employees and shareholders. *He had more information.* Changing his position on corporate loans was not hypocritical. "That's like saying you couldn't be for campaign finance reform if you took contributions," says White House communications director Dan Bartlett. "People learn from experience."[28]

All right, so Bush learned from experience about the ill effects of corporate loans. What about being on an audit committee? Wasn't that a problem? "Audit committees were different then than now," says Dan Bartlett. "They gave discretion to CEOs." When Bush was questioned about being on the audit committee at Harken when company losses were hidden by selling a subsidiary to itself, he stated, "The rules weren't as specific as one would expect and therefore the auditors and accountants make a decision."[29]

Being disciplined means holding fast to your basic, core beliefs (Bush believes in the entrepreneurial spirit of America) but being able to adjust your actions to fit new information (corporate scandals). (Figure 8.2 shows how Bush likes to get that new information.) "I'm will-

> **The whole information thing**
>
> Although he insists that "the details are important," Bush freely admits that he prefers one-page memos to thick bound treatises, oral briefings to long meetings. When he is briefed, he doesn't just sit back and listen. He engages his advisors, testing their logic and pressing them to get to the heart of the matter. Says Bush: "I like to hear someone enunciate a position, pro or con. Because if someone cannot explain a position, that generally means they don't understand the issue well enough to be part of the decision-making process" (James Carney, "Why Bush Doesn't Like Homework," *Time*, November 11, 1999, 46).
>
> He takes the time to understand things like the processes of airport security and intelligence gathering, instead of racing to the decision line on the memos set in front of him.
>
> "If there's a 10 page paper, he wants to know what are the 2 pages that contain all the content," Clay Johnson said when he was Bush's Chief of Staff in Texas (Washingtonpost.com, January 19, 2000; accessed July 14, 2002).
>
> When Bush was interviewed by *Talk* magazine in September 1999, he was asked what his most serious weakness is. He replied that it is his dislike of reading long books, especially books about policy. He told *Texas Monthly* that he hates both meetings and briefings (Ivins and Dubose, *Shrub*, New York, Vintage, 2000, 47).

Figure 8.2   Bush and information gathering.

ing," said Bush, "to work with Congress to make sure that we've got the necessary laws in place that will hold people accountable without stifling the entrepreneurial spirit."[30]

BE RESPONSIBLE

Being disciplined involves a lot more than getting up at the same time every day, getting the proper rest, and sticking to an exercise schedule. Being disciplined allows you to stay the course when you need to and helps you see when it's time to change. Being disciplined leads you to want to be responsible and accountable. It can sometimes be sort of a thorn in your side, because you have to obey its demands.

Everyone in America has a role and responsibilities.

Corporate America has a responsibility to treat its workers with respect and to give back to communities. It has a responsibility to work for clean air and cleaner water.

Mothers and Dads are responsible for being good parents to their children—the most important role they will ever have.

We have a collective responsibility to teach our children to read and know right from wrong.

We must give an honest day's work for an honest day's wages.

Respect others, respect their property, and respect their opinions.

Don't lie, cheat, steal.

We have a responsibility to extend a hand to a neighbor in need (Bush, *A Charge to Keep*, 230–31).

A president has responsibilities too. A president can speak for accountability [and] the power of faith and love (George W. Bush, introduction to *Triumphs of the Heart*, by Chris Benguhe [New York: Berkeley Publishing Group, 2000], xii).

In a long speech on family values, Bush's grandfather criticized Nelson Rockefeller for his divorce. In Grandpa Prescott's day, speaking out in public about someone's divorce was not exactly proper. Family values must have been incredibly important to him to risk people's reaction to such a speech. They sure are to his grandson, George W.: One of his three core values is family. George W. says that his grandfather's speech profoundly affected him. "There is a concept that you are responsible for your behavior. You can't shirk off your problems on somebody else. There is an individual code of honor and respect of your neighbor."[31]

Bush uses the words *responsibility* and *accountability* throughout his own book, which is, not accidentally, titled *A Charge to Keep*. He talks about accountability in the schools. He talks about the accountability of his direct staff. He talks about his own accountability. He talks about the accountability of every Texan and every American. The short story is that we need to set the goals, measure the results, praise people when they succeed, and hold people responsible when they fail.

If we disagree with anything George W. Bush has done, it's his failure to own up to some things he's less than proud of in his past behavior. (We figured we'd better come up with something we disagreed with, or you wouldn't believe the page after page of examples of how great we think this guy is.) Friends and co-workers have gone on the record in interviews as saying that, yes, he did certain not-so-wonderful things in his pre-gubernatorial life. When asked, George says,

> I did some things [in my younger days] I'm not particularly proud of today. The rumormongering has been spawned by my refusal to itemize a laundry list of those things I wish I hadn't done. They are things I wouldn't want my mother to know then. They are things I don't want my daughters to do. I think they forget that children are watching. I don't want my own daughters or any other young people to imitate anything foolish I once did or use me as an excuse for misbehavior. I hope my stand will help purge the system of its relentless quest for scandal and sensation.[32]

These are Bush's answers to the question that seems to be asked of all people in public life these days: "Did you party?" (or some more specific variation on that theme). Whether he did or whether he didn't, it was years and years ago, and come on—which one of us reading this book didn't party during our early years? How does that affect you as a leader now? How does that affect Bush as governor or as president now? Maybe it's even a good thing, assuming you're not doing it anymore. Stopping taught you discipline. (We used to think our children were super straightlaced because we saw no evidence of the stuff we'd done in high school—were we happy? Heck no. We were worried that they were nerds.) We think that past indiscretions and mistakes are no one's business but the person's own. So we don't care if Bush or any other leader partied years and years ago. We can actually even see some benefit to the person's discipline in quitting and changing. We just don't think it's anyone else's business.

Except for one problem. According to Bush's own leadership example and beliefs regarding personal accountability, if you do something wrong, you should own up to it. Other people's business or not, it goes with the territory when you're in the public eye. George, like all public figures with a deep sense of family and values, thought long and hard about the position he and his family would be in if he ran for president. We hate for our mothers and our children and other people's children to hear about his partying past as much as he does. Nevertheless, being responsible means acknowledging your errors even when it'll cause the exact problems George mentioned. We are by no means saying that leaders shouldn't have private lives. We're just saying that once you become a leader, you are held responsible for your actions a bit more publicly (or a lot more, if you're president of the United States). Unfortunately, this goes for past actions as well as for current ones, even if the past problems admittedly have no bearing on your present abilities. The public and the press are always watching, always looking for a story. Don't give it to them by being evasive.

Please remember, after that long lecture, that 99.99 percent of the time (way better than most of us), George W. Bush is the model of responsibility. In June 2002, Bush transferred presidential powers to Vice President Dick Cheney for more than two hours so that Bush could undergo a routine colon screening (which delivered a clean bill of health). Two polyps had been discovered in 1998 and 1999 and the White House physician had said he didn't need to repeat the procedure before 2003. Why have another colon screening before it was needed? Bush chose to do it early to underscore the importance of colon screening for people over the age of 50 who are at risk. He chose to transfer power (and become the first president to do so under these circumstances) because, as he said, "We're at war."[33] Bush knows he's in the public eye. He knows that every responsible act he undertakes causes others to follow suit.

LEARN FROM YOUR OWN MISTAKES
AND THOSE OF OTHERS

History is a vast early warning system.

Norman Cousins

Polls conducted in Iowa and California in June 2002 indicated that Bush would win in primaries against Gore. University of Wisconsin political science professor emeritus Charles Jones believes that results in these states reflect what has happened nationally since November 2000. He says there are still risks, but if it looks the same in the autumn of 2003, "Gore will need to consider getting out of the way. God knows there's a family precedent here [for having high approval ratings and then a big loss]," Jones said. "The difference is, this guy [George W.] is a hell of a lot more alert to the danger signals than his father was."[34]

Bush, with his awareness tuned to the early warning system of history, spent so much time in the first months of his presidency pointing to troubling economic indicators that he was accused of actually talking the economy down.[35] There's no question that he learned to keep the economy in his sights from his father's lack of attention to it.

It's no surprise that George W. would learn from his father. Bush Sr.'s defeat in his run for a second presidential term was a painful loss for a very close-knit family. George W. has high regard for his father's leadership abilities, and so naturally learned and applied the lessons taught by any of his father's mistakes.

Bush also learns from general history. It's very easy, during a war, for a president to make effective action impossible. All he has to do is to give orders that set one constraint too many. One such constraint was "no U.S. casualties." In Kosovo, this meant that U.S. pilots had to fly more safely than the passengers of some small countries' airlines do. This safety was achieved by flying at an altitude that, in effect, precluded effective bombing of mobile targets. Meanwhile, small groups of Serbs with armored vehicles terrorized ethnic Albanian villages at will.[36]

President George W. Bush set no constraints for his war on terrorism. In his 2002 State of the Union address he said, "America will do what is necessary to ensure our nation's security. We can't stop short."

After all, George W. was a history major, so it shouldn't come as a surprise that he learns from general war history too. But how about this: Bush learns from *his own* mistakes. Really learns, as in sees the problem and fixes it. He has done this even for things that are really hard to change, like losing his temper too easily. Bush was well known for having quite a temper and sometimes less than full control of it. He himself says:

> His father said that George W.'s working in his administration in the White House "was a wonderful experience for both of us. He was very helpful to me and I think it toughened him for the real world." Joe O'Neil, a Midland friend, said, "He made the transformation during the campaign from hot head to heir apparent" (quoted in J. H. Hatfield, *Fortunate Son: George W. Bush and the Making of an American President* (New York: Soft Skull Press, 2001), 87).

Based on my work in my dad's campaign, reporters and my opponents spent much of my 1994 campaign waiting for me to blow up. It never happened. They expected I would react the same way when they criticized me as I had when they criticized my father. But there is a big difference between a loyal son and being a candidate. One is a follower, the other is a leader.[37]

Bush describes his change so matter-of-factly, as though it were no big deal for him to make it. The difference in him was apparently glaring, though: In the 1994 televised, face-to-face debate against Ann Richards, during the campaign for the Texas governor's office, Bush didn't lose his temper once. His cousin Elsi Walker couldn't believe it was him. She sent his mother a flabbergasted telegram, "WHAT HAS . . . WHAT DID HE DO?"[38]

It takes real leadership genius to learn from yourself. We all say, "I guess I only learn by making mistakes," or "I learn best from painful experience." Saying it is one thing; actually changing your behavior is a very different thing. Bush is disciplined enough to examine his mistakes, determine a more successful course for the next time, and actually steer that new course.

Bush disciplines himself to learn from his own and others' mistakes. The mistakes that are easiest to learn from are those of the person whose life, beliefs, and actions most closely parallel his own—his father, George H. W. Bush. Son George W. vetoed a very popular patient protection bill when he was governor of Texas. Just as with his father's presidential veto of the popular Fair Housing Act, Bush the Younger was condemned left and right. He knew the veto was the right thing to do because the bill, though it contained some wonderful provisions, also included a whole host of mandates and regulations not related to patient care. George W. wanted to save the good things from the bill, so even as he vetoed it he turned to the insurance commissioner and asked him to develop tough rules to protect patients and health care providers. The commissioner could implement such rules through the Department of Insurance. (In Texas, the insurance commissioner has broad power to enact rules governing insurance to make sure customers are being treated fairly.) The patient and provider rules that the commissioner developed were ultimately heralded as better protections than those originally proposed in the vetoed legislation.[39]

As noted earlier, Tom Schieffer, former president of the Texas Rangers, observed that Bush "does not second-guess himself about decisions. . . . George is very good at addressing problems as they come across his desk and then moving on to the next one. When he makes mistakes, he doesn't dwell on them, he tries to learn from them."[40]

WHERE DID BUSH'S DISCIPLINE COME FROM?

Bush likes sameness in his personal life. It's a lot easier to be disciplined when some things remain constant:

- He takes his own pillow when he goes out of town.
- He likes to run on a track he's used countless times before.
- He prefers the old to the new, the tried to the untested. He makes sure he has his favorite foods available—peanut butter and jelly sandwiches.[41]

He doesn't like mess, conflict, or controversy.[42] Bush can't control everything that happens around him, but by creating some consistency, keeping his life orderly, sticking to his core values, and saying it straight, he cuts way down on the amount of mess, conflict, and controversy that does arise.

Like all successful people, Bush has overcome a lot of obstacles. He's had his share of difficulties in business: lots of dry wells and plenty of losses in baseball. He lost his first race for public office. He saw his father lose more than one race, including one really heartbreaking one. On that fateful election night, when George H. W. was told that the exit polls looked bad, he said, "Well, we'll just see how it goes." The next morning, Barbara, in her usual, unflappable way, said, "Well, now that's behind us. It's time to move on." George W. said that all the Bush children saw firsthand that you could enter the arena, give it your best shot, and leave with your dignity intact.[43]

What has really shaped Bush's discipline—more than the desire to create sameness and avoid mess, more than overcoming obstacles— are people, places, and things. As a

> "I will be guided by President Jefferson's sense of purpose, to stand for principle, to be reasonable in manner and above all, do great good for the cause of freedom and harmony" (George W. Bush, speech in Texas House after winning the presidential election, December 13, 2000).

man with a core value of family, Bush has obviously inherited a great
deal of his disciplined behavior from his family's example. His frugal-
ity, his gifts to charity, and his desire to abide by a strict set of principles (values) come from his mother. They are called "Barbara's Principles." Mrs. Bush was a passionately attentive mother who raised her
children according to a set of rules. The Bush children were expected
to look beyond themselves and be mindful of the needs of less fortunate people, to keep their whining to themselves, and to never take
themselves too seriously.[44] He learned to get things done early from
his family, too. Friends who were at the Bush house one summer said
that they saw all the presents wrapped for the upcoming Christmas.[45]
In addition to family, Bush learned discipline from a great many other
people, places, and things. Here's a quick tour of the rest of the
"School of Be Disciplined" that is George W. Bush's life:

- *Phillips Academy.* "Andover was a formal place. Much different
  from my schools in Texas," said Bush. "It stood me in good
  stead as I went from its rigid structure and rules to the free life
  of college."[46]
- *Harvard.* Uncle Jonathan Bush and other older members of the
  Bush-Walker clan who had watched W.'s progress had come to
  the same conclusion: Harvard Business School would instill discipline into the 27-year-old. Why? Harvard Business School's
  coursework is painstakingly analytical and detailed; it sets priority on probing into minute institutional dysfunctions, followed
  by rapidly developing point-by-point countermeasures. W.'s average week included writing a 1,500-word paper and attending
  several management classes that each involved teamwork, study
  groups, and cooperative problem solving.[47]

  Early in Bush's time at Harvard Business School, Professor
  Harry L. Hansen warned him and his fellow students that they
  would be inundated with more work than they could handle.
  Hansen had a higher purpose than assigning punishing amounts
  of work; the real goal, he explained, was to force students to
  learn how to separate what was important from what wasn't and
  then focus on it.[48]

- *Texas Air National Guard.* Bush learned the value of precision and single-minded focus and attention while in flight training. "The need for precision and accuracy was drilled into us at every opportunity. Colonel Udell quizzed us every day, went over the same information, time and again. 'You don't miss,' he said. 'You don't use improper procedures. You plan your attack to be successful, and you execute it to be successful. Nothing else is acceptable.' Why?—You might be flying in formation within 3–5 feet of another jet fighter at 350 knots (more than 400 miles per hour). You might be flying at night. You might be flying in difficult weather. One mistake and you could end up in a very expensive coffin."[49]

- *Oil Business.* "In the oil business, slow and steady investment brings rewards. Some people in the oil business hit grand slams, but like baseball, success in the energy business is a game of singles," said Bush.[50]

- *Texas Rangers. Runners World* asked Bush, "When you owned the Texas Rangers, was Nolan Ryan a role model for you in terms of your dedication to fitness?"

  His reply: "Yes he was—and still is. He and I are about the same age and after he pitched a game, I'd go down to the locker room and he'd be doing this intense workout right after the game. And I mean intense. Then, the next day he'd do another incredible workout. I really admired Nolan a lot. He ran quite a bit too and was in unbelievable shape which was why he was able to pitch so long."[51]

- *Governor of Texas.* Short legislative sessions force discipline and focus. The Texas legislature meets for only 140 days every 2 years.[52]

WHAT HAPPENS TO BUSH'S DISCIPLINE IN A CRISIS?

After everything we've learned about George W. Bush's discipline, you might think that in a crisis, the speed of change, the vast amount of information needed to make the right decision, and the complete up-set of his super-ordered world would just cause him to go to pieces. Not so.

The Millon Inventory of Diagnostic Criteria (MIDC), a personal-ity profiling tool, was used to discover Governor George W. Bush's personality-based leadership strengths. It showed him to have self-confidence in the face of adversity.[53] After the 9/11 attacks, there was something tremendously reassuring about the way Bush saw a politi-cal opportunity in the disaster to establish himself, once and for all, as the legitimate president. That was good for the country and good for Bush; rarely have we more desperately needed a leader who himself believed that he was equal to the task.[54]

The confidence displayed by the leader in a crisis inspires confidence in the followers. Here are a few common-sense lessons from the com-mander-in-chief, whose followers were really counting on him:

- Stay the course.
- Handle the chaos and lack of sameness that go with a crisis.
- Keep your sense of humor and take care of yourself so you can be at your best.
- Stay flexible to allow quick change in times of crisis.

Stay the Course

Stay the course: Keep your core values, keep your vision, keep hiring people smarter than you, keep leaving 'em alone, keep talking straight, keep building alliances, keep holding people accountable, keep rely-ing on your instincts. These actions, which constitute the leadership genius of George W. Bush, allow him to maintain his credibility. How could we possibly perceive a leader as credible if he falls apart when a problem arises?

Throughout the notable crises of his life, Bush has proved time and again that he could stay the course. Was it easy for him? Probably not, but as M. Scott Peck says, "Life is difficult. This is a great truth be-cause once we truly see this truth we transcend it." Peck goes on to challenge us: "Life is a series of problems. Do we want to moan about them or solve them?"[55] Bush is a master at solving instead of moaning. Only solvers can stay the course in the face of a goal like wiping out terrorism. Most said it was almost impossible—and on top of that, no timetable could be set. This is a recipe for craziness, for a disciplined guy like George. In a crisis, sure bets and timetables are not usually part of the deal. The ambiguity is offset, though, by staying the course—focusing on the goal itself.

For months after the 9/11 terrorist attacks, with only one or two exceptions, each of Bush's meetings focused exclusively on what the nation needed to do, both abroad and at home, to:

- Strike back against the perpetrators.
- Cope with the threats to its security.
- Rebound from the physical and economic damage.

His brother Jeb said, "George has not changed . . . . He could still talk about the family things . . . under this enormous pressure."[56] All of Bush's leadership actions work together—that's the genius again. He maintains his core value—family—because he's disciplined enough to do so. Some leaders get so bound up in their immediate crisis goals that they can't see or think about anything else.

Bush's ability to stay the course was also toughened by well-meaning people who didn't look at the long-term effects of *not* staying the course. Bush had to keep fighting off people who wanted him to stray from his course in the name of an emergency. In the days immediately following 9/11, aides debated if he should return to the White House in the customary helicopter or a more secure motorcade. Bush made the call: "We're going back the way we normally go back." (It was an emergency situation, so they did use three identical choppers to serve as decoys. Modifying a bit when needed allows you to stay the course and still make the well-meaning worriers comfortable.)

Remember that determined look that everyone commented on after Bush's post–9/11 address to Congress? That was the look of a man who is confident because he knows his course. What's more, Bush stays the course with apparent ease. Though certainly not of the magnitude of 9/11, the presidential campaign (the longest in American history) seemed like a crisis at the time. Bush showed impressive resiliency throughout the post-election ordeal, again staying the course in all his leadership actions.

Handle the Chaos and Lack of Uniformity That Go with a Crisis

The lack of sameness that accompanies a crisis absolutely causes problems for a disciplined leader. No matter how much you control, some things will get away from you. It's not the getting away that's remarkable with Bush; that happens to everyone at some point in a crisis. It's how he handles it after it's gotten away from him.

War is the worst crisis a president can face. War creates a fog in which sameness disappears and chaos takes over. The leader must make decisions with only half the necessary information, and all the initial reports turn out to be wrong. "Tom, get these people together," Bush told Ridge after 9/11. "We need to get to the bottom of this."

But the bottom kept falling out before they could get there. Health officials were confounded by a germ weapon never before unleashed on a civilian population; law enforcement officials were stymied by bioterrorists who were either linked to the September 11 attacks or merely pretending to be. Military officials faced a Taliban army whose tanks they could blow up but whose will was much harder to degrade. Although the public continued to show great support for the president, each new setback tested that faith and support. "The American people are going to have to be patient," the president declared in October, "just like we are."

When Bush tried to prove that progress was being made, the focus and lift of his earlier speeches was all but gone. It suggested the toll these days had taken on him. What Bush has called his destiny and life's purpose is also his terrible burden. "We've got a great response mechanism in place," he said—even though each time health officials responded to a ring of infection, they found they had drawn the circle too tight. "We've got a strategy to fight the war on the home front," he said—but no one could explain what the strategy was, and with good reason. Events were moving so quickly that one day's rumor was the next day's headline, and no one wanted to lock in a plan and then be caught off guard again. There was persistent dispute over whether the anthrax terrorists were domestic militants or Islamic extremists, which made nailing down a strategy all but impossible and surely unwise. Bush kept saying we're handling it, go about business as normal.

At that point it fell to Cheney to merge the messages and declare that there was "a new normal" now—one with room for courage and fear, joy and loss; one in which we attend birthday parties and funerals on the same day. Unlike Bush, Cheney had been warning Americans that life is different now and is probably going to stay that way for the rest of our lives. The question, of course, is how different. Bush soon began helping Americans chart the dimensions of the new normal.

To help Americans regain some stability, he had to measure American strength and stamina. He found it to be not all that different from his own. For all his faith and focus on this crisis, he was looking at the same contradictions as the rest of America was: we are under attack, yet we must not panic; we sense that everything has changed, but we need to do what we did before, as though ignoring threat were a patriotic duty. The tension embedded in this task was quite obvious in the White House, too, as staff argued about what tone a deeply worried but naturally optimistic president ought to set.[57]

In fact, the right tone ended up being honesty. Through the clamor and fog, Bush kept communicating with Americans. He told people the truth: The goal is to wipe out terrorism; the fight is going to be long, but there's no way to tell how long; we're going to have to be patient; and the only way the goal will be met is if we go about our business. Our daily business will be carried on with an ever-evolving increase in security—again, be patient. We can't create everything we need instantly when the nature of the game is constant change.

Just because you handle one bout of chaos well doesn't mean that it won't pop up somewhere else. That's the nature of chaos. In August 2002, Bush had been debating the "to get Saddam or not to get Saddam" question for several months. How did he wrestle with it? He stayed his course ("get Saddam") and let his staff and his party squabble. He let the alliances he'd built in September and October 2001 melt away, as one by one they disagreed with his plans. Bush felt it was more important to stay the course. In June 2002, in a speech at West Point, he said, "If we wait for threats to fully materialize we will have waited too long." By August he was saying, "We will look at all options and we will consider all technologies available to us and diplomacy and intelligence."[58] It's not easy to stay the course when the decisions you make are life-and-death ones. Bush was torn between two very right ways of doing things. He was leaving his staff alone and they were torn. Though he didn't want to wait, he knew he had to. It was a summer that looked like chaotic decision making, or worse, no decision making. Bush has been criticized before for waiting; in September 2001, he waited to attack the Taliban until all the ducks were in a row. He waited and it was the right move.

On September 12, 2002, Bush took his decision to the United Nations. He had his ducks in a row again. In that speech he stated that either the UN Security Council would impose stringent rules on Saddam Hussein, to guarantee disarmament and an end to repression (and lead to Saddam's collapse); or the United States, with its allies and the approval of Congress, would take military action. Gone were the muddling along, the futile negotiation over arms inspections, the endless discussions about lifting the sanctions on Iraq, the months of Democratic delaying tactics. When Bush was ready to force the issue, he did. The *Weekly Standard* declared:

President Bush's speech to the United Nations yesterday wasn't a home run—it was a walk-off grand slam. Thorough, compelling, and firm, Bush struck exactly the right tone, laid out an irrefutable case against Saddam, and established a list of conditions that Saddam cannot meet while still retaining power. The corner has been turned. Not only the public, not only Congress, but the world is now coming President Bush's way in pursuing regime change in Iraq.[59]

Keep Your Sense of Humor and Take Care of Yourself So You Can Be at Your Best

Soon after 9/11, Andrew Card, Bush's chief of staff, said that the president was making "sure that there is a balance to his effort—and that includes taking care of his mind and body and spirit." Bush stuck to his exercise regimen, watched his diet, and made sure he got a decent night's sleep. One of the few things he changed was getting to the office just before 7:00 A.M. rather than just after.[60] He not only did the things he knew were necessary to deal with the crisis, he made sure other people knew he was doing them. Many people who share Bush's preference for sameness will flip out in an unfamiliar situation. It was crucial for Bush to let the press and public know that he was taking care of himself just as he'd been doing before the crisis.

Bush let people know it himself. He called a friend three weeks after 9/11 to assure that person that he was fine. The evidence he gave? He'd run his customary 3 miles in 21 minutes, 30 seconds—a rate of 7 minutes and 10 seconds per mile. That pace was deliberately faster than he'd been doing in recent years, and it grew faster still. Later Bush said that he'd done a mile in less than seven minutes. By challenging himself to exceed expectations in a familiar activity, he was proving to himself how strong he could be.[61]

Bush also maintained his sense of humor. On September 13, 2001, Bush and his top advisors gathered in the Treaty Room of the White House so they could grill him to prepare for his first prime-time news conference since the attacks. They sprayed him with questions: Should Americans be afraid? What will the United States do in Afghanistan after the Taliban is defeated? It was the second prep session of the day, and Bush was getting impatient. Then came yet another question: How could he possibly leave the country the next Wednesday to take a scheduled trip to China? Bush clenched his jaw and said, "Well, Mrs. Bush and I want to encourage Americans to go out shopping," he said. "And I broke a plate last week."

Stay Flexible to Allow Quick Change in Times of Crisis

You've heard it before, albeit applied to calmer times: Don't change on a whim. Weigh the pros and the cons and then make changes when you need to. After 9/11, though his core values and his vision remained steadfast, Bush did reorder responsibilities to emphasize the "wipe out terrorism" goal. Some of the quotidian political activities, such as party fund-raising, were curtailed. Karl Rove, the president's chief political strategist, continued to make sure that key constituencies weren't forgotten; but for the first time in Bush's political life, Rove and Hughes no longer attended the president's most important meetings. Vice President Dick Cheney, with his skill in foreign policy, was front and center. Bush took the role of the outside player, the public spokesman, the emotional leader of the administration and the nation. Cheney became the inside man, the operations guy. Think of a train: "The President," said an advisor, "is the engineer. Cheney is the guy shoveling the coal."[62]

The president who had apparently wanted to go it alone in the world, and had scant regard for "nation building," said after 9/11 that "we should not simply leave [Afghanistan] after a military objective has been achieved." He foresaw a role for the United Nations in "the stabilization of" a new government in postwar Afghanistan. As a candidate, Bush couldn't name the president of Pakistan; after 9/11, he spoke easily and fluently of General Pervez Musharraf and other crucial Muslim leaders.

Bush used to campaign against Washington bureaucrats, and he promised to balance the budget by keeping government spending in check. After 9/11, he began creating new federal agencies and pushing for new investigative powers. He proposed billion-dollar bailouts and unemployment programs that put the federal budget in the red for the first time in five years. "We're in a very different time," explained Karen Hughes, his presidential counselor, in the fall of 2001. "He's always talked about the need for an active but limited government. This is one of those times when an active government is important."

It's also a time for speed. Bush took months to decide whether to provide federal money for stem-cell research; now he makes decisions about war and terrorism on an almost hourly basis.[63]

In a time when everyone from church leaders to CEOs to baseball players seems corrupt, voters are comforted by the Bush they saw standing amid the World Trade Center rubble: confident, decent, secure.[64]

BEING DISCIPLINED: A TIMELESS PRINCIPLE OF LEADERSHIP

The experts think that discipline is key to leadership. Bush's actions bear them out. David McCullough, the author of *John Adams* and *Truman Time,* said:

Bush has done extremely well in dealing with 9/11. I admire the control he's shown in the handling of the crisis. He has been clear and decisive but also restrained. One senses almost the air of chess moves on the part of the Administration.

Truman said, "We can never tell what's in store for us." How in the world could George W. Bush have ever known that he would have to face the worst day in our history or that we would see in him the kind of vitality and crispness—of prose and decision—that he's demonstrated?

He has risen to the occasion about as well as any public servant ever has. He's not afraid to express very fundamental, heartfelt, almost inexplicable devotions, devotion to his country, devotion to God, devotion to old verities.[65]

Frank Bruni, a presidential campaign reporter for the *New York Times,* noted that "Bush's resistance to letting himself be consumed by his obligations kept him from being overwhelmed by them."[66]

Dr. Howard Gardner, a Harvard professor and expert in cognition education, said, "I think that throughout [Bush's] life he has not done any more homework than he has to."[67] This doesn't sound much like

THE EXPERTS SAY

What the Experts Say

If an organization is to meet the challenges of a changing world, it must be prepared to change everything about itself except beliefs as it moves through corporate life. The only sacred cow in an organization should be its basic philosophy of doing business.

Thomas Watson, Jr., author and business analyst[68]

I do first things first.
I work smarter, not harder.
I try to do only A's, never B's and C's.
I have confidence in my judgment of priorities and stick to them in spite of difficulties.
I make use of specialists to help me with special problems.
I try not to think of work on weekends.
I relax and do nothing rather frequently.

Alan Lakein[69]

What the Leaders Say

It takes enormous courage to say "We just don't do that here. No matter how much money we can make." It seems so impractical. But the truth is that just such a decision may be the defining moment. It can distinguish you from everyone else in your business and inspire everyone in your operation.

Commissioner Robert Watson, retired National Commander of the Salvation Army[70]

I don't let anybody waste my time. I am not rude, but I can let you know in a very tactful, humorous way that your time is up.

Diedre S., office manager[71]

an accolade until you read John Naisbett, the futurist and analyst, who said, "In a world that is constantly changing, there is no one subject or set of subjects that will serve you for the foreseeable future, let alone the rest of your life. The most important skill to acquire now is learning how to learn." Bush knows how he learns best—just the facts, bullet points, verbal briefings rather than written ones, listening to others debate—and he asks those around him to feed him the information he needs in that form so that he can learn quickly and easily.

Jim Collins says,

Confront the brutal facts, yet don't lose the faith that you'll meet your goals in the end. This is the Stockdale Paradox: Have unwavering faith of making it regardless of difficulties and at the same time have the discipline to confront the brutal reality when you need to change. There is no worse mistake for any leader than holding on to false hopes.[72]

Collins wasn't speaking directly about Bush, but he'd surely give the seal of approval if he knew Bush. Bush makes black-and-white decisions based on principles that do not change. Often his apparently contradictory stances are the result of new information and/or learning from past experience, but the principles underlying the decisions are always the same.

If he does make a change (which he might, after weighing the pros and cons), he's regularly criticized for doing so. Bush is no stranger to criticism, so it's fortunate that he weathers it well, just as he weathers failure well. Failure creates discipline. "Storms make oak trees take deeper root," said George Herbert, a seventeenth-century metaphysical poet. Metaphysicians investigate the world by the rational discussion of its phenomena rather than by intuition. The genius of Bush is that he can combine his discipline with trust in his intuition.

Charles Swindoll, an expert on maintaining a positive attitude, is the author of the famous saying, "Life is 10 percent what happens to you, 90 percent how you respond to it." That is certainly Bush's motto. Always the optimist, George's favorite quote comes from Tom Lea: "Sara and I live on the east side of the mountain. It is the sunny side, not the sunset side. It is the side to see the day that is coming; not the side to see the day that is gone."

Knowing that how the day will go is based largely on your response to it gives you the discipline to stay the course. Calvin Coolidge, 30th president of the United States, said, "Nothing in the world can take the place of persistence. Talent will not; nothing is more common than unsuccessful men with talent. Genius will not; unrewarded genius is almost a proverb. Education will not; the world is full of educated derelicts. Persistence and determination alone are omnipotent." Persistence and determination are

> Failed in business, age 22.
> Ran for legislature—defeated, age 23.
> Again failed in business, age 24.
> Elected to legislature, age 25.
> Sweetheart died, age 26.
> Had nervous breakdown, age 27.
> Defeated for speaker, age 29; defeated for elector, age 31; defeated for Congress, age 34; elected to Congress, age 37; defeated for Congress, age 39; defeated for Senate, age 46; defeated for vice president, age 47; defeated for Senate, age 49.
> Elected president of the United States, age 51.
>
> Career summary for
> Abraham Lincoln

sustainable, though, only if you take time daily for rest. Steven Covey calls it *renewal*. It's Covey's "Habit 7: Sharpen the Saw—The Habit of Renewal" (see Figure 8.3 to see how Bush scores on Habit 7).

Sharpen the Saw is a daily process of renewing the four dimensions of our nature:

1. *Physical*. We build physical wellness through proper nutrition, exercise, and rest.
2. *Mental*. We increase mental capacity through reading, writing, and thinking.
3. *Spiritual*. We develop spiritually through reading inspirational literature, through meditating and praying, and through spending time in nature.

Physical
- Exercises every day
- Knows how much sleep he needs and gets it every day

Mental
- Takes quiet respite time daily
- Reads a wide variety of books

Spiritual
- Reads the Bible
- Participates in White House prayer daily
- Prays alone
- Participates in Bible study group
- Spends vacations working outdoors on his ranch

Social/Emotional
- Has friends over for dinner and weekends
- Spends a great deal of time with immediate family
- Shares regular phone calls and get-togethers with his parents and siblings

Figure 8.3   Bush scores high on Habit 7—renewal.

4. *Social/Emotional.* We mature socially and emotionally by making consistent, daily deposits in the emotional bank account of our key relationships.

These four dimensions sustain and increase our capacities and help us discipline our mind, body, and spirit. This daily private victory is a victory over self. Not only does the daily private victory stimulate growth, but it also helps us achieve it.[73]

HOW TO BE DISCIPLINED

Planning to Use Your Day Productively

We all have 86,400 nonrefundable seconds every day. Your day may be easier than Bush's or harder. Herman Edwards's day is harder—only during football season, but that's half the year. Herman, the New York Jets' head coach, has a grueling schedule that goes from 4:30 A.M. until midnight, with no days off until Thanksgiving. His days have to be incredibly productive because all his work is measured by results (sound familiar?) and he has only 16 Sundays in which to get those results. In fact, Herman is hired to get just one result: win. Herman will be fired if he doesn't get that result, and may actually be fired even if he does win. The Tampa Bay Buccaneers' head coach took them from a joke to a playoff team in four of five consecutive years, and then was fired because he didn't get them to the Super Bowl.[74]

You don't have Herman's job, but you still look at Bush's schedule (see Figure 8.1 at the beginning of this chapter) and think, "There is *no way* I can even dream about taking two hours in the middle of the day, at the end of the day, or any day to exercise. I know the benefits, but I just don't have time. There is no way I could go home at 6:00 P.M., and if I did I'd be working instead of playing when I got home." We're here to tell you that you can if you really want it. If you're disciplined enough, you can get there. At the very least, you can improve your current situation pretty dramatically.

Bush wants it and Bush is disciplined enough to make it happen. There is no argument from the White House that this president's way of doing business is different from anything Washington has seen for years. The Clinton administration seemed to thrive on chaos; Bush's is self-consciously calm, efficient, focused, and results-oriented. "He doesn't want our time to be White House time all the time," says Chief of Staff Andy Card. "He wants people to have a life. This does not have to be all consuming." Bush wants to dictate the terms of the job, not let the job dictate to him—which is remarkable, given the job in question! He urges advisors to go home to their kids. Even Cheney is out by 7:00 P.M. most nights. A staff member in the elder Bush's administration used to leave his office light on and jacket draped over his chair to make it appear that he'd been working all night. That kind of stagecraft isn't effective in the son's halls, says Mary Matalin, who has worked for both Bushes. "There is no guilt associated with being able to make a respectable departure," she says.

Bush's take-it-slow-and-easy approach is yet another rebuke to his predecessor. Clinton came to office promising to work for the people "until the last dog dies." In Clinton's world, working hard meant exhausting oneself—something the president and his staff did regularly, especially in his first term, when leaving the White House before midnight was viewed as proof of a lack of commitment. Clinton's sheer effort was a key part of his message.[75]

Not so President Bush. "I don't like to sit around in meetings for hours and hours and hours," he said during the campaign. "People will tell you, I get to the point." Meetings should be crisp and should end with decisions. Talking matters less than doing.

It's a widely held belief that success equals working all the time; that successful people always work long hours. A CEO who is wiser than he knew (the boss of one of the authors) felt just the opposite. His belief was that if you had to work more than the prescribed hours, you were obviously a poor time manager. Rather than leaving the office light on to pretend we were there late, we had to sneak work home. We were literally forced to become better time managers to survive the daily disapproval of our CEO.

What can you do to force yourself—to be disciplined enough—to start reducing your work hours? (Start with 15 minutes a day and work up.)

We really mean it: Force yourself. Set your departure time in the morning. Know that it's coming all day. Work toward it all day and then leave at that time, no matter what. Even if you're not done. Go and don't take anything with you. The first day, if you have to, come in 15 minutes early the next day to take care of what you left. Only do this one day, and then only if what you left will cause you to lose credibility or lose your job if it's not done by the time the person who needs it shows up in the morning.

Bush tells us what he needed to focus on to avoid losing credibility or losing his job:

> I became the face and voice of the Texas Rangers. I worked hard to sell tickets. I traveled the Rangers' market. I spoke to civic groups and chambers of commerce. I did thousands of media interviews touting baseball as a family sport and great entertainment value. I got to know all the hot dog vendors and the ticket takers and the ushers by first name. They were an important part

of making sure our fans felt welcome and at home. I signed thousands of autographs, brought guests to the ballpark and sat in the seats with the fans every night. I sat in the front row, not in the owners' box. I wanted to be close to the game and the fans and sometimes I paid a dear price—as seasons wore on and the Rangers fell behind I had a lot of frustrated fans yelling, "Hey Bush, more pitching!"[76]

Planning the tasks to include in your day is easy when you have a vision. That, of course, brings us back to the heart of Bush's genius—his clear vision.

- What specific task do you need to focus on and do each day to achieve your vision?
- What tasks do you need to delete because they're not helping you meet your vision or the organization's vision?
- What tasks do you need to delegate because they're not helping you meet your vision, but they still have to be done to meet the *organization's* vision?

There are whole books on prioritizing, planning, and organizing for efficiency. Read them and use the ideas that work with your style and job. Simply setting a timer won't do it for you beyond the first 15 minutes (depending on how undisciplined your hours have gotten, that is. It's a bit like weight loss: If you have a lot to lose, you can drop more than 15 minutes). Without the discipline of setting and sticking to a schedule—start time, end time, meetings starting and ending on time, doing the work that's crucial today instead of procrastinating—all the prioritizing ideas in the world won't help you use your day most productively. That wiser-than-he-knew CEO did one of the authors one of the biggest favors of that author's life—he forced the issue of fitting it all into "a certain amount of time." What you do during that certain amount of time has to be the priorities, the tasks that will actually help you achieve your vision, because there's just not enough time for anything else.

People are going to ask you to work more hours than you now

have planned. They are also going to ask you to do tasks that don't help you meet your vision. You—the new disciplined you—are of course going to say no. This will be much easier if you take Russell Baker's advice and get an agent in Wisconsin (see Figure 8.4).

Know When to Hold 'Em—Stay the Course

You stay the course because of your core values and the vision that's based on them. When you hire people smarter than you and leave 'em alone, they'll help you stay the course, because they're disciplined too. You'll feel accountable to them. They'll be measuring your results.

You read in Chapter 3 that Governor Bush held the role of final decision maker on each individual capital punishment case, so he had to review each case thoroughly. He set personal standards for deciding whether to allow the execution to proceed. He said that in every case, he would ask:

- Is there any doubt about this individual's guilt?
- Have the courts had ample opportunity to review all the legal issues in this case?

This is a "hold-'em" rule, and hold-'em rules aren't always the easiest. By consistently applying the same standards each and every time, Bush had to let a changed and repentant woman die and commute the sentence of a cold-blooded, unrepentant killer.

For the disciplined person, the difficulty isn't usually in staying the course. It's in dealing gracefully with the criticism of those decisions to stay the course. We found an entire book criticizing Bush's lack of interest in the environment and conservation when he was governor (*The Dirty Truth: The Oil and Chemical Dependency of George W. Bush*). Expect that kind of criticism when you stay the course. Everyone else has a course, too, stressing the things that are priorities for them. If yours aren't theirs, they'll criticize. You can help them see your course by giving it to 'em straight. Whether you try to win them over or

One of the worst mistakes I ever made was throwing away a brochure from an agent who, if you retained his services, would say "no" for you.

Suppose a long-forgotten acquaintance phoned you and said, "Congratulations, you are invited to a benefit performance of the new Broadway hit and an after-theater buffet reception at which you will mingle with famous stars and tickets are only $250 apiece, and do you want to accept?"

All you had to do was say, "You'll have to call my agent in Wisconsin," and when the call was made, this fellow would say, "No."

"No" is one of the hardest words in the language to say, not only to acquaintances, friends, and family, but also to perfect strangers.

Some years ago, having agreed to make a speech to a group I'd never heard of, I was dismayed to find that I was to share the platform with Dean Acheson, one of the most polished public speakers in the land. During the misery of the meal beforehand, I asked Acheson, "Why do I get into situations like this?"

"For the same reason I do," he said. "They always invite you so far in advance and it's so much harder to say 'no' than 'yes' that you always end up agreeing to make the speech in hope that in the meantime you may die and not have to go through with it."

Here was Dean Acheson, a former secretary of state and one of the finest diplomats of the age, yet even he found it hard to say "no" to a strange program chairman. He'd learned that a "no," whether between nations or people, is never the end of the matter, but always the opening of a long, difficult negotiation in which terrible pressures will be brought to bear.

"Yes," on the other hand, brings instant relief. The bride at the altar who might have said "no" but didn't has escaped family pressure to get a husband before she wilts with age and has freed herself of the difficulty of articulating her vague sense of uneasiness about the man beside her. Later there may be pain, but for the moment, her "yes" has relieved her of the ordeal that "no" would have produced.

What this poor creature required was an agent in Wisconsin. Imagine the sequence:

"Will you marry me, honeybunch?"

"Unfortunately, my contract with my agent in Wisconsin gives him the legal right to deal with all questions requiring a yes or no answer."

Aspiring groom on phone to agent, "Will my honeybunch please be my wife?"

Agent: "No." (Hangs up.)

Diplomats do not need such an agent. Their immediate answer to whatever is suggested is "no." This signals that they are ready to start 30 or 40 years of making things miserable for each other, thus providing themselves with lifetime jobs.

Figure 8.4   Russell Baker's advice on agents.

Adapted from "Call Now for a Firm No," by Russell Baker, Pulitzer Prize–winning *New York Times* columnist. We first read this piece in its entirety in Baker's syndicated column in the *Cleveland Plain Dealer* in the late 1970s.

not, do deal gracefully with criticism by using the following formula for responding to criticism:

- Agree in part.
- Request specific feedback.
- Use assertive communication.

Practice using the formula for responding to criticism to write out responses to these situations:

1. You hear that your customer wants to give a project that you've bid on to a competitor. You have been working with this customer for two months. You think you have a quality product and a good price and really want to do the work for the customer. How will you approach your customer? What will you say in view of the fact that she has not criticized you directly?

2. An employee says you were too strict in your handling of a problem he had in getting work done for a customer. He makes a derogatory comment about your ability to help him do his job. What is your response?

3. At your last performance appraisal, your boss told you that you could be doing a "better job." You want to ask her to be more specific. Knowing that she does not like to be put on the spot, how will you do this?

4. Your spouse complains that you just don't do the house chores like you did when you were first married, and that he is tired of doing all the work. How will you address this issue and turn a potentially negative situation into a problem-solving opportunity?

Know When to Fold 'Em— When You Need to Change

For months Bush argued, "We don't need a Cabinet-level position for homeland security." But then he was given information that caused him to reweigh the pros and the cons and see that there was indeed a need for a Cabinet-level Homeland Security slot.

The first key regarding need to change is to actually know when *not* to stay the course. You already know the steps, but here's a quick recap:

1. Be open enough and observant enough to recognize a potential need to change course. Discipline is not the same as intractability or stubbornness.
2. Get the information needed to weigh the pros and cons. What will happen if you change? What will happen if you don't change? Who will be affected by a change? What are the reasons or arguments for changing? What are the reasons or arguments for staying the course? Has this situation ever arisen before? If so, how was it handled then? How did it turn out? What can you learn from that experience?
3. Make the decision.

Describe the new situation and explain to everyone involved why you made the change. Explain it orally, and face-to-face if possible. This is one of those things that just can't be written if you want it to be perceived as "straight." Write it out if you like, but be there so they can hear it from your lips and later read it for reference.

The second key is to proclaim the change loudly and enthusiastically. Be sure that this enthusiasm shows in your face, your body, and your words. We saw this when Bush made the homeland security decision; he put his whole heart into the new department. Despite his being so set against this move previously, he cut some of the naysayers off at the knees by showing everyone that he really was committed to this changed direction. He didn't just say it, he showed it. Lots of your co-workers don't like change, but your enthusiasm will help them get on board.

These two keys only work when you are open enough to changing your course that you actually can change. Being disciplined can easily lead you to avoid brutal facts, and hold on to false hopes in the name of staying the course. It's a delicate balance, maintained by (1) knowing enough about yourself to know that you tend to hold on too long; and (2) being observant so you see the *potential* need for a change, even if you still think you should be staying the course. If you've hired people smarter than you, left 'em alone to do their jobs, and asked them to give it to you straight, observation won't be a problem. They'll tell you about anything you don't notice.

How do you recognize holding on too long? Look at the stages of change:

- Denial.
- Resistance.
- Adaptation.
- Involvement.

Think of a recent change you experienced. Pick one that was no big deal, not earth-shattering (like you need a new pair of jeans: They're frayed, your knees are showing, in fact you can actually see your underwear in the back because the seat is worn out—but you love these jeans, they fit you perfectly, you don't want to break in a new pair, they're so old you're sure they don't even make that style anymore— but they are practically disintegrating on your body, you really need a new pair). What was the first thing you did?

- Claim that your old, decrepit jeans are fine (denial).
- Put off the shopping trip until you've called the manufacturer to see if you can get the same style; discover that you can't, but put off the shopping trip again until you've exhaustively reviewed catalogues for the new style that is the most similar to the old one (resistance).
- Go shopping and try on a bunch of jeans until you finally find a pair you like (adaptation).
- Jump into the car and tell everyone you meet that you're shopping for new jeans that will be even cooler than the style you used to love (involvement).

If you deny and resist a change as minor as replacing your favorite jeans, it's likely you won't be open to changing your course even when you should. Increase your ability to change by monitoring the next several changes (small or large) that come your way. With larger, more important matters, we tend to go through all four stages of change (as opposed to skipping some stages, as you might have done in the jeans example). Actually, change researchers say that we don't skip stages; we always experience each of the stages, but some go by so fast that we don't notice we've been through them. For the next change you experience:

1. Write the four stages on a piece of paper and put a date next to the first stage, *denial*, when you first hear about the change.
2. If on that day you are already learning about the new thing and moving forward, you can put that same date next to *resistance* and *adaptation*. (It's unlikely that you'll be doing this step; if, like many of us, you even resist getting new jeans, you'll probably have to wait a few days to fill in more dates).
3. Know that you're in the denial stage. Know that you need to get to involvement. (To be honest, adaptation and involvement look like a lot more fun than denial and resistance, don't they? So if this change is going to happen, let's get there as fast as possible.) Every day, look at that piece of paper and plan to make that the day when you can truthfully say, "Yes, this change is going to happen. There will be no reprieve, no change of heart. It's a done deal." That's the day you put a date next to *resistance*.
4. Know that you're in the resistance stage. Know that you need to get to involvement. Every day, look at that piece of paper and plan to make that the day when you notice yourself glancing at the manual for the new software, looking over people's shoulders who are using it, clicking on a few menus when everyone else is at lunch. That's the date you fill in next to *adaptation*.

You know the drill by now. The day you fill in a date next to *involvement* is the day you realize, while doing something else, "Hey, this is really benefiting me because . . . ."

By looking at those stages every day, and knowing where you're going next, you are pushing yourself toward your goal. Disciplined people know all about that. The very same stay-the-course goal orientation that got you into this mess can get you out.

Creating a Culture of Discipline

"There is a difference between having a culture, having a discipline and having a culture of discipline,"[77] says Jim Collins. You can create a culture of discipline by your example and by expecting it of the people you work with. Of course, those people will know that you expect it only if you give it to 'em straight. Bush does, as he said in a magazine interview:

> *Runners World:* What's your response to people who say they are too busy to have enough time to exercise?
>
> *Bush:* I say they don't have their priorities straight. These are the same people who say they don't have enough time for their families. I don't take that as an acceptable answer. I believe anyone can make time. As a matter of fact, I don't believe it—I know it. If the President of the United States can make time, they can make time.
>
> Exercise is so important that corporate America should help their employees make time. Offer flex time. There should be flex time for families and there should be flex time for exercise. A healthy work force is a more productive work force. We have to do a better job of encouraging that in America.[78]

Give it to 'em straight about staying the course. Give it to 'em straight about being responsible, sticking to a schedule, and changing when you need to. Give it to 'em straight about what to expect in a culture of discipline during a crisis; sometimes the discipline gets lost in a crisis, but it's how they get their discipline back that's important.

Give 'em the culture of discipline in the hiring interview, on their first day, and every day after that.

Maintain strength so that those around you can be resolute. If you want to maintain this kind of strength, to get the benefits of a culture of discipline, but think that this doesn't sound like you, think about George W. Bush before 9/11. He was simpler and plainer than most of his predecessors, and that seemed to be one of the reasons many Americans voted for him. He was an easygoing, unthreatening man for easygoing times. Well, that's not how it all turned out; he's had to show us what else he could do. This has turned him into one of the most interesting presidents in decades.[79]

CHAPTER 9

Intuitive Wisdom

Trust Your Instincts

❦——————❦

But the inside story of the President's handling of the war so far shows that what he lacks in experience, he has made up in instinct.

James Carney and John F. Dickerson[1]

The dictionary defines *intuition* as "[t]he immediate knowing or learning of something without the conscious use of reasoning; instantaneous apprehension."[2] In this discussion, we use the words *instinct* and *intuition* interchangeably.

Up to now, our exploration of leadership has been on fairly solid, conventional ground. Topics like values, vision, communication, and collaboration are the "usual suspects" that we round up when examining leadership. Having been raised on Western rationalism and the scientific method, we especially like it when the skills of leaders are sensible and readily explainable. We want our leaders to be logical. We expect the boss to bless an ingenious business proposal with, "That makes sense" rather than with "I have a good feeling about it." Rarely do you hear a leader say, "I really don't understand anything you just said. But it feels right, so let's do it."

Imagine your financial advisor saying, "I think we should go heavily into the stock market."

To which you respond, predictably, "Why is that?"

He pauses, and then, after putting on his turban, responds, "I have no evidence for it. Just a gut feeling." After a moment of shock, you disappear through the wall of his office like one of those frightened cartoon characters.

Now, imagine the same scenario, but this time you resist the temptation to flee in terror and instead calmly ask your financial advisor, "Can you help me understand, intellectually and logically, why we should invest more at this time?"

The advisor politely clears his throat and responds, "The intellect has little to do on the road to discovery. There comes a leap in consciousness, call it intuition or what you will, and the solution comes to you and you don't know how or why."

Well, that does it, you think to yourself. There's nothing to do but wait for the men in white coats to take this guy away.

However, you should know that the statement this lunatic just made is a verbatim quote from arguably the smartest man in the twentieth century, Albert Einstein.[3] For Einstein, intuition was more important than knowledge. The sages of the East have endorsed—and used—intuitive reasoning for centuries: Intuitive understanding will help keep you out of trouble until the end of your days.[4]

BUSH TRUSTS HIS GUT

Much of Bush's success as a leader is explained by his willingness to trust his gut. Many people are discouraged from following their inner wisdom, but not Bush. When asked about his father's influence in this regard, Bush answered, "He said I should follow my own instincts."[5] Likewise, Bush says of Lieutenant Governor Bullock, "[H]e trusted my instincts, he knew when I made decisions, I would do what I thought was right for Texas."[6]

Many of Bush's critics claim that he is not well-read. They say he does not spend enough time reading policy statements and studying long briefs. They claim that he is an intellectual lightweight who rarely engaged in political debates in college or grad school. Bush stood this argument on its head, making "fun of people too invested in learning, which he saw as a poor substitute for horse sense, and railed against the Northeastern elite."[7]

Bush's honesty about intelligence and learning is downright refreshing. Rather than faking understanding, he will unashamedly admit that he isn't following. At one large conference, Bush turned to New Mexico Governor George Johnson and said, "What are they talking about?"

"I don't know," Johnson replied.

"You don't know a thing, do you?" Bush shot back.

"Not one thing," said Johnson.

"Neither do I," said Bush and the two high-fived each other.[8]

Johnson recognizes that Bush has the courage and good sense to admit what he doesn't know and get briefed on it, rather than trying to save face by faking it, only to be caught short and embarrassed later.

Bush's political success, in spite of his dubious credentials as an intellectual, would make perfect sense to Lao-tsu, the Eastern sage, who stated: "The more stuffed the mind is with knowledge, the less able [a man is to] see what's in front of him."[9]

GEORGE GETS IT

Bush prepares for his meetings, as any conscientious leader would, by reading summaries and talking to key stakeholders. Staff members report that during meetings, he has an uncanny ability to be completely present rather than lost in thought and theories. Bush relates this ability to "be in the moment" to his days as a fighter pilot: "[I]t didn't matter where you've been, where you were going or what you were doing, when you put a burner on, you are focused on the moment . . . . It took a great deal of concentration to fly those jets."[10] The result of this concentration, as Karen Hughes noted, is that "he always asks the best questions, the ones that get right to the heart of the matter."[11]

Vance McMahan echoed Hughes's opinion. As related in Chapter 2, during a Texas drought, he watched as Bush listened to all the rational discussion, hypothesizing, and various scenarios and then cut straight to the chase: "Tell me how much water we have, how much water we're using and how much water we need."[12]

This same ability to be in the moment and to be intuitive accounts for Bush's tremendous people skills. He has made up for any lack of book learning by using his own political antennae for reading people. A Yale classmate commented on this:

> Some guy might go to Yale and say I got the greatest book-learning education. I think George really thrived on people and thrived on the environment. He was the kind of person who knew what was going on, he wasn't the kind of person who was over in the library trying to perfect his paper on the British revolution of 1420.[13]

Frank Bruni, a journalist who traveled with Bush during much of the presidential campaign, made a similar observation: "I think that on some instinctive level, Bush sensed little disturbances in the atmosphere around him and calibrated his actions accordingly. Politicians are seducers—at least the good ones are—and Bush was practiced in the art of seduction."[14]

BUSH PAYS ATTENTION

Bruni's phrase, "sensed little disturbances in the atmosphere," also reflects Bush's ability to be intensely present and "in the moment." People who are lost in their own thoughts will miss subtle clues and occurrences. They're too wrapped up in themselves to listen to their instincts. The same present-in-the-moment quality that allows Bush to remember the name of everyone in the room also makes him aware of their body language and nonverbal cues. "His inherited skills—subtle, like any personal touch, but distinct—were always evident, especially his photographic memory,"[15] a classmate at Yale commented.

Good instincts come from clearing the mind and paying attention. Information overload and the need to control can be deadly to sharp instincts. Jimmy Carter, a supremely decent and bright man, fell into both traps. Bruni is aware of the trap, as well, noting that "Presidents before Bush had proved that an excessive attention to detail and a temptation to micromanage the affairs of government did not always work."[16]

All of us have had the experience of being with someone who is intellectually brilliant but clueless about people and everyday living; the very intelligent, well-educated people who don't have the common sense God gave a small soap dish. The poster child for this type of person is the hyperintellectual scientist-geek who wears different-colored socks and forgets his own phone number ("why should I memorize it when I can look it up in a phone book?"). In sharp contrast, Bush's genius lies in knowing instinctively what is important to the people in the room. His cousin John Ellis put it simply and well: "George got it, you know what I mean? He was on top of it."[17] In a nutshell, this ability to read and understand people is the genius of George W. Bush.

Molly Ivins dislikes Bush so much that praise from her is the ultimate compliment, and she agrees with John Ellis. When it comes to reading people and "getting" what is important, at the intuitive level, Bush is a master. Ivins writes, "Bush's resume in office may be slim, but he has worked in and around campaigns for years, knows a lot about the political side of politics, and is good at it."[18] Fred McClure, who served both Reagan and the elder Bush, takes it a step further, saying flat out that the son's instincts are better than the father's.[19]

What exactly does it mean to have "better" instincts? In part, it means being able to understand how one is perceived by others and to shape those perceptions. Staff members will tell you that Bush is forever asking, "How's it playing?" Biographer Minutaglio believes that "this process was intuitive at first, then apparently deliberate, and some of his father's highest-level advisors would say that it would make the first son a far better politician than his father."[20]

Another dimension to good instincts is good timing. Bush has an uncanny instinct for when to fight, when to concede, when to run, when to wait it out, when to start a venture. Ivins says that Bush has "been lucky in his timing. But Bush's wife, Laura, says it's not luck: 'If George is good at anything, it's timing.' And in politics, timing is everything."[21]

INTUITION AND CRISIS

The events of September 11 pushed Bush to rely even more heavily on his good timing instincts. He was faced with huge decisions and often had very little information to guide him. An entire nation of Americans was crying out for action, for the president to do something in the face of the atrocity. Bush knew this and heard some of his military advisors echoing the same sentiments. He also heard his father and Secretary of State Powell warning him not to take any action until he has built an international coalition. What should he do? What would you have done?

As a man of faith, Bush prayed and listened for God's response. Of course, the American press was suspicious. With their highly cynical and nonreligious view of the world, they wondered about the "God" approach. Those close to Bush will tell you, however, that his faith has only steadied him and even heightened his leadership abilities. He stepped up to the challenge, believing that it was God's plan for him to lead at this time and that he was ready: "I accept the responsibility."[22]

Within days of the terrorist attacks, it was evident that Bush's faith had strengthened and focused him, to the point where Bush's father said to Tom Brokaw, in an NBC interview: "This thing about faith, I mean, this is real for him. This is real. Here's a man that's read the Bible through twice. And it's not to make it holier than thou or not to make a political point. It's something that is in his heart."[23]

INTUITION AND FAITH

Bush will continue to make some observers nervous because of his faith and his reliance on faith. People who have faith understand that it is possible to know things directly. It's not a scientific view of the world. Rather, it's a view that says, "I don't understand how I can know the answer, but somehow I do." An example of this occurred when Bush met with Russia's Putin. The two leaders met for the first time in Ljubljana, Slovenia, in June of 2001. Within hours of meeting him, Bush declared that Putin was a man he could trust. How did Bush know? "I looked the man in the eye," he said, and "I was able to get a sense of his soul."[24] Of course, the news media had a field day with this comment. It was picked up by late-night talk show hosts, Internet pundits, and many others. Soon the whole world was telling jokes about what happens if Bush meets someone who is visually impaired or wearing sunglasses, and so on.

Jokes aside, Bush's remark speaks volumes about how faith guides his leadership style. He uses Judeo-Christian reference points like "soul" to determine if someone is trustworthy. Even when asked about it directly, Bush makes no apology for his faith-based leadership style:

I could not [have been] governor if I did not believe in a divine plan that supersedes all human plans. Politics is a fickle business. Polls change. Today's friend is tomorrow's adversary. People lavish praise and attention. Many times it is genuine; sometimes it is not.

Yet I build my life on a foundation that will not shift. My faith frees me. Frees me to put the problem of the moment in proper perspective. Frees me to make decisions that others might not like. Frees me to try to do the right thing, even though it may not poll well. Frees me to enjoy life and not worry about what comes next. I've never plotted the steps of my life, certainly never campaigned for one office to try to position myself for the next. I am more spontaneous than that. I live in the moment, seize opportunities, and try to make the most of them.[25]

At the end of this statement, Bush himself brings up the theme of living in the moment. Experts tell us that intuition works best when a person is present and calm, rather than preoccupied and anxious. The Quakers knew this and advocated quieting the mind so that one could listen to the still, small voice within. Bush's faith helps him to be calm, present in the moment, and confident that his intuition is reliable.

This calmness of mind was especially evident in the fall of 2002. Advisors told Bush that he needed to refocus on domestic issues, like the sagging economy and markets. The debate raged between the partisan leaders: foreign issues and the war on terrorism versus domestic issues and the economy. One advisor who worked for both the elder and younger Bushes said of G.W.'s administration, "They need a stronger message, stronger team, stronger everything."[26] But despite the varied opinions of advisors, Bush remained calm.

If Bush is distracted by the debate going on all around him, he doesn't show it. If the debate is swirling inside his mind, he doesn't show that either. He has struck old allies in recent weeks as calmer than they expected, given the challenges ahead, and several said he was more relaxed than they had seen him since the summer of 1998, when he was first being mentioned as a candidate for the G.O.P. nomination. But he is clearly aware of the intense conversation that is sweeping his party this summer. As one of his allies says, "He understands it instinctively."[27]

INTUITION: A TIMELESS PRINCIPLE OF LEADERSHIP

Clearly, some of the experts whom we've chosen to represent the timeless principles would take issue with our choice of intuition as one of those principles. One such expert is J. Edward Russo, author of *Decision Traps*, a book that describes flaws in decision making and prescribes techniques to avoid them. Russo believes that intuition is the unconscious matching of a current situation with a past one. In the

THE EXPERTS SAY

What the Experts Say

Knowledge gained from direct experience and active searching, once stored in the subconscious, becomes the basis for leaders' intuition, insights and vision.

James Kouzes and Barry Posner[28]

We have it from the great French jurist Saleilles that a judge makes his decisions intuitively and then devises the fine legal reasoning to justify them—after the fact. So it is with the leader—whether he is a businessman, administrator, politician, clergyman, or teacher.

Robert Greenleaf[29]

A powerful inner guidance system, intuition has always been—and will always be—with us to provide the focus and clarity we need to make our own best decisions.

Patricia Einstein[30]

The role of intuition in creativity, problem solving, and interpersonal relationships is vital, yet it is frequently discounted and mistrusted by those who do not understand it.

Frances E. Vaughan, author of *Awakening Intuition*[31]

What the Leaders Say

Intuition only works well when you use it confidently. You must practice using it until it becomes mastered.

Tom Graves, manager of marketing strategy, Inland Paperboard and Packaging Corporation[32]

Our subjective responses . . . are more sensitive and more rapid than our objective responses . . . . [I]ntuition must be allowed full rein and allowed to play.

Jonas Salk, discoverer of the polio vaccine[33]

past, for example, we may have been burned by risky investments. So now, when offered an excellent opportunity, we turn it down because we have "a bad feeling about it." The problem, as Russo describes it, is that the "aspect or characteristic of the past situation on which we're matching may or may not have any relevance in the current situation. Your 'match' might be based on relevant or incidental parallels. Sometimes it will be one, sometimes the other."[34]

If Russo's view is accurate, why should we value intuition? Why would we include it as a timeless principle of leadership? Quite simply, we wouldn't. If intuition merely involved guesswork, it wouldn't be valuable to leaders—or any of us, for that matter.

We argue that intuition is more than that. In the view of many Western experts, and certainly the Eastern sages, it goes far beyond guesswork. Joel Yanowitz, head of Innovation Associates in Waltham, Massachusetts, has worked with many company leaders on enhancing their intuitive skills. He says, "Leaders today have to deal with multiple challenges and opportunities, develop compelling visions, and take effective action in a complex environment. Intuition is a necessary tool for tackling these and other imperatives. As such, we believe it's part of the skill set leaders need to be successful."[35] Peter Senge, author of *The Fifth Discipline*, agrees with Yanowitz. Leaders "cannot afford to choose between reason and intuition, or head and heart, any more than they would choose to walk on one leg or see with one eye."[36]

This is all well and good, but where is the evidence for us skeptical Westerners supporting the case for intuition? Are we supposed to take these pronouncements only on faith? No. Researchers like John Mihalsky and Douglas Dean, of the New Jersey Institute of Technology, have studied the use of intuition by leaders and found that "80% of CEOs whose profit doubled over a 5 year period were found to have above average intuitive powers."[37]

Successful leaders whom we have interviewed agree with the results of this study. Robert Bernstein, chairman of Random House, noted, "In business, only intuition can protect you against the most dangerous individual of all—the articulate incompetent."[38] Bob Lutz, ex-president of Chrysler, said of his decision to go with production of the Dodge Viper, "It was this subconscious, visceral feeling. And it just felt right."[39] Paul Kussell, CEO of Shepard Clothing, remarked, "I am not impulsive, but I think my intuition gets better as I get older, because I see it coming from my experience. When you accumulate enough experience, the gut feelings are more accurate."[40]

Sonia Choquette, consultant and author of four books on intuition, told us that nearly half of her individual consultations are with business leaders, all asking for intuitive guidance on business issues. When we asked if this was some sort of New Age phenomenon, she laughed and replied, "Not at all. Some of these clients are tough SOBs. But what they have in common is a real passion for their business. Intuition, in my experience, doesn't work well if it is based on fear or greed. It works when it is based on love. These guys—and gals—love their businesses."[41]

Harvard professor Daniel Isenberg studied how 16 senior corporate managers use intuition in their leadership roles. The top five uses for intuition were:

1. To help them sense when a problem exists.
2. To rapidly perform well-learned behavior patterns.
3. To synthesize isolated bits of data and experience into an integrated picture.
4. To check results of rational analysis.
5. To bypass in-depth analysis and come up with a quick solution.

We agree with Isenberg's results and have found much the same in our own work: Top leaders with whom we've worked value intuition. This, however, represents a paradigm shift for Western leaders. Some leaders, like the ones quoted at the beginning of this section, have embraced intuition as one of the tools in their leadership kit. They gain a competitive advantage from well-honed intuition, especially considering today's challenges of information overload, constant change, and the need for rapid decision making. Many others, though, are still working from the "old" paradigm; namely, that logic and reason are the only tools available. Bush is clearly in the former camp. He trusts his intuition and relies on it as a valuable leadership asset.

HOW YOU DEVELOP INTUITION

Intuition comes easier to some of us than others, as discussed in Chapter 2. Some of us are big-picture thinkers, whereas others are detail-oriented thinkers. The former naturally trust their intuition; the latter trust what they can see, touch, taste, smell, and hear. Carl Jung, the great Swiss psychologist, called the former group *intuitives* and the latter group *sensors* (because they rely on their traditional five senses). Both groups have the same potential for tapping into the power of intuition. As Jonas Salk said, "Intuition is an innate quality, but it can be developed and cultivated."[42] Everyone has intuition. The task is to develop it and trust it. Sensors, however, tend to dismiss any information that is not grounded in empirical reality. Their mantra is "Just the facts, ma'am," like Detective Joe Friday in the old television show *Dragnet*. In fact, if you've been reading this chapter and thinking, "Intuition is a lot of hogwash," then you are most likely a sensor by birth: hard-nosed, practical, no-nonsense, down-to-earth. (And you'd probably like *Dragnet*.)

If you divide a roomful of people into two groups based on their natural preference for intuiting or sensing, and then ask each group to talk about an apple, you will get very different stories. The sensors will describe the apple: "It's a Granny Smith, the color is green, there are a few bruises on it," and so forth. The intuitives will say: "An apple is the fruit that started all the trouble in the garden of Eden. It is also famous for assisting Newton in his discovery of gravity. The Beatles chose to name their record company Apple Records because . . . ." Sensors tend to be literal; intuitives tend to be figurative. Aristotle revealed his preference for the latter when he said that great thinkers are masters of the metaphor. Sensors don't have nearly the taste for metaphors; "give us the details," they say.

Developing Intuition for Intuitives

Techniques for developing your intuition differ depending on your natural preference. Consider first the intuitives. These individuals typically have already developed some skill in intuiting. They use their imaginations actively and trust their abilities to find patterns in what others may see as random events. They tend to take in information and then play with it in their heads. If you are naturally intuitive, the following tips will further strengthen your intuitive abilities.

1. To boost your intuition, become a master in your field. In other words, gain as much practical experience and knowledge as you can. An article in *Psychology Today* stated that "researchers have found that intuitive people share one essential trait: They are experts in particular, if in some cases limited, fields of knowledge . . . . Mastery of a field, these psychologists argue, is what makes intuitive thought possible."[43] Edward Toppel, author of *Zen in the Markets*, would agree: "Intuition allows you to take advantage of all the hard work you've done."[44] So, read books, attend seminars, dive in; get all the detailed knowledge you can about your subject.

2. A second practice that intuitives must adopt, if they are to maximize their intuitive potential, is organization. What?! Wouldn't organization wreck the "flow" for the intuitives? Wouldn't it cramp their style? Don't all intuitive geniuses work in messes? That is the stereotype of the intuitive: the mad scientist or brilliant author working in the wee hours of the morning with test tubes or papers scattered all about. In reality, though, disorder will hinder your intuitive skills, according to Sonia Choquette: "Chaos creates an emotional anxiety that shuts down all intuitive ability."[45] Bush is a good example of this paradox. Even though he is highly intuitive, and often the initiator of a "big, bold idea," Bush is ruthless about starting and ending meetings on time, using written agendas, having organized office space, and keeping priorities clear (see Chapter 8). All this order allows him to be fully present in the moment because the distractions have been removed.

Developing Intuition for Sensors

All that is fine for the intuitive types, but what if you are the original skeptic from Missouri, the "Show-Me State"? You've never trusted intuition. You're still not sure that there's anything to it, but based on what you've read, you're willing to try. There are exercises that will help. Just as push-ups will build your muscles, these exercises will loosen up your intuitive powers.

1. A simple one to start with is the use of metaphors and analogies. Ask a provocative question such as, "How is leadership like electricity?" Then free-associate all the connections. Call out whatever idea comes to mind, no matter how silly it seems. For example, in a session on fund-raising for a local charity, a group was brainstorming ways to raise money. One person said, "Well, if we want to get some money we could rob a bank." It was just a joke, of course. But it sparked an idea in another person, who picked up on it and said, "You know, my brother-in-law was over last weekend and he said the bank he works for is looking to back a charity project, for good PR." The end result? The charity and the bank connected and planned a very successful campaign. Literal thinking probably wouldn't have taken them from "rob a bank" to a successful fund-raising idea, but intuition allows you to make those illogical leaps.

2. Another excellent technique for loosening up the intuitive mind is called *rapid writing*. Pick a topic that you are curious about—say, a business problem—and write it at the top of a blank sheet of paper; for example, "hiring and retaining the best people." Then begin writing about it. Here's the catch: Your pen has to keep moving. Even if you are writing, "I don't know what to write next," that's fine; just keep writing. After a while, you'll begin to break through the critical part of the mind that censors original and offbeat ideas. You'll write things that surprise you. In fact, that's a good test of whether you're doing the exercise correctly: Are you surprised by some of the things you've written? You put them on paper so quickly and with so little thought that they never even registered in your conscious mind as your pen raced across the page.

3. Yet another way to tap into the intuitive side of the brain (mentioned in Chapter 2 on vision) is to draw pictures of a problem rather than using words. Geniuses throughout the ages, from Leonardo da Vinci to Edison to Einstein, all doodled. There is something very powerful about trying to draw a problem and its solution. Rational

thinking is associated with the left brain, whereas drawing is a right-brain activity. Better yet, put on classical music while you are drawing. The combination of the two will put you solidly in the right brain where intuition resides.

4. Speaking of the place where intuition resides, what about tapping directly into the unconscious through dreams? Einstein once remarked, "Why is it that I get my best ideas while shaving?" Shaving is often a zoned-out, dream-like state. It's no wonder that good ideas emerged while he was in this trancelike state.

Many people who trust their intuition and want to tap into it sleep with paper and pen by the bedside (better yet, with a hand-held recorder, so there is no need to turn on the light). A songwriter friend of ours used this technique and awoke one morning and turned on his recorder, only to hear a gorgeous song that he had recorded in the wee hours and totally forgotten about. He finished the song during the day, recorded it, and is still cashing royalty checks from radio and television airplay of that song.

5. Sensors' thinking tends to be linear, going logically from one idea to another. Intuitive thinkers tend to see patterns in seemingly unrelated events or information. If you're a sensor, and you want to string together different ideas, go back to the exercise from Chapter 2:

> Choose a business problem and explain it briefly to five different people at different times. Ask each person for his or her advice on what to do. When you've collected the five responses, challenge yourself to find a pattern in their responses. What did all the answers have in common? Is there an underlying message in this information from five very different sources?

6. Most experts will tell you that intuition can be strengthened, but few believe that there is a single best method. We disagree: The single best method for strengthening intuition, by far, is learning how to quiet the mind. That's what most of the preceding techniques have in common (after all, we were speaking of finding common themes). When the rational mind is calm, then intuition (the still, small voice

within) can surface. People quiet their minds in different ways. Bush has prayer meetings in the White House every morning. He jogs every day. Both of these activities help calm the restless mind. Every major religion fosters techniques for quieting the mind, because spiritual masters have always held that this is the way to God ("Be still and know that I am God").

A simple technique for quieting the mind is breathing meditation. Many books are available for the serious student, but the basic process is simple: Sit comfortably with your back straight and put your attention on your inhalation and exhalation of breath. When your mind gets active ("this is stupid . . . nothing's happening . . . what's the point? . . . did I feed the cat yet? . . . I have too much to do to sit here and waste time . . . ") and you notice that you are thinking, just return your attention to the breath. Yoga, which has seen a tremendous increase in popularity recently, is focused on breathing as well.

Long-time meditators can quiet the endless interior whirring and chattering of the mind. In this state, you become much better able to be present in the moment: less distracted, more focused.

Bush associates have told us that this is the experience of being with him. He looks directly at you, makes eye contact, reacts spontaneously, and is very much present in the moment. There is no single greater way to tap into intuitive wisdom than paying attention to what is going on right now. Given Bush's knack for keeping it simple, he might well sum up this chapter as follows:

There are three things you must do to sharpen your intuitive skills:
Pay attention.
Pay attention.
Pay attention.

It doesn't get much simpler than that!

Getting Results

Hold People Accountable

I believe results matter.

George W. Bush[1]

Y ou now know everything you need to know to become president of the United States. So what are you waiting for? Oh, yes, one final thing: You have to bring home the bacon. Lots of people—Ann Richards and Al Gore, to name two—didn't think George could do that. They underestimated him. They didn't fully appreciate that Bush is relentless about results.

In dealing with his staff, he understands the importance of preaching results. Don't talk to me about great ideas, lofty notions, big plans. Where's the beef? Get me some results. Bush is clear that the way to get results is to hold people accountable. When people know that they are accountable, they produce. Bush makes this point clear to all his staff. Why else would he name his King Air campaign plane "Accountability 1"?

HOLDING STAFF ACCOUNTABLE

As we noted earlier in this book, when Bush ran the Texas Rangers, he emphasized results. "We would let the baseball people make the baseball decisions," Bush said. "We didn't tell our managers whom to play at third base, but we held them accountable for their decisions."[2] Bush believes that his experience in baseball helped shape his leadership ability: "I didn't intend it or think about it at the time, but in retrospect, baseball was a great training ground for politics and government. The bottom line in baseball is results: wins and losses."[3]

Here is another example where Molly Ivins admits that Bush got results with the Texas Rangers. "Bush paid $640,000 for 2 percent of the franchise, with a clause in his contract that would make that 2 percent 11 percent—if investors recovered their initial investment. They did, as the Rangers quickly became one of the most profitable sports franchises in the country."[4] (When Ivins throws Bush a crumb of praise, we must assume it's well earned.)

BUSH ON EDUCATION

Bush was relentless as to results when he was governor of Texas. When he first took over, his focus was clearly on education, and specifically on reading. He had a vision that every schoolchild would successfully learn to read.

> I wanted [the educators] to know the Governor was interested in results, not excuses. No more claiming they would have done a better job if only Austin had allowed them to do things differently. I know there is a vigorous debate going on right now about the best way to teach children. My interest is not the means, it is the results. If drills get the job done, then rote is right. If it is necessary to teach reading all day long—fine by me.
>
> The state of Texas and the Governor will not dictate how you should teach. But we will take our responsibility to measure your progress very seriously. We expect the TAAS reading scores to show contin-ued improvement toward our goal—that every child must read on grade level.[5]

Because of Bush's focus on results, the Texas achievement scores did improve across the board: in every subject; at every grade level; tested over five years. Further, a national study cited Texas as a national leader in school improvement.

Ivins has had to admit that "education is one area where George W. Bush deserves real credit . . . . Republicans and Democrats alike praise him for his diligence and accessibility on all education issues."[6] She goes on to say that the Texas Achievement of Academic Skills test (mentioned above and in Chapter 3)

> is the foundation of the "accountability system" in Texas schools and has indeed been helpful for that purpose. TAAS was instituted by Skip Meno, Ann Richards' education commissioner, in 1991. The program was still considered an experiment when Bush came in, and many feared he would scrap it. He has instead supported and strengthened it. The good news is, and again Bush deserves credit for this, the [legislature] appropriated money for summer-reading programs for "at-risk" kids, which means "poor" in education jargon.[7]

If one had to select a motto for Bush's leadership style, it might well be "Results." Over and over again, Bush makes it clear that he is interested only in results, not excuses or grand schemes.

Later Bush took aim at the Texas education system in general, telling the education commissioner that he wanted the curriculum completely overhauled. As usual, Bush stressed results: "I would never claim to be an expert in the details of developing a curriculum. I did know the results I wanted: [a] clear, straight-forward outline of high academic standards for Texas schools."[8]

One way in which Bush helps his team produce results is by giving them clear performance goals. Studies show that leaders who are indecisive about goals, or who micromanage goal achievement, damage the creativity and morale of their employees. Bush motivates his people by showing them the target and then getting out of the way.

BUSH ON REFORM

After education, Bush went after the Texas juvenile prison system. Aiming to reduce juvenile crime, Bush turned the facilities into "boot camps." The offenders "get up early, exercise regularly, and help maintain the facility. Every hour of their day is structured and productive." (This program would definitely keep one of the authors on the straight and narrow.) The results? "Law enforcement officials and juvenile judges have credited our tougher laws and different approach with substantial results: violent crime has decreased 38 percent and overall juvenile crime has decreased 7 percent—the first decline in a decade."[9]

When Bush tried to use this same results-oriented approach with drug and alcohol rehabilitation, he met with stern resistance from the responsible state agency. They said that the "Teen Challenge" approach Bush favored didn't meet the requirements for a treatment program. The agency compiled a 49-page list of violations, ranging from torn shower curtains to frayed carpets. In response, Bush said, "I'm results-oriented, and I worry about the state being so process-oriented that we stifle good programs. We need to judge programs on results, not on forms and process."[10]

MAKING IT EASY

If a program is to be judged on results, the judges need to see some data. That's why Bush continually pushes his people to provide facts and numbers. "One of the things President Bush wants to do is start collecting more reliable data, and so we're exploring now how to do that without being accused of tilting things in favor of faith-based groups,"[11] said Jim Towey, White House director of Faith-Based and Community Initiative Programs.

Bush's focus on results obviously affects the way his staff members talk about their efforts. Rather than merely claiming, "We're doing well," or "We've had good success with [blah]," they pepper their reports and conversation with numbers and facts that reflect their boss's high regard for measurement. Witness Towey's description of a successful rehabilitation program in New York City:

> I was at The Bowery Mission in New York City, and they have a nine-month program with a 7 percent recidivism rate, in other words, if you get into their homeless program, you're going to get off drugs, get a job, save money, get an apartment, and not come back. That's a very impressive program.[12]

Good leaders make it easy for their team to get results. They pave the way for success using the tools of decisiveness and clarity. Bush says of himself, "I am a decisive person. I get the facts, weigh them thoughtfully and carefully, and decide."[13] If there is a single complaint that resonates loudest from disgruntled workers, it is that their leaders can't make up their minds, or that they make a decision and then change it the next day. When Bush discusses his decision-making process, he often mentions "chief executives" because business is his background. Bush says, "[M]aking decisions is what governors and chief executives do. I try to do so thoroughly, thoughtfully, and fairly. I have assembled a top-quality staff that gets me accurate information and comprehensive briefings. I base my decisions on principles that do not change."[14]

When Bush makes a decision, he then acts decisively as well. Using a baseball analogy—apt in relation to Bush—*Time* magazine remarked, "When the President does decide to take a swing, he swings hard. By delivering his reform package with presidential seal and prime-time flourish, Bush hopes to propel it through Congress quickly."[15] In fact, when Bush ran the Texas Rangers baseball team, Tom Schieffer, the team's president, said,

> He does not second-guess himself about decisions. George is very good at addressing problems as they come across his desk and then moving on to the next one. When he makes mistakes, he doesn't dwell on them, he tries to learn from them. He thinks it's important to be decisive and provide some leadership.[16]

Decisive action is good because it provides both clarity for workers and a sense of urgency. Good leaders light a fire in the belly of their troops.

REWARDS AND PUNISHMENT

Bush knows how to use the carrot and stick to get results. When proposing reforms for the federal government, Bush said we must:

- Enforce the Government Performance and Results Act (GPRA) by recommending higher levels of funding for programs that work. Agency inspector generals, Bush said, will certify the accuracy of GPRA reports, and the Office of Management and Budget will factor the results into budget decisions.
- Establish a federal Sunset Review Board to recommend elimination of programs deemed unnecessary or duplicative.
- Convert at least half of all federal service contracts to performance-based contracts.
- Create performance incentives in the federal civil service system to reward achievement and attract job candidates from the private sector.
- Allow competition from the private sector for at least half of the 900,000 federal jobs not identified as inherently governmental under the Federal Activities Inventory Reform (FAIR) Act.[17]

Bush said these reforms would save $88 billion over five years.

Importantly, these reforms send a clear message to federal employees: produce or perspire. Though basically a cheerleader, Bush won't hesitate to use the stick. Bush insists on bringing in the right people. Teams need to feel that everyone is capable and pulling their weight. When this is not the case—when one person continually fails to produce or measure up—a leader must act or team morale will suffer. Schieffer says that executives working for Bush in the Rangers organization were free to run their operation as they saw fit, but were held accountable for the results. During Bush's tenure with the Rangers, he did fire field manager Bobby Valentine and general manager Tom Grieve. Schieffer believes that, although lots of reasons could be given for their release, the primary reason was, "We hadn't won." Schieffer adds, "If the day-to-day operations had not gone well, I wouldn't have been president."[18]

Bush can use the carrot as well. Bush has reassured federal government workers that the reduction in workforce can be handled through attrition and early retirements rather than layoffs. Moreover, Bush is a master of boosting morale by expressing his sincere appreciation of workers' hard work and dedication. He values them and tells them so. As noted in Chapter 5, Albert Hawkins, Bush's budget director in Texas, said that Bush realizes people "don't come into the public service expecting to get any stock options."[19] Bush understands and appreciates workers who seek the less tangible rewards that come from simply helping others. He also understands the importance of recognition; Bush initiated the "Texas Stars" program to recognize employee excellence in meeting the targets set by the state's performance-based budgeting system.

Both Schieffer and Hawkins agree that Bush has the ability to make his staff feel good about working for him. (The same cannot be said of Gore. During his campaign, some staffers said they liked his political views but not working with him.) All the research shows that motivated employees are generally more productive employees, and productivity equals results. Bush inspires people by using the combination of skills and techniques we've been discussing, and also, as Schieffer concludes, because "[h]e has such a good spirit about him, and he is interested in people."[20]

In the Oval Office, Bush's results orientation plays well. He is happy to work with leaders of either party, so long as they get results. Bush brought with him to Washington a remarkable ability to woo political adversaries like Bullock, the long-time Democratic lieutenant governor of Texas. The two of them formed a remarkably effective bipartisan team based on a simple ethic: Get results for Texas. Like his father, Bush classifies politicians into two breeds. On the one hand, there are "good men" and women who can get things done; on the other hand, there are obstructionist poseurs. Bush recognizes that good people can hail from either party. It's why Bush gives out his highest praise to liberal archenemy Ted Kennedy: "He can get things done."[21]

September 11 certainly demonstrated the need for decisive action and clear results! Bush received high praise from Edward Luttwak, senior fellow at the Center for Strategic Studies, who said, "You can thus measure Bush as a wartime President by one simple criterion. He basically told the Secretary of Defense, Please fight and Please win. He set no constraints. And by these lights, I rate George Bush very highly . . . . [H]e has acted right."[22]

RESULTS: A TIMELESS PRINCIPLE OF LEADERSHIP

Should the principle of accountability and results be considered a timeless principle of leadership, and a part of Bush's leadership genius? Do great leaders really have to hold their people accountable and pave the way for excellent results?

Yes, according to the research done by Bruce N. Pfau at Watson Wyatt Worldwide (www.watsonwyatt.com/research/, discussed in Chapter 3). In fact, Pfau's study provides evidence that holding employees accountable for performance—by rewarding them for outstanding results and terminating chronic nonperformers—is the largest single contributor to a company's stock performance, even ahead of hiring excellent people. The HCI study showed an average 16.5 percent increase in the stock price of companies with leaders who do all of the following:

- Reward employees for good work.
- Refuse to accept sub-par performance.
- Offer excellent pay and benefits.
- Link pay to company performance.
- Promote the most competent employees.
- Help poor performers and terminate chronic nonperformers.

THE EXPERTS SAY

What the Experts Say

An effective leader is not someone who is loved or admired. He or she is someone whose followers do the right things. Popularity is not leadership. Results are.

Peter Drucker[23]

The first requirement of leadership is to ensure that the organization is competitively viable. In a business setting, trust begins by demonstrating the competence required for an organization or team to prosper and grow.

Robert Bruce Shaw[24]

The concept of win-win suggests that managers and employees clarify expectations and mutually commit themselves to getting desired results . . . . Holding people accountable for results puts teeth in the win-win agreement.

Stephen Covey[25]

The only way to deliver to the people who are achieving is to not burden them with the people who are not achieving.

Jim Collins[26]

What the Leaders Say

Servant leaders must be value driven and performance oriented.

C. William Pollard, chairman of the ServiceMaster Company[27]

"Get results"—Donald Rumsfeld's two-word mantra.

Jeffrey Krames[28]

You'd get no argument from Jim Collins. He too believes that re-sults are key to top leadership. In *Good to Great*, he considers the question of how to recognize extraordinary leaders. He answers it this way: "Look for situations where extraordinary results exist but where no individual steps forth to claim excess credit."[29]

Collins calls these CEOs "Level 5" leaders. He cites as examples Darwin Smith and Charles Cork. (*Note:* "Darwin Smith" is the an-swer to the Kimberly-Clark quiz question in Chapter 2.) "Who!?" you ask. And that's exactly the point. These leaders, who took their orga-nizations (Kimberly-Clark and Walgreens, respectively) from average to extraordinary never grabbed headlines, or wrote autobiographies, or appeared on *Oprah*, or attended big Hollywood parties. But, oh boy, did they help their people get results!

Collins says that Level 5 leaders display "compelling modesty, are self-effacing and understated. In contrast, two thirds of the compari-son companies (the 'also-ran' firms) had leaders with gargantuan per-sonal egos that contributed to the demise or to continued mediocrity of the company."[30] Interestingly, when Collins speculates on how the personalities of the Level 5 leaders develop, he says,

> A strong religious belief or conversion might also nurture de-velopment of Level 5 traits. Colman Mockler, for example, con-verted to evangelical Christianity while getting his MBA at Harvard, and later, according to the book *Cutting Edge*, became a prime mover in a group of Boston business executives who met frequently over breakfast to discuss the carryover of religious values to corporate life.[31]

George W. Bush had both experiences: conversion to a deeper faith in Christianity and participation in a men's Bible study group. (He also attended the Harvard MBA program but appears not to view it as a religious experience.)

Lest it sound as though these Level 5 leaders are mostly interested in discussion groups about spiritual principles, Collins emphasizes a very different image of them: "Level 5 leaders are fanatically driven, infected with an incurable need to produce sustained results. They are resolved to do whatever it takes to make the company great, no matter how big or hard the decisions."[32] Again, the parallel to Bush's case is obvious. He is relentless about results, even in the face of such uphill battles as turning around the Texas Rangers, beating the popular incumbent Ann Richards, reforming the Texas educational system, or defeating a terrorist enemy that can't even be definitely located. Bush is the proverbial dog with a bone. He doesn't let go until the job is done.

Leaders in corporate America realize that results must be a top priority. At Hewlett-Packard, they expressed it this way:

> In our economic system, the profit we generate from our operations is the ultimate source of the funds we need to prosper and grow. It is the one absolutely essential measure of our corporate performance over the long-term. Only if we continue to meet our profit objectives can we achieve our other corporate objectives . . . . [P]rofit is not something that can be put off until tomorrow; it must be achieved today. It means that myriad jobs [must] be done correctly and efficiently. The day-to-day performance of each individual adds to—or subtracts from—our profit. Profit is the responsibility of all.[33]

In the hierarchy of corporate needs, profit comes first. Like water, food, or oxygen to a person, it's a necessity, not a luxury. Profit is not the purpose of these great companies, but it is necessary to achieve the purpose. When a firm becomes profitable, it has the freedom to think of employee fulfillment and community involvement. Firms that are struggling place their focus, quite obviously, on revenues and expenses. Eking out some earnings becomes the overriding concern, and rightly so. Then there are companies like American Century in Kansas City, mentioned in Chapter 1, which has succeeded so brilliantly that its founder, Jim Stowers, was able to donate more than $1 billion to cancer research. In Portland, Oregon, the United Way named its highest service award after Jim Rudd, chairman of Ferguson Wellman Capital Management. He and his colleagues have reached a level of success where they naturally want to give back in the form of community service and philanthropy.

HOW TO GET ACCOUNTABILITY AND RESULTS

Do you want to be known as a leader who is known for results? With a side benefit of building trust? Read and heed:

1. **Have a clearly articulated strategic direction that will enable you to succeed against competitors.** In business or politics, a clear strategy is important. In Texas, Bush ran on four campaign planks, though clearly education was his deep passion. In the presidential race, Bush chose to work closely with Rove in setting strategy. Sometimes the strategy was bold and risky, as when Rove convinced the "Bush for President" team to campaign less aggressively in the primary, to make it look as if Bush's victory was a foregone conclusion. Sometimes it was more conservative, as in the weeks that followed the terrorist attacks of 9/11. Whatever the implementing strategy, the people working with Bush are never in the dark about the overall direction.

   Tip: Use the ideas in Chapter 2, "Where Are You Going?" to help you craft a compelling vision.

2. **Help followers focus on a few key priorities and clearly stated goals.** Bush focuses well. He has a knack for keeping it simple, which allows his staff to zero in on key objectives. The same is true of the culture at General Electric:

   > At GE, we spend a great deal of time articulating the outputs we expect from our businesses and people. Most of our time is spent agreeing on the improvement we expect in each critical area. Once that is done, we trust our people to find a way to

make those targets. In other words, our efforts go into gaining clear agreement on the outputs rather than the means of achieving the outputs.[34]

Tip: Prioritize goals and focus only on the top two or three.

3. **Recognize and reward successes and take action on employee problems.** Having grown up in the business world, Bush is thoroughly steeped in the notion of pay for performance. He is bringing it to government at the federal level with many of his legislative reforms. He is also aware of the effectiveness of cutting one's losses. When the original managers at the Texas Rangers organization didn't pan out, Bush fired them. The HCI study mentioned earlier shows clearly that rewarding employees appropriately is crucial to results.

Tip: Be specific when you praise employees; tell them exactly what they did to merit the recognition.

4. **Gain widespread agreement on necessary roles and accountabilities.** Simple as it may sound, some leaders have never gotten clarity and buy-in about roles and responsibilities at the top levels. One group of senior executives, after nearly five years of working together, finally sat down and, at our prompting, worked out their job responsibilities. Obviously, results came much easier when their roles were clear.

Tip: Take the time necessary with the entire team to discuss, negotiate, and agree on roles and responsibilities. Write down the final agreements and send copies to all team members.

5. **Hold people accountable to the highest standards of performance.** Using "stretch" goals is somewhat different from the idea of rewarding people for great performance. Stretch goals are a way of life at GE, and more firms are adopting them every day. In *Built to Last,* Collins and Porras talk about the power of Big Hairy Audacious Goals: BHAGs seem impossible, but they are also compelling, inspiring employees to say, "Yes, we can do it!"[35]

Tip: Set the example for the team. Let them know your stretch goal and that you'll be stretching along with them.

6. **Create a sense of urgency and a drive to succeed.** Bush has said, "I'm a patient man," but he sure can make decisions fast when he has the information he needs. His ability to move quickly and decisively contributes to the sense of urgency. His natural drive to succeed also contributes to a clear sense of "let's get it done!"

    Tip: Along with stretch goals, set clear deadlines and hold employees to them.

7. **Make decisions on tough issues in a timely manner.** In our experience working with leaders, no single act is more damaging than delaying a decision. It frustrates the daylights out of followers. The earlier quote from Bush on decisiveness couldn't be clearer: "I am a decisive person. I get the facts, weigh them thoughtfully and carefully, and decide."[36] White House staff people to whom we've spoken confirm that Bush likes to move on decisions.

    Tip: Use the model in Chapter 6, "Encourage Collaboration," to decide how many stakeholders to involve in the decision. Then follow Bush's example: Decide and move on!

8. **Give people the resources and autonomy they need to be successful.** Bush is known for his hands-off management style. One of the quickest ways to kill motivation and creativity in staff members is to micromanage their projects. Bush hires smart people, trusts them, and leaves them alone.

    Tip: Ask your employees, "Do you have the resources and freedom to do the job?" Then make sure that they get both.

9. **Invest in and support the development and education of employees.** Ingenious leaders know that learning is continuous. Employees need to continually develop their skills and abilities. If employees sense that their current leader won't support them in this way, odds are that they will move on.

    Tip: Find excellent articles that relate to the team's work and circulate them to everyone. It's cheap and stimulates good discussion and often new approaches. (Just make sure you obey all the relevant copyright laws . . .)

Bush has learned these principles so thoroughly that he now uses them instinctively.

If you secretly feel that people underrate you; that you've never been given your due; that you could be David to someone's Goliath; that you could be a Level 5 leader . . . what are you waiting for? George W. Bush is your role model. He was an average student, a party guy, and a mediocre athlete—and look what he did with that modest talent! Parlayed it into becoming president of the world's most powerful nation. Not bad, eh? So, the next time someone underrates your honcho abilities, answer just as George would: "I love to be underrated." Then take the principles in this book, study them, learn them, practice them, and become that person's boss. George would no doubt be proud of you.

Notes

Introduction

1. Quoted in James Carney, "Why Bush Doesn't Like Homework," *Time*, November 15, 1999, 46.
2. Kathleen Parker, "Bush and Unborn Children," *Chicago Tribune*, October 2, 2002, sec. 1, 19.
3. Frances Hesselbein, Marshall Goldsmith, and Richard Beckhard, eds., *The Leader of the Future* (San Francisco: Jossey-Bass, 1996), 221.

Chapter 1 What Do You Stand For?

1. George W. Bush, *A Charge to Keep* (New York: Perennial, 1999), 104.
2. Ibid., 177.
3. Ibid., 184.
4. Ibid., 186.
5. Ibid., 225.
6. Frank Bruni, *Ambling into History* (New York: HarperCollins, 2002), 261.
7. Bush, *A Charge to Keep*, 180.
8. Ibid., 181.
9. Ibid., 182.
10. Ibid., 178.
11. Quoted in Bill Minutaglio, *First Son: George W. Bush and the Bush Family Dynasty* (New York: Times Books, 1999), 106.

12. Ibid., xi.

13. Mark Crispin Miller, *The Bush Dyslexicon* (New York: W. W. Norton, 2001), 112–13.

14. Bruni, *Ambling into History*, 116.

15. James Carney and John Dickerson, "A Work in Progress," *Time,* October 22, 2001, 40.

16. Bush, *A Charge to Keep*, 194.

17. Bruni, *Ambling into History*, 172.

18. J. H. Hatfield, *Fortunate Son: George W. Bush and the Making of an American President* (New York: Soft Skull Press, 2001), 95.

19. Bruni, *Ambling into History*, 172.

20. Bush, *A Charge to Keep*, 229.

21. Ibid., 235.

22. Ibid., 235.

23. Ibid., 151.

24. Ibid., 29.

25. Richard Barrett, *Liberating the Corporate Soul: Building a Visionary Organization* (Boston: Butterworth-Heinemann, 1988), 192.

26. James C. Collins and Jerry I. Porras, *Built to Last* (New York: Harper Business, 1994), 73.

27. Jac Fitz-Enz, *The 8 Practices of Exceptional Companies* (New York: AMACOM, 1997), 71.

28. Jack Bogle, *Common Sense on Mutual Funds* (New York: John Wiley & Sons, 2000), 425.

29. Ted Goodman, *The Forbes Book of Business Quotations* (New York: Black Dog & Leventhal Publishers, 1997) 684.

30. Richard Barrett, "The Value of Values: Why Values Are Important in Organizations," www.corptools.com; accessed October 16, 2002.

31. Collins and Porras, *Built to Last*, 222.

32. Quoted in Robert Howard, "Values Make the Company: An Interview with Robert Haas," *Harvard Business Review*, September–October 1990, 135.

33. Collins and Porras, 223–24.

34. John P. Kotter and James L. Heskett, *Corporate Culture and Performance* (New York: Free Press, 1992), 45.

35. Charles D. Ellis, "Will Business Success Spoil the Investment Management Profession?" *Journal of Portfolio Management*, Spring 2001, 14.

36. Kenneth H. Blanchard, *Managing by Values* (San Francisco: Berrett-Koehler, 1998).

37. Beth Michaels and Dale Primer, Focus Consulting Group, Glenview, Illinois; 847-729-3508.

38. Delroy Alexander, "The Fall of Andersen," *Chicago Tribune*, September 1, 2002, 1.

39. Molly Ivins and Lou Dubose, *Shrub* (New York: Vintage, 2000), 107.

40. Ibid.

41. Frances Hesselbein, Marshall Goldsmith, and Richard Beckhard, eds., *The Leader of the Future* (San Francisco: Jossey-Bass, 1996), xiii.

42. James Carney, "Why Bush Doesn't Like Homework," *Time*, November 15, 1999, 47.

Chapter 2   Where Are You Going?

1. George W. Bush, *A Charge to Keep* (New York: Perennial, 1999), 44.

2. Ibid., 118.

3. Dick Kirschten, "Bush as Boss," *Government Executive Magazine*, July 1, 2002, 16.

4. Bush, *A Charge to Keep*, 180.

5. Frank Bruni, *Ambling into History* (New York: HarperCollins, 2002), 245.

6. Ibid.

7. Aubrey Immelman, "Getting Inside the Bush Mind," *St. Cloud Times*, December 17, 2000, 17.

8. Bush, *A Charge to Keep*, 205.

9. Ibid., 208.

10. Ibid., 204.

11. Ibid., 122.

12. Ibid., 67.

13. Bill Minutaglio, *First Son: George W. Bush and the Bush Family Dynasty* (New York: Times Books, 1999), 229.

14. Bush, *A Charge to Keep*, 104.

15. Ibid., 136.

16. Ibid., 107.

17. Ibid., 236.

18. Elizabeth Mitchell, *W: Revenge of the Bush Dynasty* (New York: Hyperion, 2000), 76.

19. Eric Pooley, "Bush in the Crucible," *Time*, September 24, 2001, 11.

20. George W. Bush, statement to the nation, September 11, 2001.

21. Douglas Waller, "Ready for the 50-Year War?," *Time*, January 7, 2002, 21.

22. Prov. 29:18.

23. J. H. Hatfield, *Fortunate Son: George W. Bush and the Making of an American President* (New York: Soft Skull Press, 2001), 89.

24. Ibid., 91.

25. Robert Rosen, *Leading People* (New York: Penguin USA, 1997), 45.

26. Robert Greenleaf, *On Becoming a Servant Leader* (San Francisco: Jossey-Bass, 1996), 337.

27. Ben Cohen and Jerry Greenfield, *Ben & Jerry's Double-Dip* (New York: Fireside, 1988), 86.

28. Phil Jackson, *Sacred Hoops* (New York: Hyperion, 1996), 98.

29. Katrina Brooker, "Meet the (Sort of) New Bosses," *Fortune*, May 28, 2001, 76.

30. Charlie Feld, "Leadership Challenges," *Fast Company*, October 2000, 348.

31. Quoted in Frances Hesselbein, Marshall Goldsmith, and Richard Beckhard, eds., *The Leader of the Future* (San Francisco: Jossey-Bass, 1996), 82.

32. James C. Collins and Jerry I. Porras, *Built to Last* (New York: Harper Business, 1994), 73.

33. Jim Collins, *Good to Great* (New York: Harper Business, 2001), 98.

34. Collins and Porras, *Built to Last*, 237.

35. Bush, *A Charge to Keep*, 241.

36. Quoted in Hesselbein, Goldsmith, and Beckhard, *The Leader of the Future*, 103.

37. Quoted in Sandra Weintraub, *The Hidden Intelligence: Innovation Through Intuition* (New York: Butterworth-Heinemann, 1998), 92.

38. Bush, *A Charge to Keep*, 180.

39. Bill Watterson, *Calvin and Hobbes: Tenth Anniversary Book* (Kansas City, Mo.: Andrews McMeel Publishing, 2001), 8.

40. Bush, *A Charge to Keep*, 136.

41. Ibid., 84.

42. James Carney and Douglas Waller, "Bush Does His Vision Things on Arms Control," *Time*, June 5, 2000, 18.

43. Bush, *A Charge to Keep*, 44.

Chapter 3   Can I Trust You?

1. 1 Cor. 4:2.

2. Frank Bruni, *Ambling into History* (New York: HarperCollins, 2002), 229.

3. Sam Howe Verhovek, "As Woman's Execution Nears, Texas Squirms," *New York Times*, January 1, 1998, 1.

4. George W. Bush, *A Charge to Keep* (New York: Perennial, 1999), 147.

5. Ibid., 103.

6. Ibid., 149.

7. Ibid., 136.

8. Ibid., 150.

9. Ibid., 151.

10. Ibid., 160.

11. Ibid., 164.

12. Ibid., 166.

13. Ibid., 69.

14. Ibid., 75.

15. Ibid., 75.

16. Ibid., 78.

17. Ibid., 103.

18. James Carney, "Our New Best Friend," *Time*, May 27, 2002, 42.

19. Bush, *A Charge to Keep*, 65.

20. Ibid., 64.

21. Bruni, *Ambling into History*, 181.

22. Quoted by staff member in interview with authors, August 2, 2002.

23. Carney, "Our New Best Friend," 43.

24. Bush, *A Charge to Keep*, 37.

25. Ibid.

26. Bruni, *Ambling into History*, 197.

27. Marianne M. Jennings, "Professional Responsibilities, Ethics, and the Law," in *AIMR Conference Proceedings*, Charlottesville, Virginia, December 7–8, 1999, 4.

28. Frances Hesselbein, Marshall Goldsmith, and Richard Beckhard, eds., *The Leader of the Future* (San Francisco: Jossey-Bass, 1996), 190.

29. Stephen Covey, *The 7 Habits of Highly Effective People* (New York: Simon & Schuster, 1990), 178.

30. Jac Fitz-Enz, *The 8 Practices of Exceptional Companies* (New York: AMACOM, 1997), 157.

31. Phil Jackson, *Sacred Hoops* (New York: Hyperion, 1996), 21.

32. Brian Billick, *Competitive Leadership* (Chicago: Triumph Books, 2001), 13.

33. Brian Billick, James A. Peterson, and Andrea Kremer, *Competitive Leadership: Twelve Principles for Success* (Chicago: Triumph Books, 2001), 10.

34. Quoted in Hesselbein, Goldsmith, and Beckhard, *The Leader of the Future*, 251.

35. James C. Collins and Jerry I. Porras, *Built to Last* (New York: Harper Business, 1994), 4.

36. *Merriam-Webster's Collegiate Dictionary*, 10th ed. (Springfield, Mass.: Merriam-Webster, 1993), 1269.

37. Robert Bruce Shaw, *Trust in the Balance* (San Francisco: Jossey-Bass, 1998), 45–57.

38. Bush, *A Charge to Keep*, 155.

39. Ibid.

40. Shaw, *Trust in the Balance*, 63–84.

41. Bob Kemper, "Bush, Putin Sign Nuclear Arms Pact," *Chicago Tribune*, May 25, 2002, 1.

Chapter 4   Bring in the Right People, Part One

1. George W. Bush, *A Charge to Keep* (New York: Perennial, 1999), 97.

2. Ibid., 98–99.

3. Ibid., 151.

4. Karen Hughes, foreword to Bush, *A Charge to Keep*, xii–xiii.

5. Vance McMahan, after interviewing with Governor Bush for the job of policy director, quoted in Bush, *A Charge to Keep*, 28.

6. Karl Rove, quoted in James Carney and John F. Dickerson, "The Busiest Man in the White House," *Time*, April 30, 2001, 32.

7. Quoted in James Carney, John F. Dickerson, Massimo Calabresi, Mark

Thompson, Karen Tumulty, and Douglas Waller, "Inside the War Room," *Time,* December 31, 2001, 122.

8. Frank Bruni, *Ambling into History* (New York: HarperCollins, 2002), 53.

9. Bush, *A Charge to Keep,* 68–69.

10. Carney et al., "Inside the War Room," 122.

11. Bush, *A Charge to Keep,* 27–28.

12. Ibid., 106.

13. Carolyn B. Thompson, *Straight Talk for Employers* (Chicago: TSI Publications, 1996) (audiotape).

14. Larry Burkett, *Business by the Book* (Nashville, Tenn.: Thomas Nelson Publishers, 1990), 97.

15. Roger E. Herman, *Signs of the Times* (Winchester, Va.: Oakhill Press, 1999), 19.

16. Quoted in Sara P. Noble, ed., *301 Great Management Ideas from America's Most Innovative Small Companies* (Boston: INC Publishing, 1991), 33.

17. Quoted in Sara P. Noble, ed., *Managing People* (Boston: INC Publishing, 1992), iv.

18. Brian Tracy, *Hire and Keep the Best People* (San Francisco: Berrett-Koehler, 2001), 16–17.

19. Bruce Tulgan, *Winning the Talent Wars* (New York: W. W. Norton, 2001), 76.

20. Catherine D. Fyock, *Get the Best* (Crestwood, Ky.: Author, 1993), 17.

21. Roger E. Herman, *Keeping Good People* (Winchester, Va.: Oakhill Press, 1999), 41.

22. Fairfield & Woods, www.fwlaw.com; accessed July 21, 2002.

23. Carolyn B. Thompson, *Interviewing Techniques for Managers* (New York: McGraw-Hill, 2002), 131.

24. Charles J. Stewart and William B. Cash, *Interviewing Principles and Practices* (Madison, Wis.: WCB Brown & Benchmark, 1994), 155.

25. Robert W. Wendover, *Smart Hiring* (Aurora, Co.: National Management Staff, 1989), 111.

26. Jim Collins, *Good to Great* (New York: Harper Business, 2001), 50–52.

27. Bruni, *Ambling into History,* 150.

28. Ibid., 115.

29. Ibid., 200.

30. James Carney, "O Ye of Little Faith," *Time,* August 27, 2002, 1–2.

31. Thomas Beaumont, "Iowa Now Pro-Bush, Poll Says," DesMoines-Register.com, July 7, 2002; accessed October 22, 2002.

Chapter 5   Bring in the Right People, Part Two

1. George W. Bush, *A Charge to Keep* (New York: Perennial, 1999), 151.
2. Michael Duffy, Massimo Calabresi, John F. Dickerson, J. F. O. McAllister, and Scott MacLeod, "Trapped by His Own Instincts," *Time*, May 6, 2002, 28.
3. John King, "Bush Aide Karen Hughes to Leave White House," cnn.com, April 23, 2002; accessed July 15, 2002.
4. Michael Duffy, James Colbum, and Matthew Cooper, "How Bush Hires," *Time*, December 25, 2000, 90.
5. Johanna McGeary, Massimo Calabresi, Margaret Carlson, James Carney, Michael Duffy, Mark Thompson, Douglas Waller, and J. F. O. McAllister, "Odd Man Out," *Time*, September 10, 2001, 24.
6. John F. Dickerson, Matthew Cooper, and Douglas Waller, "Bush's Two Sides," *Time*, August 6, 2001, 24.
7. James Carney and John F. Dickerson, "The Busiest Man in the White House," *Time*, April 30, 2001, 32.
8. Howard Fineman, "I Sniff Some Politics," *Newsweek*, May 27, 2002, 38.
9. Howard Fineman, Tamara Lipper, and Roy Gutman, "Same as He Ever Was," *Newsweek*, September 11, 2002, 33.
10. James Carney, John F. Dickerson, Massimo Calabresi, Mark Thompson, Karen Tumulty, and Douglas Waller, "Inside the War Room," *Time*, December 31, 2001, 112.
11. Michael Elliott, et al., "We're At War," *Time*, September 24, 2001, 40.
12. Romesh Ratnesar, James Carney, John F. Dickerson, Massimo Calabresi, Matthew Cooper, Andrew Goldstein, Karen Tumulty, and Michael Weisskopf, "Can He Fix It?" *Time*, June 17, 2002, 26–27.
13. John F. Harris and Dan Balz, "A Question of Capital: Bush Makes Political Investments, But Will They Make Him?" washingtonpost.com, April 29, 2001; accessed July 12, 2002.
14. Bush, *A Charge to Keep*, 97.
15. Ibid., 60.
16. Bill Minutaglio, *First Son: George W. Bush and the Bush Family Dynasty* (New York: Times Books, 1999), 157.
17. Bush, *A Charge to Keep*, 103.

18. Frank Bruni, *Ambling into History* (New York: HarperCollins, 2002), 122.

19. Ibid., 230.

20. Bush, *A Charge to Keep*, 104.

21. Ibid., 105.

22. Ibid., 100.

23. Unit for Study of Personality in Politics, http://www.csbsju.edu/uspp/ExecutiveSummaries/Bush-Abstract.html, April 6, 2000; accessed July 12, 2002.

24. Michael Elliott, "We Will Not Fail," *Time*, October 1, 2001, 20.

25. Carney et al., "Inside the War Room," 112.

26. Keith Koffler and Brody Mullens, "Bush Pushes Hard for Flexibility in New Department," govexec.com, July 26, 2002; accessed July 26, 2002.

27. Carney et al., "Inside the War Room," *Time*, December 31, 2001, 112.

28. Michael Duffy, Nancy Gibbs, John F. Dickerson, and Andrew Goldstein, "Defender in Chief," *Time*, November 5, 2001, 26.

29. Ibid.

30. McGeary et al., "Odd Man Out," *Time*, September 10, 2001, 24.

31. Elizabeth Mitchell, *W: Revenge of the Bush Dynasty* (New York: Hyperion, 2000), 68.

32. "Bush Seeks to Reassure Investors," msnbc.com, July 22, 2002; accessed July 22, 2002.

33. Bill Saporito, John F. Dickerson, and Adam Zagorin, "Wall Street's Verdict," *Time*, July 29, 2002, 18.

34. Kelly Wallace, "Treasury O'Neill Faces the Heat," cnn.com, July 29, 2002; accessed July 29, 2002.

35. Bruni, *Ambling into History*, 171.

36. James Carney, John F. Dickerson, Karen Tumulty, and Douglas Waller, "A Few Small Repairs," *Time*, July 9, 2001, 20.

37. "A Spring Cleaning for the Bush Economic Team," Time.com, September 23, 2002; accessed September 23, 2002.

38. Tamara Lipper, Martha Brant, Michael Hirsh, Roy Gutman, Mark Hoenball, Michael Isikoff, John Barry, Stryker McGuire, and Christian Caryl, "Selling the World on War," *Newsweek*, September 23, 2002, 29.

39. Interview with Fred I. Greenstein, author of *The Presidential Difference: Leadership Styles from FDR to Clinton* (Princeton, N.J.: Princeton University Press, 2001).

40. James Carney, "Why Bush Doesn't Like Homework," *Time*, November 15, 1999, 46.

41. Leslie Yerkes, *Fun Works: Creating Places Where People Love to Work* (San Francisco: Berrett-Koehler, 2001), 111.

42. William C. Byham, Ph.D., *Zapp!: The Lightning of Empowerment* (New York: Ballentine, 1998), 52, 56.

43. Quoted in Tom Peters, *A Passion for Excellence* (New York: Random House, 1985), 362.

44. Quoted in Ken Blanchard, "Three Secrets of the One Minute Manager," *CPA Journal Online*, nysscpa.org, April 1992; accessed August 8, 2002.

45. Kevin Merida, "Shades of Grey Matter; The Question Dogs George W. Bush: Is He Smart Enough? There's No Single Answer," washingtonpost.com, January 19, 2000; accessed July 13, 2002.

46. Paul Begala, *Is Our Children Learning?: The Case Against George W. Bush* (New York: Simon & Schuster, 2000), 118.

47. Bruni, *Ambling into History*, 240.

48. Ibid., 266.

49. www.brainyquote.com; accessed October 16, 2002.

50. Amy C. Edmondson, "Learning Curve," *HBS Leading Research* 5, no. 1 (2002): 1–2.

51. Max DePree, *The Art of Leadership* (New York: Dell, 1989), 75.

52. Interview in *SAM's Club Source*, July 2002.

53. Bruni, *Ambling into History*, 224–25.

54. DePree, *The Art of Leadership*, 12.

55. Bush, *A Charge to Keep*, 61.

56. Ibid., 29.

57. Ibid., 99.

58. Ibid.

59. Quoted in Dick Kirschten, "Bush as Boss," govexec.com, July 1, 2000; accessed July 12, 2002.

60. Bush, *A Charge to Keep*, 10.

61. Kirschten, "Bush as Boss."

62. Bob Wischinia, "We Raced with Bush," runnersworld.com, October 2002; accessed September 13, 2002.

63. Elliott, "We Will Not Fail," 20.

Chapter 6   Encourage Collaboration

1. George W. Bush, *A Charge to Keep* (New York: Perennial, 1999), 241.

2. Bill Minutaglio, *First Son: George W. Bush and the Bush Family Dynasty* (New York: Times Books, 1999), 331.

3. Aubrey Immelman, "Getting Inside the Bush Mind," *St. Cloud Times,* December 17, 2002, 17.

4. Quoted in Minutaglio, *First Son,* 62.

5. Ibid., 153.

6. Molly Ivins and Lou Dubose, *Shrub* (New York: Vintage, 2000), xxi.

7. Ibid., 92.

8. Minutaglio, *First Son,* 295.

9. Ibid.

10. Bush, *A Charge to Keep,* 112.

11. Ibid., 113.

12. Minutaglio, *First Son,* 328.

13. Quoted in James Carney, "Why Bush Doesn't Like Homework," *Time,* November 15, 1999, 47.

14. John F. Dickerson, Matthew Cooper, and Douglas Waller, "Bush's Two Sides," *Time,* August 6, 2001, 21.

15. Ibid., 22.

16. Bush, *A Charge to Keep,* 185.

17. John F. Dickerson, "Bush's Furor over Der Führer," *Time,* September 30, 2002, 23.

18. Ibid., 24.

19. James Carney et al., "Mission to Europe," *Time,* June 18, 2001, 26.

20. Ibid., 27.

21. Michael Duffy, "War on All Fronts," *Time,* October 15, 2001, 32.

22. Ibid., 34.

23. Edward Gubman, *The Talent Solution* (New York: McGraw-Hill Trade, 1998), 178.

24. Richard Barrett, *Liberating the Corporate Soul, Building a Visionary Organization* (Boston: Butterworth-Heinemann, 1998), 198.

25. Tiorio, ancient philosopher, quoted on cybernation.com; accessed October 16, 2002.

26. Ted Goodman, *The Forbes Book of Business Quotations* (New York: Black Dog & Leventhal Publishers, 1997) 171.

27. Ibid., p. 172.

28. Peter Drucker, "The Age of Social Transformation," *Atlantic Monthly,* November 1994, 31.

29. Daniel Goleman, *Emotional Intelligence* (New York: Bantam Books, 1997), 160.

30. Jeff Diermeier, interview with the authors, November 5, 2001.

31. Frances Hesselbein, Marshall Goldsmith, and Richard Beckhard, eds., *The Leader of the Future* (San Francisco: Jossey-Bass, 1996), 39.
32. Harrison Owen, *Open Space Technology: A User's Guide* (Potomac, Md.: Abbot Publishing, 1992), 44.
33. Interaction Associates, www.interactionassociates.com; 617-234-2700.

Chapter 7   Give It to 'Em Straight

1. George W. Bush, *A Charge to Keep* (New York: Perennial, 1999), 182.
2. Quoted in Elizabeth Mitchell, *W: Revenge of the Bush Dynasty* (New York: Hyperion, 2000), 87.
3. Frank Bruni, *Ambling into History* (New York: HarperCollins, 2002), 27, 117.
4. Beatrice Gormely, *President George W. Bush* (New York: Aladdin, 2001), 34–35.
5. Michael Duffy, Nancy Gibbs, John F. Dickerson, and John McCain, "Fathers, Sons and Ghosts," *Time*, February 28, 2000, 38.
6. J. H. Hatfield, *Fortunate Son: George W. Bush and the Making of an American President* (New York: Soft Skull Press, 2001), 77.
7. Speech to United Nations, September 13, 2002, available on Whitehouse.gov; accessed September 13, 2002.
8. Speech at "People for Pete" dinner, August 16, 2001, available on Whitehouse.gov; accessed July 14, 2002.
9. Bush, *A Charge to Keep*, 37.
10. Eric Pooley, "Bush in the Crucible," *Time*, September 24, 2001, 48.
11. Bush, *A Charge to Keep*, 233.
12. Speech on economic recovery and job creation, August 13, 2002, available at Whitehouse.gov; accessed August 29, 2002.
13. Bruni, *Ambling into History*, 62.
14. Bush, *A Charge to Keep*, 27.
15. Ibid., 203.
16. Michael Duffy and J. F. O. McAllister, "Marching Alone," *Time*, September 9, 2002, 44.
17. Michael Elliott, "We Will Not Fail," *Time*, October 1, 2001, 18.
18. Howard Fineman, "I Sniff Some Politics," *Newsweek*, May 27, 2002, 37.
19. Bruni, *Ambling into History*, 69.
20. Fineman, "I Sniff Some Politics," 37.

21. Hatfield, *Fortunate Son*, 50.
22. Bush, *A Charge to Keep*, 181.
23. Douglas Waller and John F. Dickerson, "Remaking the Rules of Engagement," *Time*, June 11, 2001, 26.
24. Bush, *A Charge to Keep*, 178.
25. Ibid., 175.
26. Ibid., 73.
27. Byron York, "Bush's Life in Business," nationalreview.com, July 17, 2002; accessed July 25, 2002.
28. Bruni, *Ambling into History*, 182.
29. Ibid., 202.
30. Ibid., 210.
31. Bush, *A Charge to Keep*, xii.
32. Ibid., 94.
33. Bruni, *Ambling into History*, 34.
34. Ibid., 70.
35. Ibid., 9.
36. Michael Duffy, Massimo Calabresi, John F. Dickerson, J. F. O. McAllister, and Scott MacLeod, "Trapped by His Own Instincts," *Time*, May 6, 2002, 24.
37. Quoted in Dick Kirschten, "Bush as Boss," govexec.com, July 1, 2000; accessed July 14, 2002.
38. Bush, *A Charge to Keep*, 175.
39. Aubrey Immelman, "How Bush Will Govern," *St. Cloud Times Online*, July 30, 2000; accessed July 14, 2002.
40. *Our Mission and Our Moment* (Washington, D.C.: New Market Press, 2001), preface.
41. Duffy et al., "Trapped by His Own Instincts," 24.
42. Bush, *A Charge to Keep*, 81.
43. Ibid., 174–75.
44. Ibid., 33.
45. Ibid., xii.
46. Bruni, *Ambling into History*, 47, 176.
47. Martha Brant, "West Wing Story: In Defense of Paul O'Neill, newsweek.com, July 31, 2002; accessed August 26, 2002.
48. Bush, *A Charge to Keep*, 227.
49. James Carney, "Why Bush Doesn't Like Homework," *Time*, November 15, 1999, 46.

50. James Carney, John F. Dickerson, Karen Tumulty, and Douglas Waller, "A Few Small Repairs," *Time*, July 9, 2001, 22.

51. Kevin Merida, "Shades of Grey Matter; The Question Dogs George W. Bush: Is He Smart Enough? There's No Single Answer," washingtonpost.com, January 19, 2000; accessed July 13, 2002.

52. Bruni, *Ambling into History*, 13.

53. Chris Komisarjevsky and Reina Komisarjevsky, *Peanut Butter & Jelly Management* (New York: AMACOM, 2000), 146.

54. Quoted in Anthony Robbins, *Unlimited Power* (New York: Fawcett Columbine, 1986), 216–17.

55. Quoted in Tom Peters, *A Passion for Excellence* (New York: Random House, 1985), 389.

56. Jeff Shaara, *Rise to Rebellion* (New York: Ballentine Books, 2002).

57. Allan Cox, *Straight Talk for Monday Morning* (New York: John Wiley & Sons, 1990), 242.

58. Max DePree, *The Art of Leadership* (New York: Dell, 1989), 105–108.

59. Gloria Gilbert Mayer and Thomas Mayer, *Goldilocks on Management* (New York: AMACOM, 1999), 43.

60. Fred I. Greenstein, *The Presidential Difference: Leadership Styles from FDR to Clinton* (Princeton, N.J.: Princeton University Press, 2001), afterword.

61. David Brooks, "Keeping It Simple," weeklystandard.com, June 25, 2002; accessed July 14, 2002.

62. Tamara Lipper, Martha Brant, Michael Hirsh, Roy Gutman, Mark Hosenball, Michael Isikoff, John Barry, Stryker McGuire, and Christian Caryl, "Selling the World on War," *Newsweek*, September 23, 2002, 28.

63. David M. Armstrong, *How to Turn Your Company's Parabales into Profit* (Stuart, Fla.: Author, 1995), 298.

64. Noel Tichy and Eli Cohen, *The Leadership Engine* (New York: Harper Business, 2002).

65. Howard Witt, "Bush to UN: Act on Iraq," *Chicago Tribune,* September 13, 2002, 21.

66. J. Douglas Brown, *The Human Nature of Organizations* (New York: AMACOM, 1973), 62.

67. Elliott, "We Will Not Fail," 18.

68. Bush, *A Charge to Keep*, 103.

Chapter 8   If It's Noon, I Must Be Jogging

1. James Carney, John F. Dickerson, Massimo Calabresi, Mark Thompson, Karen Tumulty, and Douglas Waller, "Inside the War Room," *Time*, December 31, 2001, 112.
2. Frank Bruni, *Ambling into History* (New York: HarperCollins, 2002), 76.
3. George W. Bush, *A Charge to Keep* (New York: Perennial, 1999), 199.
4. Bill Minutaglio, *First Son: George W. Bush and the Bush Family Dynasty* (New York: Times Books, 1999), 14.
5. Dick Kirschten, "Bush as Boss," govexec.com, July 1, 2000; accessed July 14, 2002.
6. John F. Harris and Dan Balz, "A Question of Capital: Bush Makes Political Investments, But Will They Make Him?" washingtonpost.com, April 29, 2001; accessed July 12, 2002.
7. Elizabeth Mitchell, *W: Revenge of the Bush Dynasty* (New York: Hyperion, 2000), 325.
8. Bush, *A Charge to Keep*, 96.
9. James Carney and John F. Dickerson, "Easy Does It," *Time*, March 19, 2001, 38.
10. Bush, *A Charge to Keep*, 27.
11. Bob Wischinia, "We Raced with Bush," runnersworld.com, October 2002; accessed September 13, 2002.
12. Bruni, *Ambling into History*, 5.
13. Minutaglio, *First Son*, 5.
14. Molly Ivins and Lou Dubose, *Shrub* (New York: Vintage, 2000), xvii.
15. James Carney, "Why Bush Doesn't Like Homework," *Time*, November 15, 1999, 46.
16. Bush, *A Charge to Keep*, 116.
17. John F. Dickerson, Matthew Cooper, and Douglas Waller, "Bush's Two Sides," *Time*, August 6, 2001, 20.
18. Michael Elliott, Massimo Calabresi, James Carney, Michael Duffy, Elaine Shannon, Douglas Waller, Michael Weisskopf, David Schwartz, Bruce Crumley, and J. F. O. McAllister, "How the US Missed the Clues," *Time*, May 27, 2002, 24.
19. Howard Fineman, Martha Brant, John Barry, and Seth Mnookin, "Harkening Back to Texas," *Newsweek*, July 22, 2002, 22.
20. Robert J. Samuelson, "The Right Price of the Slide," *Newsweek*, July 29, 2002, 33.

21. Michael Duffy and Massimo Calabresi, "Theater of War," *Time*, August 12, 2002, 21, 22.
22. Jim Hoagland, "Bush Deserves a Bias-Free Hearing," *Chicago Tribune*, September 13, 2002, 23.
23. Jill Lawrence and Kathy Kiely, "Bush Vacation Plans Draw Heat from Leading Democrats," *USA Today*, July 24, 2002, A01.
24. Wischinia, "We Raced with Bush."
25. Carney et al., "Inside the War Room," 112.
26. May 5, 2000, interview with Barbara Walters (on ABC's "20/20"), quoted in Mark Crispin Miller, *The Bush Dyslexicon* (New York: W. W. Norton, 2001), 107.
27. Bruni, *Ambling into History*, 21.
28. Fineman et al., "Harkening Back to Texas," 22.
29. Ibid.
30. Bill Saporito, John F. Dickerson, and Adam Zagorin, "Wall Street's Verdict," *Time*, July 29, 2002, 21.
31. Mitchell, *W*, 66.
32. Bush, *A Charge to Keep*, 133–34.
33. Lawrence L. Knutson, "President Cheney—But Just for a While," *Daily Southtown*, June 30, 2002, A7.
34. Thomas Beaumont, "Iowa Now Pro-Bush, Poll Says," DesMoines-Register.com, July 7, 2002; accessed July 14, 2002.
35. Bruni, *Ambling into History*, 154.
36. Michael Beschloss, Doris Kearns Goodwin, David Kennedy, David McCullough, John Keegan, and Edward Luttwak, "How Bush Rates," *Time*, December 31, 2001, 122.
37. Bush, *A Charge to Keep*, 186.
38. Beatrice Gormely, *President George W. Bush* (New York: Aladdin, 2001), 123.
39. Bush, *A Charge to Keep*, 194.
40. Dick Kirschten, "Bush as Boss," govexec.com, July 1, 2000; accessed July 14, 2002.
41. Bruni, *Ambling into History*, 61, 65.
42. Ibid., 208.
43. Ibid., 4–5.
44. Martha Brant and Weston Kosova, "The Queen Mother," *Newsweek*, May 13, 2002, 36.
45. Minutaglio, *First Son*, 152.
46. Bush, *A Charge to Keep*, 20.

47. Minutaglio, *First Son,* 155–56.
48. Carney, "Why Bush Doesn't Like Homework," 46.
49. Bush, *A Charge to Keep,* 52–54.
50. Ibid., 64.
51. Wischinia, "We Raced with Bush."
52. Bush, *A Charge to Keep,* 113–14.
53. Unit for Study of Personality in Politics, http://www.csbsju.edu/uspp/ExecutiveSummaries/Bush-Abstract.html, April 6, 2000; accessed July 12, 2002.
54. Michael Duffy, Massimo Calabresi, John F. Dickerson, J. F. O. McAllister, and Scott MacLeod, "Trapped by His Own Instincts," *Time,* May 6, 2002, 24.
55. M. Scott Peck, *The Road Less Traveled* (New York: Touchstone, 1998), 1.
56. Bruni, *Ambling into History,* 261–62.
57. Michael Duffy, Nancy Gibbs, John F. Dickerson, and Andrew Goldstein, "Defender in Chief," *Time,* November 5, 2001, 24, 30.
58. Michael Hirsh, Martha Brant, Tamara Lipper, and Mark Hosenball, "Hawks, Doves, and Dubya," *Newsweek,* September 23, 2002, 28.
59. Fred Barnes, "Bush Indicts Saddam," TheWeeklyStandard.com, September 13, 2002; accessed September 13, 2002.
60. Michael Elliott, "We Will Not Fail," *Time,* October 1, 2001, 19.
61. Bruni, *Ambling into History,* 12–13.
62. Elliott, "We Will Not Fail," 20.
63. James Carney and John Dickerson, "A Work in Progress," *Time,* October 22, 2001, 41–42.
64. Howard Fineman, "Living Politics: Bush Finds He's No Longer Boss Cousin," newsweek.com, July 22, 2002; accessed July 17, 2002.
65. Quoted in Beschloss et al., "How Bush Rates," 122.
66. Bruni, *Ambling into History,* 263.
67. Quoted in Harris and Balz, "A Question of Capital."
68. Quoted in Stuart Crainer, *The Ultimate Business Library* (New York: AMACOM, 1997), 284.
69. Alan Lakein, *How to Get Control of Your Time and Your Life* (New York: Signet, 1993), 158–60.
70. Robert A. Watson and Ben Brown, *The Most Effective Organization in the U.S.* (New York: Crown, 2001), 200.
71. Quoted in Marcus Buckingham and Donald O. Clifton, *Now Discover Your Strengths* (New York: Free Press, 2001), 96.

72. Jim Collins, *Good to Great* (New York: Harper Business, 2001).
73. Steven Covey, *The 7 Habits of Highly Effective People* (New York: Simon & Schuster, 1990).
74. Devin Gordon, "Coach Til You Drop," *Newsweek,* September 2, 2002, 48.
75. Carney and Dickerson, "Easy Does It," 38.
76. Bush, *A Charge to Keep,* 203.
77. Collins, *Good to Great,* 120.
78. Wischinia, "We Raced with Bush."
79. Bruni, *Ambling into History,* 265.

Chapter 9   Intuitive Wisdom

1. James Carney and John F. Dickerson, "Inside the War Room," *Time,* January 7, 2002, 112.
2. *Merriam-Webster Dictionary* (New York: Simon & Schuster, 1974), 377.
3. James Ware, *The Psychology of Money* (New York: John Wiley & Sons, 2001), 242.
4. Bennett Goodspeed, *The Tao Jones Average* (New York: Penguin, 1983), 146.
5. J. H. Hatfield, *Fortunate Son: George W. Bush and the Making of an American President* (New York: Soft Skull Press, 2001), 94.
6. George W. Bush, *A Charge to Keep* (New York: Perennial, 1999), 130.
7. Frank Bruni, *Ambling into History* (New York: HarperCollins, 2002), 120.
8. Ibid.
9. Goodspeed, *The Tao Jones Average,* 74.
10. Hatfield, *Fortunate Son,* 45.
11. Bush, *A Charge to Keep,* xiii.
12. Bruni, *Ambling into History,* 245.
13. Bill Minutaglio, *First Son: George W. Bush and the Bush Family Dynasty* (New York: Times Books, 1999), 86.
14. Bruni, *Ambling into History,* 197.
15. Hatfield, *Fortunate Son,* 31.
16. Bruni, *Ambling into History,* 240.
17. Minutaglio, *First Son,* 59.
18. Molly Ivins and Lou Dubose, *Shrub* (New York: Vintage, 2000), xv.
19. Minutaglio, *First Son,* 268.
20. Ibid., 153.

21. Ivins and Dubose, *Shrub*, xix.

22. Bruni, *Ambling into History*, 256.

23. Ibid.

24. James Carney, "Our New Best Friend," *Time*, May 27, 2002, 23.

25. Bush, *A Charge to Keep*, 6.

26. Michael Duffy, "Marching Alone," *Time*, July 11, 2002, 45.

27. Ibid.

28. James Kouzes and Barry Posner, *The Leadership Challenge* (San Francisco: Jossey-Bass, 2002), 111.

29. Robert Greenleaf, *On Becoming a Servant Leader* (San Francisco: Jossey-Bass, 1996), 32.

30. Patricia Einstein, *Intuition: The Path to Inner Wisdom* (Rockport, Mass.: Houghton Mifflin, 1996), 45.

31. Frances E. Vaughan, *Awakening Intuition* (New York: Anchor, 1979), 64.

32. Quoted in Sandra Weintraub, *The Hidden Intelligence: Innovation Through Intuition* (New York: Butterworth-Heinemann, 1998), 119.

33. Quoted in Weintraub, 127.

34. Ibid.

35. Ibid.

36. Peter Senge, *The Fifth Discipline* (New York: Currency/Doubleday, 1994), 81.

37. Weintraub, *The Hidden Intelligence*, 89.

38. Quoted in Goodspeed, *The Tao Jones Average*, 75.

39. Quoted in Alden M. Hayashi, "When to Trust Your Gut," *Harvard Business Review*, February 2001, 6.

40. Quoted in Weintraub, *The Hidden Intelligence*, 118.

41. Sonia Choquette, telephone interview with author, October 2, 2000.

42. Quoted in Weintraub, *The Hidden Intelligence*, 27.

43. *Psychology Today*, October 1989, 49, quoted in Stauffer, "Your Managerial Intuition," 4.

44. Quoted in Robert Koppel, *The Intuitive Trader* (New York: John Wiley & Sons, 1996), 103.

45. Sonia Choquette, *The Psychic Pathway* (New York: Crown Trade, 1995), 68.

Chapter 10 Getting Results

1. George W. Bush, *A Charge to Keep* (New York: Perennial, 1999), 30.

2. Ibid., 202.

3. Ibid., 205.

4. Molly Ivins and Lou Dubose, *Shrub* (New York: Vintage, 2000), 36.

5. Bush, *A Charge to Keep*, 75.

6. Ivins and Dubose, *Shrub*, 122.

7. Ibid., 125.

8. Bush, *A Charge to Keep*, 211.

9. Ibid., 212.

10. Ibid., 213.

11. Quoted in Shannon Pearson Smith, "President Bush's Faith-Based and Community Initiative Is Designed to Help Your Church Increase Its Involvement in the Community," *Church Executive*, August 2000, 37.

12. Ibid., 2.

13. Bush, *A Charge to Keep*, 140.

14. Ibid., 166.

15. Romesh Ratnesar, "Can He Fix It?," *Time*, June 17, 2002, 26.

16. Dick Kirschten, "Bush as Boss," *Government Executive Magazine*, July 1, 2000, 43.

17. Ibid., 42.

18. Ibid., 44.

19. Ibid., 45.

20. Ibid., 46.

21. James Carney, John F. Dickerson, Massimo Calabresi, Mark Thompson, Karen Tumulty, and Douglas Waller, "Inside the War Room," *Time*, December 31, 2001, 116.

22. Quoted in Jeffrey A. Krames, *The Rumsfeld Way* (New York: McGraw-Hill, 2002), 126.

23. Frances Hesselbein, Marshall Goldsmith, and Richard Beckhard, eds., *The Leader of the Future* (San Francisco: Jossey-Bass, 1996), xii.

24. Robert Bruce Shaw, *Trust in the Balance* (San Francisco: Jossey-Bass, 1997), 108.

25. Stephen Covey, *Principle-Centered Leadership* (New York: Simon & Schuster, 1992), 192.

26. Jim Collins, *Good to Great* (New York: HarperCollins, 2001), 53.

27. Quoted in Hesselbein, Goldsmith, and Beckhard, *The Leader of the Future*, 247.

28. Jeffrey Krames, *The Rumsfeld Way*, 167.

29. Collins, *Good to Great*, 37.

30. Ibid., 38.

31. Ibid., 37.

32. Ibid., 39.

33. Ibid., 48.

34. Robert Bruce Shaw, *Trust in the Balance*, 49.

35. James C. Collins and Jerry I. Porras, *Built to Last* (New York: Harper Business, 1994), 73.

36. Bush, *A Charge to Keep*, 140.

Index